MINORITIES IN THE MIDDLE

SUNY Series in Ethnicity and Race in American Life
John Sibley Butler, Editor

Minorities in the Middle

A Cross-Cultural Analysis

Walter P. Zenner

State University of New York Press

Published by
State University of New York Press, Albany

Printed in the United States of America

For information, address State University of New York
Press, State University Plaza, Albany, N.Y. 12246

Production by E. Moore
Marketing by Theresa A. Swierzowski

Library of Congress Cataloging-in-Publication Data

Zenner, Walter P.
Minorities in the middle : a cross-cultural analysis / Walter P.
Zenner.
p. cm. — (SUNY series in ethnicity and race in American
life)
Includes bibliographical references and index.
ISBN 0-7914-0642-3. — ISBN 0-7914-0643-1 (pbk.)
1. Ethnic relations—Cross-cultural studies. 2. Minorities—Cross
-cultural studies. 3. Discrimination—Cross-cultural studies.
I. Title. II. Series.
GN496.Z46 1991
305.8—dc20 90-39846
CIP

10 9 8 7 6 5 4 3 2 1

FOR LINDA

CONTENTS

PREFACE

The idea for this book about trading minorities grew out of many different experiences. Both my parents were children of Jewish merchants in German small towns. My father started as a plastics manufacturer in Germany and became a broker for new and used plastics machinery in the United States. During my childhood in Chicago, my mother and my aunt owned a Continental-style confectionary. So I saw a small ethnic business firsthand.

I lived in ethnically diverse neighborhoods for most of my life, and I have been aware of division of labor along ethnic lines. As a refugee from Nazi Germany and as a resident of American cities, I felt and observed the effects of anti-Semitism, racism, and the tensions between people of different classes. Many of my ideas about trading minorities crystallized while doing research among Syrian Jews and Arabs in Israel and the United States. That, together with teaching courses on ethnicity, anthropological approaches to business, and the ethnology of Jews, led me to the present study of the relationship of occupational specialization to ethnic conflict.

I have many people and institutions to thank for their assistance. I began this study with a summer grant from the Research Foundation of the State University of New York. I first presented this work at various seminars at the State University of New York at Albany (SUNY), the University of Haifa, the former Research Institute for Ethnic and Immigrant Studies of the Smithsonian Institution, and the YIVO Institute for Jewish Research. As a research fellow at the Annenberg Research Institute in Philadelphia, I was able to prepare the final draft for publication.

An earlier version of the introduction and chapter 1 was published as "Middleman Minority Theories: A Critical Review" in the *Sourcebook on the New Immigration*, edited by Roy S. Bryce-Laporte, Delores Mortimer, and Stephen Couch, published by Transaction Books 1980, pp. 413–426. Chapter 6 is a revision and elaboration of "American Jewry in the Light of Middleman Minority Theories," *Contemporary Jewry* 5: V: 11–30 (1980). The former is printed with the permission of the Smithsonian Institution and Transaction Books; the latter by permission of the Association for the Social Scientific Study of Jewry.

The comments, suggestions, criticism, and encouragement of many colleagues—especially those working on middleman minorities and related field—have been very important to me over the years. These include Judith Blau, Edna Bonacich, Laurel Bossen, the late Werner Cahnman, Donald T. Campbell, Robert Carmack, Erik Cohen, Michael Curtis, Mark Granovetter, Ron Helfrich, Robert Jarvenpa, William Jordan, Robert LeVine, Ivan Light, the late Paul Meadows, Hans Panofsky, Edward Riegelhaupt, William Roff, Sammy Smooha, and anonymous reviewers of this manuscript.

I also appreciate the assistance in manuscript preparation which I received from Gail Grouper, Jennifer Jones, Betty Kruger, Etty Lassner, Joanne Somich, and Steve Wells. I would also like to thank Brad Fisher for his editing of a previous draft, as well as Rosalie Robertson and the staff of the State University of New York Press for their editorial work.

Finally I would like to thank Rachel, Abigail, and above all, Linda, for their support and encouragement of my work over the years.

Introduction

In recent decades, social scientists have given much attention to interethnic relations and the problem of racism as it refers to dominant Europeans and conquered peasant peoples of color. Much less stress has been placed on that subtler racism which affects stigmatized groups in middle economic positions. Yet these ethnic groups have been and continue to be the object of some of the most violent attempts at final solutions of ethnic and class conflicts in this century. Just within the past 30 years, we have witnessed the partial expulsion of Asians from Kenya, the total expulsion of this group from Uganda, and the expropriation and forced exodus of many Chinese from Vietnam. Many such events during modern time are discussed in this book and constitute some of the cruelest interludes of the twentieth century.

Theories which seek to explain the phenomenon of the middleman minority are at the juncture of ethnic symbolism, economic specialization, social status, and power. In fact, one could say that this is one point in which class and ethnic conflicts coalesce. It is also the point in which the interpretation of events has a direct bearing on the economic and political spheres.

In trying to define middleman minorities it should be evident that we are marking out a field for inquiry on which comparative social scientists will contend with each other. It is, therefore, not surprising that agreement about which groups are, indeed, such minorities is incomplete or that definitions used by different authorities are contradictory. The early discussions of this kind of minority consisted of descriptions of the Jewish status in Western Europe, sometimes mixed with casual comparisons of the Jews as merchants and moneylenders with other groups in Europe and elsewhere. Since many of these groups are referred to as Jews of the New World or the Jews of the South Seas, we could class these as "Jews-of" theories. Later social scientists developed the concepts of people class, stranger, pariah people, trading minorities, penalized minorities and middleman minorities.

The minority part of these concepts implies both subordination and being fewer in number than other groups. Of course, in certain places and during certain periods, the minority may constitute a numerical majority. The number of Chinese in western Malaysia is fairly close to that of the politically dominant Malays, and the Chinese are the majority in Singapore.

The middleman concept is more complex, but brings us directly to the paradox of the middleman-minority position, namely frequent economic success combined with political impotency and with charges against the minority of having hidden power. But who are these middlemen?[1]

The members of these minorities can be seen as intermediaries between the ruling elite and the masses—in peasant societies—as merchants, government contractors, and even as government bureaucrats. In economic terms, they are middlemen between the producers and the consumers. Even doctors, lawyers, and other professionals can be seen in these terms. They are seen primarily as merchants, moneylenders and the like, rather than as organizers of productive enterprises. Whether middleman-minority members become economic leaders or entrepreneurs in industrial society is one of the questions to which theorists address themselves.

Several definitions are currently in use. The first defines an ethnic group as a middleman minority if a substantial and disproportionate number of its members are engaged in trade and finance.[2] Another sees them as buffers between the ruling class and the masses, whether as providers of luxuries to the elites or as extractors of wealth from the masses on behalf of the rulers—hence, the use of the terms *intermediaries* and *middlemen.*[3] The third usage sees *petit bourgeois* or small-business activity, either in the form of self-employment or family firm, as defining the essence of the middleman.[4] In this instance, while concentration in the service sector—rather than as industrial producers—may be present, it is the mode of employment which is the key.

As with other synthetic concepts used in the social sciences[5] —such as peasantry or the revitalization movement—each of the several definitions and alternate terms—such as status-gap minority and trading diaspora—has its merits.

The first definition has the advantage that it does not make any statement about the nature of stratification in the society under consideration, nor does it prejudge the way in which members of the ethnic group are perceived. It thus serves to aid in comparison of differing groups in a variety of settings and at different evolutionary stages.

The second definition is particularly useful in the study of feudal and colonial settings, in which both merchants and retainers may fill the chasm between the upper and lower strata of society.

The third term is used by those who concentrate their attention on immigrant and other ethnically based enterprises in advanced industrial societies.

The first definition is the one which will be used there, but the characteristics pointed to in the other two definitions will be kept in mind.

The problem of definitions and typologies is that they imply an ideal type which is rarely approximated in reality. Some would argue that this invalidates the exercise, or they would, at least, use such definitions and types cautiously. Obviously, social scientists must be sensitive to the problems inherent in demarcation of a phenomenon and must proceed with care. Still, such conceptualizations have value in forcing one out of a narrow mold of historical and cultural particularism. It compels us to compare. In the realm of cross-cultural and cross-temporal comparisons, we can begin to develop more general hypotheses and principles, leading to the formulation of theories.

The middleman-minority concept is particularly attractive because it combines an interest in ethnicity—generally seen as a primordial factor—with the search for socioeconomic explanations of social phenomena. We must look for similarities between groups on the basis of their social positions and compare the relationship of the ethnic minority to the surrounding society. Considering the tendency to see ethnic groups separately from the class structure of the society, this is an important contribution to the study of ethnicity and stratification. Middleman minorities—which are often penalized minorities—also combine the paradox of relative economic success and even affluence with ultimate powerlessness which permits their victimization. The very persistence of ethnic groups of this type in advanced societies challenges notions about the significance of class and integration in modern times.[6]

As suggested, social scientists use existing prototypes in developing concepts. Arguments over definitions often relate to the fact that different social scientists begin their generalizations from different standpoints. Thus, Weber's "pariah people" concept is an outgrowth of his contrast of Jews and Protestants in early modern Europe, while Bonacich's modifications to the middleman-minority concept stem from an interest in Asian immigrants in contemporary North America. My own interest in the middleman phenomenon emerged from an interest in applying contemporary social science to the study of medieval and modern Jewish communities. The Jewish examples can be used to test ideas and hypotheses derived from other societies while, at the same time, they may shed light on non-Jewish groups as well.[7]

The danger in using particular ethnic groups as a prototype is manifold. One drawback is that one may use comparison to identify one group with the others, while still ignoring differences. Comparing overseas Chinese with diaspora Jews in terms of similarities alone is an example of this.[8]

Another danger lies in treating those who fit under one ethnic label, but live in different countries, regions, and historical regions, as a single unit. The idea that Jews have a unitary economic history is an example of this.[9]

Falling into some of these pitfalls is inevitable because of limitations of space. Through a variety of extended comparisons, one may provide the means with which to overcome some of these problems. These comparisons will provide a kaleidoscope with which to view the different factors which are part of the middleman phenomenon.

In chapter 1, a brief history of the development of middleman-minority theories will be presented, followed by a summary of issues and conclusions reached by those who have studied middleman minorities in the past. This chapter will argue that explanations which seek to explain the middleman phenomenon primarily through economic interpretations will not suffice and that emphasis must be placed on the interpretations and image manipulations used by both the minority and the majority in their interaction. More detailed comparisons of minorities in terms of one social function—that of moneylender—will be discussed in chapter 2. This discussion ties social roles to the concept of the stranger, and also examines the economic aspect of the middleman role.

In chapter 3, the idea of majority hostility will be related to images and ideologies employed against middleman minorities, especially those ideologies which have spread throughout the world. This is related to the idea of image manipulation and cultural strategies. The focus will be placed on anti-Semitism as the major one of these ideologies. Since the diffusion of the image of the Jew as middleman is so widespread, it raises questions about the comparability of different groups as separate from underlying anti-Semitic stereotypes. Rather than viewing host-hostility as something which is independently invented in each society, I will suggest that we should supplement functional explanations with the history of ideas.

In chapter 4, the attribution of ethnic solidarity to middlemen will be looked at with regard to three large groups: Ashkenazic Jews, overseas Indians and overseas Chinese. This uncontrolled comparison will provide an opportunity to examine cultural differences as well as similarities. Chapter 5 considers Protestant middlemen whom Max Weber has contrasted with the Jews. In chapter 6, American Jewry will be analyzed in terms of the foregoing discussions. This will provide an occasion for looking at strategies for changing group images and at the possible occupational changes confronting this middleman-minority concept at the crossroads of assimilation and survival.This will be followed by a brief conclusion.

Chapter 1

Middleman Minority Theories

Historical Background: The Classical Theories

The thinking which entered the social sciences often started in the conventional wisdom of early modern Europe.[1] Just as the different images of city and country formed the basis of urban sociology, so the various stereotypes of Protestant, Catholic, and Jew, as well as Scot, Englishman, and Irishman affected the way in which European thinkers formulated theories about the links between economic roles, religion, and ethnic identity. The late medieval specialization of Jews in Europe as pawnbrokers, old-clothesmen, and peddlers, and the startling success of a few Jews in rising to become court bankers and great financiers was a noteworthy phenomenon in the eyes of such observers as Voltaire, Kant, and Karl Marx. As is well known, the connections which these intellectuals made between Jewishness and economic participation of Jews was founded in the anti-Jewish prejudices of the times.[2] Despite this, the suggestions which they made about the relationship of ethnicity to occupational choice formed the basis for the first formulations of theories about the middleman-minority phenomenon.

By the nineteenth century, the features which had entered social scientific thinking about middleman minorities were: (1) the observation that a disproportionate number of Jews were engaged in petty trade, moneylending, and related activities; (2) a negative evaluation of these activities, especially the secondhand trade and pawnbroking; (3) a view that these activities were either to be extirpated as antisocial or were obsolete; and (4) a perception of the similarities between Jews and other trading minorities.

In this chapter, the most important of the theories will be discussed briefly. The prejudices which typified the precursors, such as Voltaire, continued to cast a shadow on some of the later theories, although a variety of attitudes toward trade, capitalism, Jews, and other trading minorities can be found among these thinkers.

In 1875, Wilhelm Roscher, an economic historian, formulated an explanation of the ups and downs of the Jewish status in medieval Europe. He saw the Jews as pioneers of international trade in Western Europe who were subsequently displaced from their preeminent positions by Christians when the national economies of these countries had matured. Roscher suggested the applicability of this hypothesis of the introduction of foreign traders into a previously underdeveloped economy and their subsequent ouster by native competitors to situations of their groups, such as the Chinese in Southeast Asia. His thesis has formed a basis for other middleman-minority theories.[3]

Several of the pioneers of modern sociology addressed themselves to the questions surrounding the presence of commercially specialized minorities in society. This was especially true of the German sociologists—such as Toennies, Sombart, Weber, and Simmel—who were influenced by Marx and Roscher among others. The Jewish question during the late nineteenth and early twentieth centuries when these sociologists flourished was at the forefront of social problems in Germany, and it was entangled with other issues such as the relationship of capital to labor. Generally, these figures did comment on the role of Jews in Europe, although their approach was always comparative.

Weber's use of the term *pariah,* for instance, implied that there was something which Jews shared with certain Indian castes. In addition, his contrast of Jews and Puritans is central to this delineation of the relationship between Protestantism and the rise of modern capitalism. The role of trade in breaking up the folk community and natural economy of the early Middle Ages and bringing about the impersonal relationships characteristic of the contemporary period was a central theme in the view which these writers took of Jews, Protestants, Florentines, and others.

These theorists have focused on two important strands of explanations of middleman minorities. One stresses the situation of minority-majority contacts, while the second emphasizes the attributes of the minority.

Toennies and Simmel have dealt with the particular form of ethnocentrism which arises when strangers from outside, often bearing goods, enter a closed community. They deal with the interaction between those outside of the intertwined kinship networks of the community and those within them. The stranger enters, but lingers. He or she is close, yet distant; intimate, but objective; comes today and stays, or returns tomorrow, rootless and innovative.

The very fact of trading activity introduced new ways into the community, and traders have a way of being impious and flippant.[4] This focus on the middleman as stranger has continued to have a significant influence on social scientific theory in general, as witnessed by the reprinting of Simmel's essay in the United States and on theories dealing with middleman minorities in particular. Some who feel that Weber has mislabeled such groups as *pariahs* see Simmel's conception as appropriate.[5]

In their work, Sombart and Weber stress the culture of the middlemen rather than the context. They can be seen as advocates of a cultural configurational or national-character approach to explaining ethnic specialization. In the case of Weber, the term *religious character* might be preferred since he emphasized the role of the ethical teachings of religious traditions. Sombart saw a wide variety of factors including race, religion, and the role of migration in explaining entrepreneurship. Both Sombart and Weber were concerned more with the economic activities of the groups under consideration and much less with the interaction between the majority and the minorities.

While the issues in the debate between Weber and Sombart about the role of Judaism and the Jews in the emergence of modern capitalism are to some extent passe, there are several reasons why consideration of the works of these two sociologists continues to be relevant. While Sombart's reputation as a major figure has declined—partly as a result of his anti-Semitism and sympathies with Nazism—his works have continued to be reprinted. There is no doubt that his book, *The Jews and Modern Capitalism,* was a major stimulus for research into the economic history of the Jews. Weber, of course, is still seen as a giant figure of twentieth-century sociology and a pioneer in comparative studies of economic ethics and religion. In addition, both wrote book-length works on the Jews and devoted a large part of their discussion to the place of this classic middleman minority in the structure of modern capitalism. This problem also is discussed in their writings on the economy and society.[6]

Finally, they took differing stances on whether the Jews, as a middleman minority, have been capitalists in the full sense of the word or represent a special variation—pariah capitalists. This issue continues to concern researchers into entrepreneurship and middleman minorities, although it has been refined. In large measure, the ambivalence or hostility toward capitalism which Weber, Sombart, and their contemporaries had is shared by contemporary social scientists, even though the contempt for Jews which was rife during their time has passed.

Sombart attributed the rise of capitalism to a Jewish cultural configuration which was borne by the Jewish race—that of a rational, wandering desert people. While the racial overtones of Sombart's anticapitalist and anti-Semitic work have been excised, the association of the middleman with migration and sojourning survives in later theories.

Sombart saw the Jews and Judaism as being among the prime movers of modern capitalism. The word "among" is important, since Sombart, in each of his works on capitalism, wrote as if the subject of each book—whether it was migration, Judaism, or luxury—was a primary cause. To Sombart, capitalist enterprise was a synthesis of the ability to mobilize other human beings for a particular task, enterprise, or undertaking with talent for manipulating money and maximizing economic gain. Sombart sees several factors—including race, religion, and migration—producing such enterprises. To him, the Jews combine all three, although other people—such as the Florentines and the Scots—are seen in a similar light.[7]

Sombart's debate with Weber concerned the relative contributions of Judaism and Puritanism to the rise of capitalism. Sombart was of two minds regarding this. Sometimes, he identified Puritanism with Judaism. On other occasions, he stressed the antagonism of Puritanism to the capitalist ethic.

He did, of course, see the roots of capitalism in the cold, objective, calculating manner which he attributed to the Jews, seeing the desire to remain separate as a stance of otherhood. His evaluation of capitalism was generally hostile; he disliked the unlimited lust for gain and the calculating bourgeois spirit, while still admiring the boldness of entrepreneurs. Unlike Weber, Sombart does not distinguish between varieties of capitalism in general and Jewish capitalism in particular.

Weber's assertion of a qualitative distinction between modern rational capitalism—founded on the universalistic economic ethic of the Puritans—and pariah capitalism—rooted in the dualistic ethic of Judaism—has shaped much subsequent thinking about middleman minorities.[8] Weber's term *pariah,* often combined with *pariah capitalism,* has been widely applied to middleman minorities, even by social scientists who do not have any interest in the differences between Jews and Puritans, but who merely use it as a synonym for minority business. This term has also drawn the fire of Jewish economic historians who correctly point out the important differences between Jews in medieval Europe and outcastes in India.

To Weber, modern rational capitalism was characterized by a unique organization of labor and corporate structure, which is differentiated from other forms of capitalism. The latter are based on consumer credit, irrational speculation, the accumulation of booty, and colonialism. The pariah capitalism of the Jews is one of these forms.

Weber claimed that the reason why the Jews, despite their relatively rational religion, failed to develop rational capitalism was because their religion reinforced their status as a pariah people. He defines the term as follows:

> In our usage, pariah people denotes a distinctive hereditary social group lacking autonomous political organization and characterized by prohibitions against commensalism and intermarriage, originally founded upon magical, tabooistic, and ritual injunctions. Two additional traits of a pariah people are political and social disprivilege and a far-reaching distinctiveness in economic functioning.

Weber goes on to compare Hindu castes—particularly outcastes—with the Jews since they share the traits of segregation based on religious principles, religious obligations, and future salvation as a result of their present low estate.[9] Elsewhere, he elaborates on the economic relationship which such people have with nongroup members. He sees them as living in dispersed communities, segregated from their neighbors but tolerated, possibly even privileged, because of their usefulness to the latter.[10]

To Weber, it was the pariahhood of the Jews which prevented their economic activity from giving rise to modern, rational industrial capitalism. Ritual segregation, a dual ethic in business, and fulfillment of ritual obligations as the goal of Judaism differentiate it from Puritanism, according to Weber. While Judaism is "this-worldly," it does not see one's economic activity as the arena in which one proves one's goodness. Thus, Judaism leads the businessman to be opportunistic. Usurious loans to Gentiles, driving a hard bargain, and tax farming, as well as booty capitalism, are all permissible activities.

Puritans, especially Quaker businessmen, Weber writes, had a very different view. Economic activity was a religious vocation. Honesty—especially toward nonbelievers—was not only the best policy; it was a duty. This led to treating all people rationally—as exemplified by a fixed-price system—while the view of economic activity as a religious calling made it central to one's life. Judaism lacked this view and thus could not lead to modern capitalism.[11]

Weber's influence is apparent in many considerations of middleman minorities in the social sciences. This includes the usage of such words as *marginal trading minorities, outcaste traders, pariah capitalism* and *guest peoples.*[12] In fact, Weber himself compared pariah and guest peoples, not middleman minorities. His view of a special variety of ethnocentrism being a quality of pariahs and causing them to undertake certain social roles has become a component of several later theories.

The classical founders of social science refined some of the notions which they had inherited. Like their predecessors, they were still primarily concerned with Jews. After all, the Jewish question was a prime concern of Central European society during the period of their work. They inherited a generally unfavorable image of Jews, which they generally accepted. It is noteworthy that neither Weber nor Sombart were particularly concerned in their model-building with anti-Semitism as a social problem. Only in models like Simmel's of the stranger do we find increased attention given to the mutual interaction of minority member and the majority. His model is one leading to a contextual explanation of antiminority sentiment. The image of the stranger is a product of the environment, not an inherent quality of his or her culture.

The classical social scientists, however, did extend their work beyond the Jews. They related the Jewish question to central social concerns. They formulated concepts and generalizations which could be used comparatively, like the stranger, the pariah people, pariah capitalism, and the Roscher thesis. These conceptualizations force us to consider comparison. Jewish historians have looked askance and have rejected comparison of Jews with others, but the concept of the pariah people makes them contemplate its possibility. The concept of pariah also links the stereotype of the minority with its economic position, thus maintaining a connection between ideology and culture on the one hand with power and material wealth on the other.

Historical Background: 1940 to the Present

The term *middleman minority* comes from Howard Paul Becker, an American sociologist who was influenced by the German classics. His writing on the subject can be seen as an indirect response to Sombart's association of commercial success with the Jewish race. In his various formulations, Becker endeavored to prove that those traits which may be associated with the Jews appear in other ethnic groups noted for their commercial acumen, such as the Scots, the Chinese, the Parsis, and the Armenians. In all of these groups, one finds enterprise connected to what he called a "Chosen People complex," but later was referred to as "ethnic solidarity" or a "separatist complex."[13]

Becker's comparisons placed equal stress on several middleman groups, thus focusing attention on comparison. From 1940, when his first essay appeared, through the 1950s, most writing on the subject was still entwined with socioeconomic explanations of anti-Semitism.[14] There also were some valuable sociological writings dealing with anti-Semitism and European Jewry along these lines in the 1960s. By the late 1960s, however, increasing emphasis was placed on the trading minorities of Africa and Asia, who were perceived as comparable to the Jews in terms of pariah capitalism. This new interest accompanied concern with economic development and interethnic tensions in those regions. The formulations of Shibutani and Kwan, Blalock, Jiang, McClelland, Hagen, Wertheim, and others reflect this new thrust.[15]

In 1973, Edna Bonacich wrote a provocative article in which she argued that the middleman-minority theory was applicable not only to the study of early modern Jewry in Europe and the trading minorities of the Third World, but also to Asians and other small businessmen in the United States. Through their willingness to work hard for low profits and their ethnic solidarity, they filled niches of the economy which were too expensive for the large corporations to fill. At the same time, they could arouse the hostility of their native competitors, the native workforce against whom they might discriminate when employing their co-ethnics and their customers. She thus explains widely separated phenomena such as black riots which destroyed small businesses often owned by Jews and Asians in the United States during the 1960s and 1970s, the internment of Japanese in California during the World War II, and anti-Indian riots in South Africa. While seeing communal solidarity as supporting the small businesses, she does not argue in her later articles and books that such groups are necessarily permanent minorities.[16] Her work is linked to that of other contemporary sociologists, especially Ivan Light and Howard Aldrich. It is marked by a highly critical stance toward the capitalist status quo.

Bonacich's approach is based on the assumption of several labor markets which divide the working class of capitalist societies into mutually antagonistic segments.[17] Her thinking was part of a general revival of Marxist thought in the United States and Western Europe during the 1970s. In dealing with middleman minorities, there has also been renewed interest in Abram Leon's pamphlet on the Jewish question, which suggested that the Jews in certain periods and places should be seen as a "people-class," a concept that combines ethnicity with the Marxist view of classes as groups with conflicting interests and differential access to the means of production and strategic resources.[18] Another Marxist current, that which views capitalism as having created a single-world system, is also useful in the interpretation of the roles of commercial ethnic groups.[19]

Another figure whose work integrated consideration of middleman minorities into a broader approach to the study of complex societies is Abner Cohen. For him, there is a continuous dialectical relationship between the symbols which mark different cultures and the way these symbols are used to further the political and economic interests of the bearers of those cultures. Such interest groups are based on primary relationships, whether ethnic or otherwise, and such groups are more important than the larger classes discerned by sociologists. The use of symbols to maintain group boundaries can thus be seen as a cultural strategy. In fact, many groups in traditional and modern societies find that their interests are guarded better through invisible organizations such as cousinhoods, membership in a common set of social clubs, religious ties, and informal networks, than through a highly visible, formally recognized institution. At times, ethnic groups may need to heighten their visibility as strangers to maintain their interests, while in other instances they may wish to lower their profile and appear to be an integral part of the society.[20]

An example of such invisible organization is the trading diaspora which maintained the long-distance caravan trade in West Africa in the recent past. The Hausa were one ethnic group which had such a diaspora, and they were similar to medieval Jewry in this regard.

Cohen considers the trading diaspora as a special organization in which a stable structure must allow for the mobility of its personnel. It must be a dispersed, but interdependent, set of communities. Often a diaspora is denied resort to the regular exercise of organized physical coercion, and it must find other means to maintain authority. To accomplish this, the diaspora may have stringent requirements for group membership, such as religious adherence or genealogical relations, special means of communication, and power exercised through regulation of credit.[21]

Overlapping Concepts

Cohen's terms *trading diaspora* has recently been used in Philip Curtin's comparative world history of cross-cultural trade. By cross-cultural trade, Curtin means trade between cultural areas in which not only language but the rules of trade and other features of life are radically different. Mediating such trade are mercantile communities of strangers who live in a foreign host community and come to learn its ways.

Curtin's study covers this phenomenon from its beginnings in prehistoric times until its demise with the establishment of an ecumenical trade system (for example, the European-controlled world system) in recent times. He refers to them as *trade diasporas,* but obviously Curtin's use of the term takes on different meaning from the way it was used by Abner Cohen since the latter's studies were limited to long-distance trade under colonial conditions.

In addition, Curtin notes that the social status and political power of such mercantile communities ranged from the powerlessness of pariah traders such as medieval Jews, through relatively autonomous but pacific trading communities to the trading-post empires of Europeans during the period from 1500 to 1850. Such trading posts were armed and often had their own soldiers. While some of these are included here as middleman minorities, the merchant-adventurers are less obviously so, though this will be touched on in our discussion of Scots in chapter 6.[22]

Another concept which overlaps considerably with the middleman minority is that of the ethnic enclave, developed by Alejandro Portes and his associates to analyze the Cuban community in Miami. In the ethnic enclave, most immigrants are either self-employed or employed by fellow immigrants. The conditions of employment are "paternalistic" when compared with jobs in the primary or large-corporate sector, or with the conditions in the secondary labor market. While wages and other costs are lower than in the primary market, employers take a paternalistic attitude toward their employees and help them to achieve better living conditions.

The model is Miami in the 1970s. One pictures a large city with a very high proportion of immigrants, often fiercely competing with each other. There is, within this population which may share many cultural and linguistic features, a wide range of skills and socioeconomic heterogeneity. The picture might also fit the Jewish Lower East Side and Garment District of New York City around 1900 or Chinese Singapore. The conclusions drawn by Portes about paternalistic labor relations in Miami may not apply to these other enclaves. Still, there are communities and occupational sectors where we would find that the ethnic-enclave model would overlap or replace that of the middleman minority.[23]

Inherent Biases

The movement toward social scientific models is incomplete. By now, even those who seek an ideal of a value-free social science must be aware of the impossible nature of this goal. The language which we use, the residues of historical experience which are imbedded in our perceptions, and our own political aspirations cannot be neatly separated from our scholarly activity. This is certainly the case with regard to middleman minorities.

One bias which is found in the discussion of middleman minorities is a disdain for commerce, trade, and middlemen. Even bourgeois intellectuals who are themselves the children of commercial people share this viewpoint. The prejudice is common to aristocrats and radicals, from Kant and Voltaire to American radicals of the 1960s. Many of us have a tendency to view middlemen as unnecessary parasites and hold a negative view of money that is made from money.

The metaphor of the middleman as parasite is a particularly insidious one. The idea of the guest who preys on his host has even been accepted into medical jargon. The medical analogy suggests that parasites must be eliminated by total solutions. In nineteenth-century German writings, the Jew was frequently described as a parasite engaged in nonproductive occupations. This criticism was adopted by Jewish philanthropists and Zionists who sought to transform the Jews into a productive people, engaged in a wide range of occupations. It was also adopted in such social scientific terms as *guest people, host society* and *host hostility,* which give preeminent rights to the majority. Such figures of speech were reified in the Nazi extermination of Jews.[24]

Another bias is the nationalist perspective. The nation or state is taken for granted as the unit for most social scientific studies. Even many anthropologists consider the basic culture-bearing unit as one in which language and political control over a territory coincide. Development theorists write in terms of nation-building and developing nations. From such a perspective, cosmopolitans—such as homeless diasporas, *compradore* merchants, international bankers, and multinational corporations—are suspect. There is something abnormal about middleman minorities. Affirmation of diasporas requires a positive approach to free trade and *laissez faire* capitalism and an appreciation of entrepreneurship.[25]

The importance of the relationship of a stance with regard to capitalist activity and one's view of the minority middleman has been stated quite clearly by Edna Bonacich. She views the petty bourgeois, including minority small businessmen, as both victims and oppressors in the capitalist system. She sees capitalism as exploitative and dehumanizing with few, if any, redeeming features.[26]

Another type of bias comes from the attributes of the groups studied by social scientists at the start of their research. We tend to make our definitions and models fit the prototypical group. For decades, the Jews were the archetype, but, since the late 1950s, attention has shifted to Asians and to African trading groups. Bonacich's stress on small business and self-employment in her definition of middleman minority can be related to her interest in the Japanese-Americans who, for a long time, included small-business truck farmers and gardeners. While she makes an excellent case for her definition, it certainly gives her work a different cast from that of others who are concerned with a different set of occupations.[27]

A Summary of Middleman Minority Theories

In previous sections of this chapter, the development of the study of middleman minorities was reviewed historically. In this section, the features of the different theories will be summarized. Consistent among all these theories is the question of whether the most significant independent variables are those derived from the setting in which the minority finds itself or from the character of the minority itself, as well as how these factors affect each other. In extreme formulations a racist would see only factors stemming from the personalities of the minority members, while an extreme economic determinist might ignore any factors other than those arising from the total economic context. A third focus is on the immediate situation confronting the minority and majority group members when they interact, which may synthesize the two views.[28]

The aspects of the middleman situation which draws the attention are:

1. External conditions of the larger society and the economic niches of the minority
2. The situation of the stranger/sojourner/pariah
3. The attributes of the minority: (a) culture; (b) internal cohesion; and (c) objective visibility
4. Socioeconomic explanations of anti-Semitism

Cohen more than others has focused attention on the internal organization of the minority. This kind of discussion is helpful in understanding acculturation, separatism, and assimilation as it affects middleman groups. It focuses our attention on how groups may be labeled strangers or pariahs rather than merely assuming that any ethnic group specializing in trade or consisting of those who are self-employed is considered to be alien by its neighbors.

At the present time, the interest in the relationships between ethnicity and economics is active. There have been several symposia at scholarly meetings on middleman minorities and related topics. New works in the field are appearing, and research is spreading beyond a small core of social scientists.

Refutation

Opposition and refutation of middleman-minority theories exist. Those who deny the comparability of the different groups obviously fit into this category. To a certain extent, so do those such as Sombart and Milton Friedman who see middleman minorities as simply capitalists without special characteristics.

A recent refutation of economic competition as a root-cause

of ethnic conflict was put forth by Donald Horowitz. In this argument, he presents arguments against Bonacich among others.

Horowitz marks out the field of his comparison as one in which ethnic groups are not ranked into rigid castes, although some ranking is always present. In most empirical cases, as in Africa and Asia, he claims that economic competition is limited by an ethnic division of labor. Recruitment to work in particular industries or sectors is through kin and former locals. Particular ethnic groups express preferences for jobs which usually avoid friction with other groups.

Sometimes, members of the majority group do compete directly with minority businessmen. In those cases, however, they frequently get little support from majority clients of the minority middlemen. In cases where governments give preferences to majority businesses in order to break the minority's monopoly, they, in fact, may create commercial rivalries.

Horowitz also cites many instances in which clients could have vented their anger on minority middlemen during periods of instability and chose not to. He tends to attribute hostility against commercial minorities to elites, such as university students. The latter are overrepresented in attitudinal studies. Horowitz, in general, diminishes the role of realistic economic interests as the foundation of ethnic political conflict.

In the conflict of unranked groups, he gives group entitlement a prime role. This term refers to the group's sense of its worth and legitimacy (for example, its honor). He believes that, when this psychology of group comparison is combined with the analysis of intragroup variability, the political party system, and other institutional constraints, one can explain the passionate and symbolic aspects of group conflict. Horowitz, as a political scientist, is uninterested in the reasons for ethnic occupational specializations which has engaged sociologists like Light and Bonacich. He also may overly diminish the importance of economic causes for ethnic antagonism. Still, there is considerable convergence between his views and those expressed in this book.[29]

External Conditions and Economic Niches

In explaining the particular economic conditions which give rise to the specialization of certain ethnic groups as middlemen, several social scientists have pointed to the existence of a status gap. The status gap has been defined as "the yawning social void which occurs when superordinates and subordinate portions of a society are not bridged by continuous, intermediate degrees of status."[30] A status gap in the literal sense, however, need not be present to provide for open niches in an economic system which beg for filling.[31] Several social settings have such openings which, whether or not they are full status gaps, will be discussed here.

An agrarian society based primarily on a subsistence economy may develop a status gap with the introduction of luxury goods through monetary trade. In such a setting, the feudal lords of the ruling elite disdain commercial activity and the peasantry does not possess the necessary skills. The classic case is that of Jews in the medieval-European economy prior to the Crusades.[32]

Very similar is the situation of a newly conquered colonial area, ruled by an imperial elite and in which the indigenes lack the knowledge and skills to participate fully in the export and import economies. In both of these situations, there is a situation of complementarity as the traders occupy a new niche and have not displaced others.[33]

In some settings, a particular region already has a trading group which is oriented to the old internal market. The incorporation into a wider world market, however, entails different knowledge and skills; the old trading group may be displaced by a different ethnic group oriented to a new export-import market. The Jews in sixteenth-century Poland are typical of this situation. In that period, they played an increasing role in the export of grain, while Christian merchants were not as involved in this trade. Jews were, however, excluded from trade with Muscovy.[34]

In advanced capitalist societies, large corporations such as supermarket chains may close retail outlets in remote rural areas or in impoverished urban slums. In state socialist economies, similar openings appear because of deficiencies in the state monopoly. There, black and gray markets appear. While ethnic specialization in the Soviet countereconomy has not been studied, the Soviet Georgians and the Jews have played prominent roles.[35] A debate continues as to whether the status gaps of preindustrial and colonial societies are comparable to the vacant niches in modern capitalist and socialist economies.[36]

Status gaps may be filled either through the immigration of traders, which is comparable to importing contract labor, or through the rise of an indigenous commercial class. Different societies have followed a variety of strategies in filling these gaps. It is presumed by some authors that indigenous entrepreneurs are more nationalistic, while those who immigrate are more oriented to an international market.[37]

From the perspectives of native and alien traders, the situation may be one of competition rather than complementarity, especially when one variety of skillholder has displaced another. After the Jews filled the initial status gap in medieval Europe, they were, in turn, displaced by a Christian bourgeoisie. In other situations, minority and alien traders may continue to have advantages over the natives. It is often unclear as to who is objectively a minority member or an alien, but it is in such situations of transition in which members of each group are concerned with their own group's merit.[38]

Situation of the Stranger/Sojourner/Pariah

Those who become traders and other middlemen are often distinguished from both the ruling elite and the masses by some ethnic markers, including religion, race, language, or some previous status. They are thus strangers to the majority.[39] A problem in trying to make generalizations in terms of strangers and related concepts is that they depend heavily on the perceptions and folk categories of both minority and majority groups. In some areas, people from the next village are as foreign as are people from another country. When making generalizations, positivistic social scientists are often loath to deal with these native perceptions on their own terms. We prefer a single category such as *ethnic, race,* or even *stranger* to trying to equate the relationships between *infidel* and *believer* under medieval Christendom, Islam with castes in South Asia, and *brown-yellow* relations in Indonesia. In speaking about sojourning and settling, one must disentangle the complicated motives of migrants from the complex perceptions of permanent residents. It is important to realize that terms such as *stranger* are a type of shorthand.

Social thinkers have introduced the concept of the stranger in terms of a model of an isolated folk society beginning to be connected to a larger world through trade.[40] The outsider has advantages in monetary dealings precisely because he does not face the same kinds of demands for reciprocity which confront members of the group. This reduces the stress of commerce which threatens the "folk" moral order, and the trader, in turn, is threatened by the moral demands of this society. His opportunism and mobility aid him in remaining objective. Often, he belongs to a different ethnic group than do his clients. On this aspect, Brian Foster wrote, "The ethnic difference has the effect of reducing the conflict inherent in face-to-face commercial transactions."[41]

The fact that the trader is a stranger gives him a paradoxical advantage. He is attractive as a confidant because he is socially distant. He is more likely to keep a secret and aid the natives in doing certain things without the knowledge of the latters' sometimes antagonistic kin. A variety of roles from moneylender to court physician are thus open to the stranger. Especially important for the trader in this aspect are credit relationships. At the same time, he is stigmatized and barred from competing for authority and prestige.[42]

If the trader treats his clients as objects, he and his fellows may be treated similarly. While medieval cities took varying degrees of wealth into account in assessing taxes of citizens, all Jews were obliged to pay the same tax, regardless of economic position.[43]

Still, the tension and conflict arising from commerce are not eliminated by traders belonging to a different ethnic group than the people surrounding them. The tension is simply shifted from the interpersonal level to another in dealing with it. Shifting the conflict to the level of interethnic relations is made possible by the police power of the state.[44]

Societies with governments can back up the definitions which develop. They may encourage the separatism of the minority. The definition of a caste hierarchy in India is one example. Another is the way in which traditional Christian and Muslim states have tolerated infidels but suppressed heretics. Modern colonial and national governments allow the importation of labor and control stranger groups through designated leaders. They make laws and rules preventing them from owning land or entering civil service. They limit eligibility for citizenship and thus may actually facilitate the creation of a class of sojourners.[45] Through inhibiting contact or facilitating assimilation they may create or disperse a class of strangers. The alien minority can serve the elite as taxpayers, tax collectors, concessionaires, or providers of credit and luxury goods. Because the strangers are relatively weak and lack authority (although not always power), they provide the rulers with deniability for wrongdoing and a ready scapegoat. They are given protection, except when their services as scapegoats are needed. Their relationship with the elite makes them ready servants of power, yet, as strangers, they are suspected of treason. The strangers' proximity to power may also offend the honor of the legitimate elite and mass majority members.[46]

The insecurity of the strangers' position—especially when their original intention was only to sojourn in a particular place—makes it unlikely that they will invest extensively in land or in heavy industry. In a period of economic nationalism, this subjects strangers to the charge of sending money out of the country and exploiting the natives. A problem in dealing with the liquid investments of minorities is the difficulty in defining liquidity because investments in diamonds, stocks, or even truck farms can all be considered as relatively liquid.[47]

For those leaders who are interested in mobilizing their peoples to produce more, to invest in the local economy, and to achieve both economically and intellectually, there is a disadvantage in importing strangers who may be considered as pariahs or infidels. Persons with such stigmas are not considered to be models for majority elite behavior. For example, no Pole before World War II would model himself after a Jew. On the other hand, if the economic innovators—even members of religious and ethnic minorities—can sell themselves as being integrally native, then their behavior is likely to provide a model. The difference between stranger and native is not absolute and is a question of cognition as well as objective features.[48]

ATTRIBUTES OF ALIEN MIDDLEMEN

Cultural Attributes

In the preceding section on the situation of the stranger, the position of middlemen was considered generally and primarily in terms of how others view them. Ethnic groups, however, may be, in part, responsible for their persistence as middleman minorities and may bear cultures which assist in their adaptation to these niches.[49] The cultural patterns which have been attributed to middleman groups by different authorities are not always consistent, one with the other. As we have seen, Weber and Sombart differed as to the attributes of Judaism and Puritanism. The patterns discerned are discussed below even though they may be contradictory.

Middleman minorities tend to assimilate slowly because of their separatist complex. The most important constituents of this are (1) ritualistic segregation of the group, including a ban on marriages with other groups, rejection of mixed offspring, and restrictions on eating with outsiders; (2) loyalty to their original language which continues to be used, especially through special schools; and (3) a double standard of morality. The latter is expressed in dealings with outsiders, such as lending to them with interest, unscrupulous selling practices, and providing outsiders with illicit means for gratifying their appetites, while at the same time, denying the same means to ingroup members.[50]

Particular group practices are related to the separatism and ethnocentrism of the group. For instance, members of the Ibadi sect of Islam from the Mzab in southern Algeria and the island of Jerba off Tunisia have become merchants in the northern regions of their respective countries. They do not, however, allow their wives to accompany them. The men from these areas spend most of their working years away from home, returning for brief visits, and finally retiring to their hometowns. They are classic sojourners with the pattern enforced by religious and cultural norms.[51]

Ideologically, such patterns of self-segregation are supported by various beliefs, such as the castes of India and a "chosen people" complex. A strong attachment to the old home and desire to return to it may be included, even though groups may have strong migratory tendencies. This provides the groups with high morale, self-esteem, and sublimation of any feelings of vengeance which may result from rejection. For many individuals, religious and ideological reasons may be the motivation for following the group's modal occupation. For most others, of course, the economic adaptation they have made dictates commitment to the group. If circumstances alter, however—such as a Jewish banker being offered the opportunity to become a Christian nobleman and landowner—they may switch groups.[52]

The preferred family form is the patrilineal, virilocal extended family. This permits the formation of family firms and the use of the unpaid labor of relatives. Such a family form is usually supported by a strong familistic value system. This is an important constituent of group solidarity. If such a family is indeed associated with middleman minorities generally, the role of women must be taken into account. The relationship of gender has not been considered much in research on trading minorities, though in West Africa and other parts of the world, women have played a significant role in trade.[53]

Economic behavior has been a key element in the discussion of middleman minority culture. In addition to the dual standard of morality and the family firm, other traits have been suggested as affecting economic behavior, including:

1. Rational and unfair economizing behavior, such as price-cutting, saving, hard work, austere living, postponement of gratification and willingness to work for lower socioeconomic returns to other groups in the society[54]
2. Future orientation and high achievement motivation[55]
3. An orientation to life marked by restraint and self-control[56]
4. Economic activity viewed as a necessity, but not as the goal of life[57]
5. Specialization in labor-intensive occupations requiring only moderate amounts of capital and utilizing credit provided by family and other ethnic group members[58]

Despite the fact that cultural attributes are considered by many to be a major factor in the creation and persistence of these minorities, they have been studied in a superficial manner. We have not advanced much beyond Weber and Sombart. Up to now, we have dealt primarily with the economic behavioral manifestations, rather than delving more thoroughly into the residues of past experience and the total world outlook of members of these ethnic groups.[59]

Ethnic Cohesion

Intimately tied to the cultural attributes of middleman minorities is the degree of ethnic solidarity displayed by these groups. Both those who favor cultural theories and those advocating contextual and situational explanations for the phenomenon of middleman groups see the internal cohesion of the groups—expressed in their segregation, their high degree of morale, and their capacity for mutual aid—as important variables. For the culturalists, these are independent variables.

One task in considering ethnic solidarity is to define the parameters of this aspect more clearly. Another task is to specify those factors which contribute to the breakdown of the solidarity of these minorities and the degree to which this affects middleman roles.

The specific ways in which this solidarity may be manifested include:

1. Ban on out-group marriage;
2. Residential self-segregation;
3. Use of kin and ethnic ties for preferential economic treatment and organizing capital, especially with regard to hiring and credit;

4. Occupational specialization by ethnicity;
5. Leisure-time association with coethnics;
6. Establishment of language and cultural schools for children (or sending children home for schooling);
7. Active participation in ethnic religion and nonparticipation in majority rites;
8. Tendency to avoid involvement in local politics, except where the ethnic group is directly affected; and
9. Maintenance of formal ethnic community organizations.[60]

Several of these characteristics overlap substantially with cultural traits attributed to middleman minorities, such as the separatist complex. They may be seen as the social manifestations of the world outlook of the minority members. There are circumstances, however, in which the government that rules a territory enforces residential and other forms of segregation with regard to the minority and rules them through a formal organization of its own creation. Governments may discourage the participation of minority members in local politics by denying them citizenship. Thus, outward manifestations of solidarity must be examined closely as to their origin and function.[61]

Of central importance, of course, are those aspects of solidarity which help the minority maintain its economic position in the society's division of labor. Occupational specialization is supported by monopolies, preferential hiring, and credit, as well as by resistance to out-group marriages, often reinforced by residential segregation. Such economic mutual aid is usually first directed at family and kin. As we have seen, the family firm is often a basic unit for middleman minorities.

After kin, people from one's hometown are preferred, followed by other subgroup members from region, dialect group, caste, sect, and so on. While there are exceptions, the primary basis for ethnic solidarity is the family and the locality of origin.

Beyond the family firm lies a broad range of formal and informal economic groupings and networks which may be ethnic markers. When properly supported by socialization, kin groups and, to a lesser extent, locality origin groups help diasporas and others resolve the dilemmas of enforcing authority and trust without resort to physical coercion. This basic dilemma of the dispersed minority must be solved if it is to carry on business. This is especially true when it involved long-distance trade, credit, and communication are involved. Some groups have been very effective in maintaining economic monopolies by perpetuating group loyalty discipline along extrakin lines. Those groups which belong to closely knit religious sects are often among the most successful.[62]

While the ethnic solidarity of middleman minorities is often seen as an important factor in both their success and their vulnerability to attack, this characteristic does not necessarily distinguish them from the elites. Such particularism is not confined to precapitalist formations and to pariah capitalists, but it is found in the higher reaches of finance and multinational corporations, such as in the city of London and in old Wall Street banks and brokerage houses.[63]

Early writings about middleman minorities implied that these groups have much cohesiveness, but did not examine the dynamics of how such groups may lose solidarity and assimilate. The usual patterns are the ones which assume that group solidarity and the status gap lead to competition, host hostility, and a final solution of genocide or expulsion. But assimilation of some minorities has occurred over time.[64]

Still, to overcome the tradition of overstressing the unity and exclusivity of middleman minorities, phenomena like self-hate, apathy, and other manifestations of assimilation on all levels must be considered. In fact, substantial facets of structural and behavioral assimilation would be met by reversing trends toward group solidarity. These include increasing intermarriage, residential integration, loss of occupational specialization, educational and expressive integration, and loss of special ethnic rituals and separate organizations.

Minority members who do assimilate develop positive preferences for the ways of the majority elite, including disdain for their own traditions and marrying nonminority members. For such assimilation to become established, the society must encourage these minority members by such means as merit selection for jobs and patronage for talented individuals who are not kin. If the middleman roles are still needed, however, it is likely that one middleman minority may be replaced by another which does similar things. Social as well as physical mobility and assimilation can help explain the peaceful succession of middleman minorities in many places. As one group leaves the less prestigious positions in society, it is succeeded by others.

Objective Visibility

Slowness to assimilate may be due to attributes of the minority group, but the group's visible differences from the majority, in and of itself limit assimilation. While some long-standing middleman groups—such as the Chinese in Southeast Asia and the Indians in Africa—are physically, as well as culturally, distinctive. Others—such as the Jews and the Armenians, despite prohibitions on intermarriage—are not as easily distinguished from their neighbors.[65]

The perception of separateness—whether in terms of visibility of group solidarity, as well as the actual traits and behaviors of the group—must be considered. Ethnic differences have a history, and certain differences—such as race in the United States or caste in India—are considered to be more fundamental in some places than others. At certain times, some groups may be more threatening than others, not only because of their actual behaviors, but because of their apparent connections with the enemy, whether it be the Devil or the Great Commissar. The other groups may be considered to be relatively innocuous.[66]

The minority groups themselves—whether of elite, middle, or low status—may utilize strategies to heighten or lower their visibility, while outsiders may try to heighten the perception of separation as well. Various movements among nineteenth-century German Jews—which sought to acculturate Jews to the dominant culture, ranging from advocacy of complete assimilation and conversion to Christianity or a neo-Orthodoxy which stressed general education and outward conformity combined with rigid observance to Jewish law—can be seen as efforts to lower Jewish visibility.[67] Whether we consider an ethnic group which has specialized in commerce and industrial enterprise as a group of strangers or as a native bourgeoisie must be seen in terms of its historical background as perceived by its members as well as by the majority of the population. It is not a fact that is obvious to the outside observer.

Host Hostility

Living as we do under the shadow of the Nazi Holocaust and in an age of continued final solutions of interethnic conflict, it is not surprising that we should focus on the hostility against minorities. The various factors which have been discussed—economic position, status as aliens, cultural attributes, cohesion, and the visibility of middleman minorities—are all seen as contributing to the arousal of hostility on the part of the majority. Conflict between the alien minority and the majority can be seen as a case of class conflict reinforced by ethnocentrism.[68]

Middleman-minority theories all stress the real socioeconomic position of the minority, but differ as to whether the context of the social scene or the qualities of the minority are the more salient causes of hostility. The former see the surrounding society as causing both the offensive commercial qualities of the group and the tragic situation which follows. The latter stresses the previous culture of the minority as causing it to take a vulnerable role in the economy. There is, however, sufficient overlap between intelligent exponents of each view so that particular causes of hostility are specified in both varieties of theory.

While there is a potential of conflict between the commercial principle and that of reciprocity at all times, and a disdain for commerce by other segments of the population, open conflict with and persecution of middleman minorities takes place only during certain periods. For those who see middleman minorities as a phenomenon of the status gap created in feudal or other traditional societies, this conflict emerges when the society evolves into a fully modern capitalist system. Others see conflict in the transition from an expanding economy to one which is contracting.[69]

In any case, such transitions have several characteristics

1. The transition results in the increasing impoverishment of certain classes and, thus, aggravates class conflict.
2. New classes arise in the majority group which have the managerial and entrepreneurial skills to compete directly with the middleman minority.
3. The apparent prominence and power of the minority may be seen as besmirching the honor of the majority and, therefore, as illegitimate.
4. The ruling elite and the new classes find the old middleman to be a convenient scapegoat for the troubles of the transition. The fact that the minority has a conspicuously disproportionate share of the total wealth of the society makes it a visible target for those who wish to plunder.[70]

In such a period the characteristics of the majority and minority ethnic groups affect the nature of the conflict and make for strongly anti-middleman popular movements, as demonstrated by: (1) visibility of the minority because of conspicuous and indelible markers; (2) coincidence of cultural, racial, and religious dividing lines with economic class conflict boundaries, rather than cross-cutting lines; and (3) lack of common symbols of identity, especially common foes.[71]

In these attributes, the presumed cohesion and cultural loyalty of the minority would work to maintain sharp boundaries between itself and the majority. In fact, the minority—whether Jewish, Chinese, Indian, or other—is frequently accused of failing to show proper loyalty and of not assimilating. Under conditions of sharp ethnic divisions, it is likely that assimilation of large numbers of minority members would be treated with a great deal of suspicion, since they would be seen as insincere. The other side of this dilemma is that assimilating minority members would be perceived as competitors, especially by those holding positions which are reserved to the majority.[72]

The absence of host-hostility, too, must be explained. First, general economic conditions may favor the absence of host-hostility, such as during a long period of economic expansion and prosperity. Barring such an ideal situation, other circumstances may inhibit mass animosity. A society with a relatively static status system—such as the traditional Indian caste system—may have less conflict than one which is highly competitive and dynamic.

If the degree of separation between the majority and the minority groups is minimized, or the minority lacks a separatist complex (with these two conditions often acting in conjunction), opposition along ethnic lines will be minimal. It is likely that, in such a situation, there will be the possibility for developing cross-cutting ties.[73]

When a situation of stable complementarity or ethnic division of labor persists, ethnic minorities may remain in a middleman position without provoking massive hostility. This is especially true of such minorities that persist in societies which recognize hierarchical division of labor and do not have a striving for unity. The classic example of this type are the Parsis of Western India.[74]

In all of the cases cited, there is something more than the objective criterion of group cohesion vis-a-vis a particular social setting. Within certain limits of plausibility, minorities and their leaders may try to minimize those aspects of their outward behavior which will threaten the majority. In societies seeking to homogenize they may seek to appear like natives, whereas, in hierarchical societies, they will stand out, but in a way befitting other castes. There are, in fact, trading ethnic groups who have utilized ethnic cohesion and combined it with local patriotism, such as the Susi Berber traders who form a large part of the small business community of Casablanca.[75]

In his famous essay, "The Self-Fulfilling Prophecy," Merton discusses Jewish visibility. Jews seek to lower their profiles, while anti-Semites seek to maximize the Jewish role in the economy in order to stress its potential threat.[76] The acts of both majority and minority members thus play a role in arousing or calming interethnic antagonism—but even then economic factors are basic. In this manipulation of images, various plausible ideologies and stereotypes—both homegrown and foreign—may be brought into play. Thus, theories which attribute hostility to prejudice and those stressing economic and political competition converge at this point.

The Interplay of the Components

In this final section of the chapter, a picture of how the different elements work together will be summarized. In current theory, minorities are usually seen as recent immigrants who come to Country A from their homelands. To avoid competition with the majority, they take on either undesirable or innovative roles in the economy. They are successful in doing this because their close familial, kin, ex-local, and further ethnic ties give them advantages in obtaining employment and credit. In fact, their mutual loyalty and trust are reinforced by common symbols to which they cling. They continue to socialize their children within this culture.

Generally, the sector of the economy in which they are concentrated is one which is labor-intensive and where small, though linked, enterprises are most successful. Such a sector appears at various stages of socioeconomic development, beginning with preindustrial agrarian societies and continuing into advanced capitalism. However, in the latest phase, it is found among the *petit bourgeoisie.*

After the initial entry into such a niche, and the success of the group in finding a special place within the economy, there are several outcomes depending on the way in which the group is perceived. The intensity of intergroup competition is intense. Those groups which are perceived as alien are likely to be expelled or even exterminated. If only one portion of the group is expelled, persecution may reinforce group loyalties of the ones who remain and thus continue to make them vulnerable.

The classic case of this outcome was that of Asians in East Africa. It is possible, however, that an ethnic group may be disintegrating internally and, thus, its members increasingly move beyond its specialized niche, thus increasing their competition with the majority.

This may have disastrous results in a troubled economy, as it did for Jews in pre–World War II Poland and Germany. For a minority in an expanding economy—such as among Japanese and Jews in postwar North America—it may make assimilation possible. A more-or-less static society in which groups tend to accept their status—may be relatively conflict-free, as in the case of premodern India. Assimilation, as opposed to group persistence, is most likely best for those groups which regardless of their economic roles, can find ways to be perceived as non-alien. Thus, stress should be placed on how groups are perceived by others, and the strategies which they use to show their affinity for as well as separation from their neighbors.

Chapter 2

Minority Moneylenders in Traditional Societies

In the previous chapter, middleman minorities have been considered generally without concentration on the various functions which they perform. In most of the chapters of this volume, such general discussion of particular groups will be continued. Still, each of the different occupations and specialties—whether they be peddling, production of ready-made ware, the trade in diamonds, or the processing and trade of rubber—have their own characteristics.

One particular function, however, whether as a separate occupation or combined with other vocations, has been crucial in the relationship of middleman minorities with their neighbors. That particular function is the provision of credit.

Lending money is a part of trade. In agricultural communities, for instance, shopkeepers and peddlers must provide goods to customers prior to harvest and on condition of later repayment. All levels of business are run with similar arrangements. Then, of course, there is full-time specialization in lending by pawnbrokers, bankers, and finance companies.

Moneylending was, for a long time, the major economic role played by Jews and Lombards in the economies of Western and Central Europe, as well as by Armenians, Chinese, and certain

Indian castes in other parts of the world. Certainly, the stereotype of the avaricious, almost cannibalistic moneylender, exemplified by Shakespeare's Shylock is a central part of the image of the Jew in European cultures. The merchant as creditor may be portrayed similarly elsewhere.

For these reasons, the relationship of minority credit to the economic and political position of these ethnic communities deserves our attention. The question of credit from the member of one ethnic group to another group brings us back to the description of the stranger noted in Chapter 1. Trust, intimacy, reciprocity, and hatred between the members of a small community and members of other groups are involved in this consideration.

Parts of this chapter will be speculative because the obscure origins of minority credit are discussed. While inferences can be made from the works of historians on medieval Europe or from contemporary ethnographies, no good case study illustrating the situation exists. Perhaps the synthetic "just-so story" concocted here can serve as a stimulus to further research. Here, attention is concentrated on what is loosely termed "traditional societies." These societies are based on premodern technology which includes dependence on agriculture and pastoralism, tools made from metal, extensive crafts specialization, and reliance on human and animal labor. Political authority is in the hands of a small ruling elite, centered in either courts and manors or in cities. The urban population is quite small, while the cultivators are the majority of the population.[1]

The need for money in such a society is variable. There are segments of such a society where most payments are made in kind, while other sectors utilize monetary exchange. As trade and crafts specialization increases, it is likely that the need for money will follow suit. Metal tools, wine, distilled liquors, coffee, tea, tobacco, rice, salt, spices, and sugar are items which have been purchased—first by the well-to-do, but later by peasants and pastoralists as well—in many parts of the Old World. At weddings and similar ceremonies, when one must show hospitality and generosity to one's kin and neighbors, such goods are especially in demand, and there will be a need for credit. Governments and landlords may prefer to be paid taxes and rents in cash rather than kind. Thus the need for money and trade is stimulated.

As this need increases, so the trader must extend credit. This happened in eleventh-century France, where Jewish merchants would give credit to customers who lacked cash. In many cases, the customers would leave some security with the merchant. This mode of loans led these merchants into professional pawnbroking.[2]

The conflict in traditional agrarian and maritime societies between the ancient distributive ethic of reciprocity and the new stress on maximization of monetary gain is quite sharp, both in medieval times and among peoples drawn into the modern-world system through colonization.[3] As already indicated, this same conflict persists in advanced capitalist and socialist societies.

In this chapter, five basic questions relating the stranger as moneylender to ethnic stratification will be considered.

1. Why and in what circumstances is the stranger needed to provide credit rather than kinsmen and unrelated neighbors of the same ethnic origin?
2. Why must lenders charge high interest in the settings considered?
3. To what extent does the creditor gain power, authority, and control over the debtors?
4. What is the relationship between the stranger-lenders and the ruling elite, especially the government?
5. What are the institutional alternatives to the moneylenders, and when do they become effective?

Most attention in this chapter will be on consumer credit in the form of moneylending in the rural areas and pawnbroking. These are the forms of moneylending most commonly associated with the rank-and-file of middleman minorities. In fact, they mark the way in which the minority member serves to link the rural and urban lower classes with the money economy.

The view of the lender will be the focus of attention here. He will be seen as a prisoner of his situation, rather than as a prime cause of the misery of his clients, as the opponents of minority middlemen have labeled them. The lender's role is seen as necessary to certain types of socioeconomic formations.

The Stranger as Lender

The first question is why turn to a stranger for a loan in the first place?

Borrowing can be connected to a chain of obligations which extends from close kin to distant kin and unrelated, coethnic, neighbors, and then to strangers.

In an egalitarian folk society, the primary mode of transactions would be in the form of reciprocity, and various strands of moral obligations would be dense with one's close kin. It is only with distant kin and strangers that one can borrow and lend in a direct way without some of the entanglements implicit in relations with kin. The stranger provides an additional advantage to the borrower, because he is less interested in why the borrower wants the money. The latter is better able to keep a secret and maintain a measure of privacy with strangers. One applies the *lex talionis* (an eye for an eye) to strangers, and it is distant kin and strangers from whom one borrows.[4]

The Pentateuchal laws (Deut. 23: 20–21) which permits the taking of interest from foreigners relate this:

> You shall not deduct interest from loans to your countrymen, whether in money or food or anything else that can be deducted as interest. You may deduct interest from loans to foreigners, but not from loans to your countrymen...

The Deuteronomic statute represents the pole of "tribal brotherhood," to use Nelson's description of how lending reflects the movement from a folkish moral order for the ingroup to the objective relationships of modern industrial society "from tribal brotherhood to universal otherhood."[5] The nexus of primary relationships, of course, persists even with the growth of the monetary sector of an economy. Here, too, we find a contrast of lending to kinsmen, coethnics, and neighbors, as opposed to strangers.

All lending involves some risk of nonrepayment. In the case of close relatives and friends, this risk is greater since one is less likely to foreclose on the security of a loan or otherwise force repayment when it may jeopardize other strands of a relationship. In Thai villages, tradesmen are generally more isolated in the social networks of a village than are those in other occupations. Borrowing and lending is highly charged emotionally, and social distance is one way in which to handle the tensions on both sides of such a link.[6]

A society where social bonds are loosening may actually have to prevent individuals from charging interest within the community. The Deuteronomic prohibition discussed earlier, was the result of increasing class cleavage. But the result of various measures to prevent usury and to aid ingroup debtors may actually result in the tightening of credit, such as a moratorium on debts every seven years (Deut. 15: 2–3). This moratorium was, in effect, annulled in the famous Prozbul of Hillel, which permitted the claiming of debts by creditors, even after the sabbatical year.

Difficulty in obtaining loans within the community may be handled in other ways. Social pressure may make it shameful to obtain loans from professional lenders or from outsiders, as among the Chinese traders in Papua, New Guinea. In that ethnic community, there are also sanctions on those Chinese who do not repay their loans.[7]

Despite the strains of credit within the family network, such loans are common in many places. Among Malay fishermen, seasonal interest-bearing loans may be obtained from wealthier kin. In Chiapas, Mayan-ritual kin relationships and drinking ceremonies are used to get loans. Elsewhere, kinsmen and friends may exchange capital through gifts and similar forms of reciprocity, as well as direct loans. In India's many villages, about one-third of outstanding loans were from kindred or family, according to one survey of rural credit.

Even in the industrial United States, many turn to members of their nuclear and extended families for loans. Small businesses are generally financed by the savings of other entrepreneurs like themselves or with the help of friends and family members. Such familiar transactions, however, are a major cause of quarrels with kin. It is likely that loans among kinsmen tend to be of shorter term than other loans, and there is less pressure to repay directly. As a recent popular article points out, a family loan is more than a banking transaction. The interest is emotional, and the kin relationship itself is at risk.[8]

There are means by which members of a group may extend credit and preserve primary group ties at the same time. The rotating credit association, about which much has been written, is just such a device. A rotating credit association is formed around the core of participants who agree to make regular contributions to a fund which is given, in whole or in part, to each contributor in turn. Such associations have been reported in Europe, Asia, Africa, Latin America, and the Caribbean. Rotating credit, however, is no more reliable than the least honest member of the group.

If the members are largely unknown to each other, one is likely to run off with the bank. On the other hand, where there is group solidarity, sanctions against borrowing from strangers, and group members with adequate resources, such associations may be a good basis for group enterprise, as among some overseas Chinese.[9]

Aside from freedom from entangling relationships, the absence or unreliability of other institutions, and the available cash of the stranger, there are other possible advantages in dealing with the outsider. For instance, the stranger is likely to keep secrets, including that of the borrower's impoverished state, because, for many people, pauperism is a stigma. Another advantage is special to the institution of the pawnshop: it is possible for the borrower simply to relinquish his security and not repay the loan. In this, pawnbrokers who can resell the pawn differ from banks and other lenders who must have repayment.[10]

Another reason for borrowing from strangers is derived from their weak and exposed position in many societies. Alien lenders of middle or low status will be more likely, because of their vulnerability, to defer to their clients, even if they are of low status.

This weakness is shown in different ways. The state may force moneylenders to lend at unprofitable rates, as Venice did to Jewish pawnbrokers in the sixteenth century. It may declare moratoria on loans to strangers. It may make it particularly difficult to deal with powerful borrowers for their valuable securities cannot be resold and lenders are often unable to foreclose. The state and church may cast the low-level moneylending of strangers into the category of licensed sins—or worse, along the lines of prostitution and gambling.[11]

A vulnerable lender may be desired by borrowers because such creditors may not be in a position to demand repayment. In premodern Iran, Muslim borrowers were not legally bound to repay Jewish lenders, though the latter could threaten the borrower with a boycott by other Jewish lenders.[12] During times of upheaval, minority lenders—such as the Chinese in postwar Indonesia—might also find it difficult to demand repayment.[13]

The weakness of minority lenders makes it likely that they will lend at a slightly lower rate of interest. They are less likely to foreclose on peasant land or other security. Sometimes they may substitute the receipt of usufruct rights for actual possession of the land, which, as aliens, they cannot utilize. On the other hand, a member of the indigenous elite may seek possession.[14]

The stranger should be someone who is proximate physically but distant socially. One needs the lender as someone who can be trusted. The lender also needs to know enough about the borrower to assess the risk. Yet the relationship is a hardheaded one. There must be mechanisms to maintain distance. Along with other ethnic factors—such as race, language, and nationality—religion is extremely important. Thus, Jews and excommunicated Christians provided loans in medieval Christendom, while Chinese were the lenders among the Muslims of Indonesia, Malaysia, and elsewhere.[15]

One may still ask the question, "Why must the stranger be of a separate ethnic group?" After all, there are often members of the majority groups present who are not kin.

As indicated in chapter 1, the statuses of stranger and native are manipulable. In medieval Germany, Lombards could be viewed as fellow Christians and as aliens, while Jews speaking a German dialect could be perceived as locals, albeit infidels.[16]

Even with that, however, the stranger has an advantage. If we assume that credit inherently conflicts with expectations of generosity, honesty, and fairness, then the stranger of an entirely different group is entirely outside the orbit of the group and is not even potentially kin. At the same time, the hostility toward a human who violates expected reciprocity as creditors do can be displaced from the ingroup to the outgroup.[17]

In the Indian villages of Mauritius, most shopkeepers are Chinese, who differ ethnically from their clients. By staying apart, they are in a better position to withhold credit than Indian shopkeepers are, since the latter have close kin and other social ties with fellow villagers. Burton Benedict wrote, "Close relations, such as kinship ties inhibit the creditor-debtor relationship."[18]

The Business of Moneylending

While the provision of credit to cultivators and the urban poor is a necessary social service in a monetary economy, the high price which the borrowers must pay has been blamed for the continued impoverishment of these classes. This charge is made against moneylenders, whether or not they are members of ethnic minorities. The economic arguments revolve around the degree to which high rates of interest which lenders charge are derived from an unfair advantage or monopoly profit. Alternative explanations for the high interest rates stress risk, administrative costs, and opportunity costs borne by the lenders.[19] This situation has been examined with particular regard to two types of lenders: the rural merchant and the urban pawnbroker.

The problem of monopoly profit is especially acute with regard to the "lender-cum-merchant-cum-middleman." In many rural areas in developing nations, there are no banks and few individuals who engage in shopkeeping, buying of agricultural surplus, and the like. The nonspecialized lender in such a market with relatively small volume often has a monopoly. Since the market is small, there are few who enter it. Because he is the sole supplier in many cases, he can put pressure on the small-holding cultivator to sell him his entire surplus when he lends him what the latter needs. The advantages of this connection are great.[20]

There were social as well as economic reasons for this monopolistic tendency. Social and religious prohibitions against lending on interest could be circumvented in various ways.

For instance, a shopkeeper may accept payment in kind for a monetary loan (or for goods ordinarily sold at a set price), and then he will take part of the harvest and sell it at a higher price. The creditor may also receive certain services from the debtor. Restrictions on usury or caste specialization limits the number of people who become lenders; these, in turn, tend to be related to each other. They can prevent other members of their own ethnic group or caste from competing with them. Medieval Jewish communities, for instance, restricted the number of Jews who could reside in a particular community and go into a particular business.[21]

There is a symbiotic relationship between the peasant and the lender. If the lender is a shopkeeper who supplies the small-holder with goods which he does not grow, the farmer must sell him his produce to pay off the debt. The small-holder also needs the long-term relationship with the merchant. A dealer may reduce interest charges to long-term patrons, so that a small-holder will suffer by transferring his business to another trader. The older the relationship—even beyond the present generation—the more likely that interest rates will be lower, since risks are lower. If someone transfers his business from another trader—especially if he leaves unpaid debts behind—the more fearful is the new dealer that he will be treated similarly.[22] Thus, there is a penalty in change.

Both the lender and the borrower have power over each other. Lenders may not lend to those who do not repay when they are able. For this reason, lenders must know their clientele well.

On the other hand, the lender who forecloses on the land of a peasant may face boycotts on the part of villagers, and he may be forced out. The lender with whom a borrower has a special relationship protects the latter against bad harvests and may continue to lend to him, even without interest, during periods of stress. Thus, the two are tied to one another.[23]

As this premise indicates, even when a monopoly exists, there are limits on the profits which can be derived from it. Two closely related factors are the risk of default and opportunity costs.

Opportunity costs means that the lender ties his money up in a loan, so that he loses other—often quite profitable—opportunities to invest his money elsewhere. The liquidity of those who lend to farmers is highly limited. Money loans are seasonal and are made on the basis of the cultivator's future harvests. Thus, one's principal is not convertible for that period. At the same time, the risks of nonpayment because of a bad harvest and the like are great. Delays in payment are quite common.[24]

The fact that most loans, as is the number of borrowers, are small, means that administrative costs in these rural areas are high, especially for a full-time lending institution like a bank. The lack of transportation facilities—as well as the socioeconomic relations which tie borrowers to old creditors—prevent the full use of such institutions in large market towns and cities. They prevent the rise of competition, too.

The fact that those who actually provide credit are engaged in general trade lowers the administrative costs, simultaneously perpetuating a monopoly. This also makes it worthwhile for unspecialized trader-lenders to continue, while banks and credit unions remain centered in urban areas.

The need to borrow, of course, varies on bases other than purely agricultural ones. Ceremonies such as weddings are often occasions for heavy borrowing. When the farmer is not dependent on credit for food, fertilizer, payment of taxes, or ceremonial occasions, he will not borrow frequently. Where credit is needed for these plus capital investment, the need to borrow will be great. It is likely that some peasants will actually profit from the indebtedness of others during periods of expansion. On the other hand, those who wish to enlarge their land holdings may be those most in debt.[25]

Up to this point in the book, agricultural credit has been discussed as if it is a single entity around the world. Obviously, there are wide variations.

First of all, there is a difference between the economy of a feudal manor with serfs in which rent is paid in kind, and a capitalist cash-crop economy where all must pay taxes as well as purchase goods with money. The feudal economy was accompanied by such conditions as poor transportation, an inflexible labor force, and little expansion of credit facilities. Some differences between the situations of cultivators is due to the nature of produce. Government policies—such as licensure for trade in certain products—may also affect the situation by encouraging a monopoly.[26]

A particular historical example can illustrate how these factors may impinge on each other. In eighteenth-century and nineteenth-century Bengal, peasants—especially cotton weavers—were adversely affected by the work market. To take advantage of the new technology which had arisen in Europe, peasants would have had to save through extreme parsimony and individualistic achievement. Market conditions did not permit that. Neither did the peasant's social setting which forced peasants to expend great resources on weddings.

Paradoxically, as Marshall Hodgson wrote: an expensive wedding as a group delight can be less expensive than long-term investment for individual enterprise. The peasants were also injured by British colonial law which gave moneylenders increasing power to foreclose. The uncorrupt impersonality of the British Indian courts and the negative attitude toward commercial expenditure favored the moneylenders in the short run and ruined the local cotton weaving industry.[27]

Pawnbroking shares some characteristics with the type of rural lending that has been discussed. It is also a form of short-term, high-risk lending, which must be distinguished from such aspects of banking as deposit banking and international transfer of funds, although the same person did all of these tasks in some periods. Pawnbroking is merely the transfer of purchasing power from the lender to the borrower.

As pawnbroking rarely involves capital investment, it is "barren money," devoted to consumption and cannot be used without being spent. Just as the rural lender is connected to the role of agricultural middleman, so pawnbroking is joined to the second-hand trade. Unredeemed securities must be reconditioned and sold. It is logical to see how pawnbroking and the sale of used goods could lend themselves to the requirement of the professional fence, serving as a community of thieves.[28]

The net profit of the licensed pawnbroker is low, despite the high interest which he charges. His administrative costs are high, including the often extortionate license fees of medieval cities, rent on a suitable house, the wages of servants and employees, commissions of canvassers seeking business, interest on till money, and the sale of forfeited pledges, often at a loss. His opportunity costs include the idleness of his money while holding a pledge. His risks include loss through theft, insolvency, and the loss-in-value of unredeemed pledges. Licensure, however, insured a measure of monopoly, especially when a city contracted with a special group such as Jews or Lombards.[29]

Generally, the pawnbroker's profit is low, and he lacks money for reinvestment. He may profit best from his high rate of interest, but this leaves him with little incentive for new enterprises, which generally have a low return in the short run. There are exceptional situations, however, where pawnbroking provided the capital base to move into other lines of business.

In general, the urban moneylender faces the same dilemmas as his rural counterpart. However, to be too liberal invites losses, while too much caution drives business away. He is likely to lend with no surety to those with high financial standing than to the poor.[30] (See Figure 1.)

The high costs borne by the lender and passed on to the borrower through interest charges are not understood by the latter and, obviously, exacerbate the animosity between the two. Opportunity costs in particular will be seen only as unfair profits. This point should not be overdrawn. In addition to licensed pawnshops, there are others who may lend money with lower costs in urban contexts including peddlers such as the installment sellers in twentieth-century Chicago. Pawnbrokers also thrive alongside gambling as in Las Vegas. There are situations in which pawnbroking may be sufficiently profitable to lead to reinvestment in other enterprises.

Solidarity and Moneylenders

For both pawnbrokers and rural lender-traders, costs are cut through their connections with kin and coethnics in the same or related businesses. The tobacco trade in seventeenth-century Westphalia was in Jewish hands, and the processing of natural rubber in Malaysia and Indonesia has been a Chinese monopoly. In Venice, Jewish merchants helped the pawnbrokers stay in business when the government forced them to maintain unprofitably low interest rates. Among themselves, the various trader-lenders and pawnbrokers assist each other through interest-free or low-interest loans, and through a system of trust enforced by threats of ostracism and boycott.[31] The general economic strength of these minorities reinforces their abilities to provide credit in the often credit-short sectors of the society in which they work.

Entry into the Lending Niche

As noted at the beginning of this chapter, entry into pawnbroking and other moneylending activities is, in most cases, the concomi-

FIGURE 1

Pawnbrokers' Cost of Doing Business (in New York State)

1. Security—Often two electronic security services are utilized at an expense of more than $500 per month for each location.
2. Storage—Bank vault charges are often $1000 per year. Internal vault and safe installation may cost approximately $25,000 or more.
3. Record keeping—Records of each transaction must, by statute, be written in as many as seventeen places.
4. Insurance—As much as $20,000 per location for premiums.
5. Wages—Average shop has from fifteen to forty-four employees.
6. Rent—Rent per location must compete with other storefront businesses on the street.
7. Printing and office supplies—Statute requires extensive forms and printing expense.
8. License fee—$500 per year, per location.
9. Postage—Minimum of two registered notices and usually three are sent. Postage was $.01, now $.15. Our rate hasn't changed.
10. Losses—Pawnbrokers suffer losses by changes in market (the price of gold, diamonds, or whatever is dealt with), obsolescence (as with watches and cameras), errors in judgment (mistaking cypic zirconium, fake diamonds, fake gold, and ersatz watches), and stolen merchandise. Pawnbrokers also suffer losses due to questions of title. Attorneys must defend pawnbrokers in court.
11. Auctioneers' fees—Eight to 10 percent of the sale price.
12. Advertising of sale—Must be advertised six days in three newspapers as to item, date, time, and place.

Supplied to author by Mark Kress on behalf of Pawnbrokers Association, City of New York, 1980.

tant of mercantile activities. This was the situation of Jewish pawnbrokers in eleventh-century France and of modern trader-lenders in developing nations, whether they are of the minority or of the majority. Some odd historical circumstances exist which lead to a group's entry into lending. Many Sikhs in Malaya started lending money to laborers when they served as watchmen in towns, a movement from one low position to another. In the case of medieval Jews and Lombards, pawnbroking was the result of being forced out of higher status activity.[32]

The Jews and Lombards were specialized in medieval Europe as moneylenders. The Jews appear to have entered Western Europe as traders, but they were forced into the more marginal occupations of pawnbroking and trade in second-hand goods as Christians came to dominate the emerging monetary economy. Pawnbroking was the result of displacement.

Despite the fact that Jews and Lombards are seen in some settings in their capacity as pawnbrokers, this was not the only specialty in which they appear. In some countries, they were involved in international transfer of funds and deposit banking. Even in thirteenth-century Perpignan, France, where the initial role played by Jews was in lending, they were more than pawnbrokers, and the period of moneylending was followed by one in which Jews had a variety of other occupations.

In India, and among overseas Indians, while there is also a tendency to have ethnic groups and subcastes specializing in moneylending, immigration is a feature of entry. The Pathans in South India, the Marwaris in the Bombay Deccan, and the Sikhs and Chettiars in Southeast Asia were all fairly recent immigrant groups. Chettiars from Madras may have engaged in such occupations for a long time, while the Sikhs and the Pathans began to become moneylenders only in recent generations.[33]

While the Jews, Lombards, and some Indian castes as aggregates seemed to be fixed in the role of moneylenders for long periods of time, close examination reveals a constant—albeit circular—change of occupation for the individual communities and families.

Opposition to Jewish and Lombard moneylending, opportunities in other occupations, emigration, and assimilation all caused descendants of the original moneylenders to leave these occupations. While agricultural credit and pawnbroking do not, on their own qualities, lend themselves to great expansion, opportunities for the lender may arise, and he may abandon his rural store or pawnshop and enter a new more lucrative enterprise.

Usury, Prestige, and Power

Both the pawnbroker and the rural lender fill a niche in the monetary economy which larger and more prestigious institutions are loath to fill—that of providing loans to high-risk borrowers. They can be seen both as those who profit from the hardship of others and as providers of a philanthropic service. Since the status of the recipient of the services is low, so is the prestige of the provider. As Polanyi wrote, "he who trades for the sake of duty and honor grows rich, he who trades for filthy lucre remains poor."[34]

This is comparable to the relative status of other providers of social services. The psychiatrist who has affluent clients has a much higher position than the public assistance caseworker, and the university professor's social status is much higher than that of a kindergarten teacher.[35]

This principle can be similarly illustrated with moneylenders. In medieval Flanders, the Italian merchant-bankers with their consuls and the local moneychangers were quite respectable, while Lombard pawnbrokers were social pariahs, often denied communion at church. Paintings of the period portray the moneychanger as an honorable citizen, while the pawnbroker is viewed as venal.

The pawnshop is stationary. Entering the pawnshop involves movement into the space of the broker, which, if one belongs to a more prestigious group, might be seen as lowering oneself. This was the case when Christians entered Jewish pawnshops in the Middle Ages. A recent study has shown that most such borrowers in Picardy, a region of France, were women, often accompanied by children. This could be interpreted as an unnatural dependency on Jews in a hierarchical setting.[36]

While the status of these moneylenders was low, as the history of moneylending groups indicates, it was not static. They could still achieve greater wealth, status, and power. Like middleman minorities in general, however, the contradiction between their potential wealth and the limits of their power and prestige was ever present.[37]

Moneylenders often require power in enforcing their demands, whether they are backed by the legitimate powers of the state, through courts of law or the police, or are illicitly purchased by protection. The moneylenders, however, may acquire recognition through licenses from the government.

While these licenses may be challenged—as when a medieval Christian state permitted the practice of usury—they generally provided the lender with coercive power.

The monopolies which minority lenders maintain in trade are also a form of power. This kind of power, however, is not recognized authority.[38]

On the other hand, moneylenders rarely are communal leaders, and, in modern times, are usually not elected to office. In Iranian villages, shopkeepers may be wealthy but they are suspect because of their lending activities and are rarely elected to political office. A Chinese shopkeeper in an Indian village on Mauritius who entered politics was threatened by a factional boycott. Indian village shopkeepers there generally kept out of politics. Here again, there is the paradox of economic power without political authority.

The isolated and nearly powerless position of stranger-lenders is due to this contradiction.[39] With regard to medieval Aragon-Catalonia, Shneidman wrote, "Without royal protection the Jews' money was meaningless."[40]

In fact, the Jew had to pay dearly for the protection. But "Jewishness" or alien status were not necessarily the causes for this lack of power. Native lenders could, of course, have similar difficulties. Still engaging in a dubiously legitimate practice reinforces estrangement.

By taxing the minority lenders, the officials of the ruling class profit from the taking of interest. They may become more involved by becoming silent or open partners of the lenders, such as did some medieval clerics and notables who made huge profits by acquiring bonds of loans contracted with Jews at substantial discounts. They were able to profit, in part, because they could collect outstanding debts more readily than could the weaker Jews.[41]

At times, those with greater power, may be more directly involved. In nineteenth-century western India, many of the moneylenders were Brahmins and village headmen. While less direct hostility was directed against them than against immigrant lenders from a lower—albeit nonpariah—caste (the Marwaris), they were more interested in acquiring land through foreclosure than the Marwaris.[42]

The political leader and the noble landowner may become creditors, but their relations with the debtors are different from that of alien lenders. The landowner and the politician often have many-stranded relationships, whereas the alien has a relationship with debtors based primarily on commercial transactions. Thus, the ties which the latter has are more fragile and more likely to be broken in times of crisis.

Assuming that the political and military ties continue to bind landowner and politician with peasant, the former would be more willing to pardon the debts of his underlings or seek repayment on some social basis, rather than demand monetary payment. This the trader-lender and the pawnbroker cannot do.

Of course, when the social and political ties are broken and only economic connections persist, *noblesse oblige* is likely to be forgotten.[43]

The minority moneylender is a convenient scapegoat for both the ruling elite and the masses during times of crisis. If the minority lenders cease to be useful as providers of credit and revenue, their vulnerability increases. If more revenue is sought by the state and the minority provides less credit, then it is likely that landowners and wealthy peasants will be in a better position to acquire more land. This is especially true as the monetization of economy has increased, and land has become an alienable commodity.[44]

Unless there is a thoroughgoing revolution—and in some cases, even when there is such revolution—antiusury regulations are likely to be directed specifically at minority lenders rather than at all those who lend at high rates of interest. Alsace, in 1806 and 1808, were untouched, even though Christian moneylenders in France charged even higher rates of interest than the Jews.[45]

Opposition and Reforms

Being involved in riots, decrees, and political movements aimed at moneylenders—and at middleman minorities in general—is more than an immediate situational reaction. After all, moneylending is a break in ordinary reciprocal relations between people. It is a violation of a moral order in which the accumulation of goods by some is a form of communal insurance for all.

In conjunction with the redistributive ethic, there is a strain of puritanism which seeks to restrict consumption, investment, and displays of opulence. While it is difficult to control the consumption of the ruling elites, many people feel that one must restrain the extravagance of the poor. This is especially the case when the poor are dependent on others for their subsistence.

In agrarian societies, the priestly class often functioned as the preserver of this redistributive ethic, while, in modern times, intellectuals have undertaken this task. These groups have moved beyond the immediate situation to formulate opposition to a monetary economy. They have often stressed some sort of "brotherhood" or "otherhood." It should be noted that, while having access to the ruling elites, many religious functionaries and intellectuals were less opulent than others in their families who chose more lucrative professions, thus making the former open to advocacy of a puritanical egalitarianism.

In those areas of the world—such as medieval Christendom, where lending on interest was prohibited—the moneylender was a natural target. When the lender was both an alien unbeliever and a violator of the redistributive ethic, he was doubly vulnerable.

The lender was blamed for the extravagance of the borrower as well. He was seen as leading the poor into temptation. In the fifteenth and sixteenth centuries, the Franciscan campaign against moneylenders had a particularly adverse effect on the Jews in Europe.[46]

In modern times, secular intellectual and political leaders have taken up this cause from the priestly class. These include nationalists, socialists, fascists, and imperialist philanthropists.[47]

Reform, of course, requires more than merely removing the moneylenders, for one group of lenders will just be replaced by another, perhaps even more exploitative, group. Reform measures have included regulation of interest rates, new types of lending institutions, and a total social revolution.

The third reform is the most costly, but the other two have their problems. Regulation of high interest rates has long been the subject of debate among economists. While advocates have stressed its positive effects on increasing investment, others have pointed out that a ceiling on interest rates may actually make it more difficult for small borrowers to obtain loans. It may even open up the way for loan sharks. In fact, during the great "credit crunch" of the 1970s and 1980s in the United States, many states abolished their usury laws.[48]

Institutions to replace lenders who lend for their own personal profit have included special philanthropic pawnshops—such as the *monte di pieta* operating in Italy and other Catholic countries during the fifteenth and sixteenth centuries, and modern agricultural banks. In modern industrial societies, of course, pawnshops and installment dealers or tallymen have been displaced by large corporate banking and modern forms of credit, such as credit cards, as much as they have been by reform institutions.

While there are important differences between early modern and contemporary lending institutions, there is much that they share.

1. They have been established to provide low-interest loans to those in need.
2. Because of puritanical and paternalistic motives, which include the prevention of borrowing for frivolous purposes, they attempt to guard the economic morality of the poor.
3. Due to such motives and to adopting a bureaucratic model of

organization, such institutions are often viewed as cold and distant, intruding, and cumbersome. This was found to be the case with Indian credit cooperatives and the German agricultural banks set up by the Nazis, as well as other such institutions.

4. Such institutions are less accessible. They are set up in towns and do not have the flexibility of the trader-lender. They must be subsidized, and they have high administrative costs.
5. The institution deviates from its original purpose. First, because the financial demands make it conform to the ways of other financial institutions, the *monte di pieta* would lend money to city governments, while American savings and loan associations are accused of being "redliners." Second, if they do not conform to such demands of business, they may be seen as lackadaisical and indifferent financial institutions. Third, there is the dishonesty of the officials of the institution. One expects private moneylenders to seek personal profit, but the monte and the new institution are public trusts. Still, an official of an Indian cooperative may demand a bribe, so that the loan will be processed, while another cooperative's secretary absconds with its funds.[49]

The comparison of such institutions suggests that elimination of the middleman minority does not always result in a just distribution of goods to the poor. The hopes of righting the wrongs against the poor are often dashed by the lack of the correct tools to reach this end.

Conclusions

This brief consideration of minority moneylending complies with the general themes of the middleman-minority theory, such as the importance of ethnic-economic specialization and the role of the stranger. It also brings together materials from Jewish history, economic anthropology, and economics which have ramifications regarding moneylending today, especially with regard to credit reforms in peripheral areas.[50]

In the core of the modern world, of course, universal otherhood in the form of corporate impersonality reigns supreme. In that context, even one's friendly neighborhood bank is only a branch office of a large bureaucracy, and bankers may openly and easily mingle with other members of the ruling elites. Thus, other rules prevail.

Looking at minority moneylenders is one way of viewing middleman minorities, since all those who are middlemen in monetary transactions play the role of creditor. It is not, however, the only role. Unlike Shakespeare's Shylock, the medieval Jew was more than an isolated banker consumed by his gold and promissory notes. The stranger could serve the rulers and the populace as taxpayer, physician, and official. But he also had an inner life not visible to his clients. At the same time, it is easy to see how the alien moneylender, when foreclosing on borrowers, can be seen as one with illicit power and as a "bloodsucking leech" or cannibal.

In the Hebrew language, for example, one word for "money" is *damim,* which is also a plural of *dam* meaning "blood." In a more recent—even though long ago—context, William Jennings Bryan portrayed hard-pressed American debtors as "being crucified on a cross of gold."

Chapter 3

Anti-Middleman Ideology and the Diffusion of Anti-Semitism

Since middleman minority theories are socioeconomic explanations of the ethnic division of labor and of intergroup conflict, they assume that the causes of conflict are real. Realistic explanations of prejudice, however, do not exclude irrational and emotional components. While some of this sentiment arises from a general dislike and fear of strangers, there are also special negative qualities attributed to alien traders.[1] More than pure prejudice is involved in the ideologies directed against minority middlemen.

In this chapter, I will discuss two aspects of anti-middleman ideology. The first is the relationship of such ideologies to an ethic of distributive justice. The second is an examination of how anti-middleman sentiment—especially anti-Semitic imagery—may combine with other ideologies and spread.

This chapter is exploratory in nature; it is an essay in the comparative intellectual history of the images of middleman minorities. Since the particular relationship which I am suggesting has not been investigated, the evidence which I am reviewing is much weaker than what I am presenting elsewhere in this book. It is my hope that others will be encouraged to look into the links between the diffusion of nationalism and anti-Semitism and the treatment of minorities outside of the West.

THE KERNEL OF TRUTH IN STEREOTYPES

Human beings may judge very similar behavior quite differently, although they may agree in their descriptions. It is not uncommon to say "I am thrifty, while you are stingy, and he is a miser." The different evaluations reflect more than dislike of the others, but may indicate differences in degree and in what constitutes a sound policy of savings. One study of Filipino and Philippine Chinese stereotypes has shown that there is considerable agreement between the two about the actual traits of each group with some difference in evaluation.[2]

Situational factors, of course, play a role in such estimates. The tensions between shopkeeper and buyer or between employer and his past, present, and potential employees will color judgments. In addition, there are important differences between individual attribution—such as green eyes and red hair—and judgments in which the traits of a singular person are disregarded in consideration of an aggregate.

Experiences with individuals of the target group may even contradict one's stereotype. African businessmen in Kenya characterized Asians as unhelpful and unscrupulous businessmen, but some of the Africans had been trained by Asians and had employed Asians as bookkeepers, had friendly relations with Asians, and regularly did business with them.[3] Aside from direct interaction, however, one's evaluation of the group as a whole, whether a particular profession or ethnic group, will enter into the picture.

THE DISTRIBUTIVE ETHIC AND COMPARISON

Among the peasants of Cauca Valley of Columbia, a belief has grown up to explain why some people increase their wealth. It is said that, when a baptism is to take place, some men will baptize a piece of currency rather than the infant. The infant will be in danger as an unbaptized being, while the baptized bill will continue to return to its owner, permitting him to spend it repeatedly and, thus, enrich himself at the expense of others. It is money reproducing itself. Thus do these country folk explain the rise of exchange-value at the expense of use-value. It is the dialectical opposition between the satisfaction of natural wants on one side and the limitless search for profits on the other.[4]

This dialectical opposition is inherent in the suspicion with which those of the folk society view the traders and in the opposition of priests and others to the ruling elite. As Lenski[5] suggested, priests in agrarian societies saw themselves as the guardians of the ancient redistributive ethic with its emphasis on reciprocity and charity. They criticized the massive flow of goods and services from the masses to the elite and its retainers.

The lending of money on interest was particularly offensive to upholders of the old ethic of reciprocity. Usury to them seemed to be a form of cheating and unfair profit taking. They criticized the elite for its loss of a sense of *noblesse oblige* with its concomitant generosity. Hence, Lenski includes prophetic figures such as Amos in the priestly class.

In modern society, the military and the civil servants have often looked down on businessmen. The alienated section of the intelligentsia has taken up arms against the moneymen and provided revolutions against capitalism with potent counterideologies. These intellectuals have denounced bourgeois Philistinism and advocated radical egalitarianism with great fervor. To carry out the overturn of the regime. they must form coalitions with others.[6]

This opposition can be viewed as a sincere expression of these classes or as a cynical tool for gaining and maintaining power by those wishing to oust competitors, plunder the wealthy, and turn the wrath of the masses on weak strangers. Whether the motives of priests and intellectuals have been sincere or cynical, the outcome has often fitted the model suggested by the skeptical observers.[7]

Cynical opposition often attributes the worst abuses of capitalism to the minority. It parallels the denunciation of the aggressive search for filthy lucre by lowly peddlers while praising the nobility of the wealthy ruling class. The two groups with whom the ideologists combine are, of course, the masses—who, as clients of the middlemen, are exploited and who also see their greater wealth as plunder—and the native entrepreneurs, professionals, and middlemen who are the competitors.[8]

Anti-Semitism and Anti-Middlemen Hostility

The social theorists who have written about middleman minorities have themselves been influenced by the anti-middleman sentiments of the intelligentsia and the stereotypes of middleman both in their own and in other societies. This sentiment is clear in such thinkers as Voltaire, Marx, and Sombart, but this anticapitalist mentality can be found in contemporary sociology as well.[9] The same stereotypes and prejudices about trading minorities have spread on a popular level and helped to produce similar behavior toward culturally and ethnically different traders who are perceived as being of the same mold.

Social scientists do not conceive of themselves as "historians of ideas," and they often write as if each setting is an entity onto itself. Unless explicitly part of the study, external influences are neglected. Unquestionably, antiminority violence is a product of internal tensions, but it may well be aggravated by the importation of stereotypes and ideologies.

Such diffusion is part of the dispersal of ideas associated with inventions, religious conversion, and political ideologies. Associated with the worldwide hegemony of Western culture has been the idea of the nation-state as a self-sufficient economic community. Nationalism is an idea that has conquered the world.[10] Anti-Semitism fits the nationalist conception that the nation must control its own economy and sees dangers in letting important sectors fall under the control of strangers, such as Jews. In this chapter, we will concentrate on anti-Semitism and its application to non-Jewish middlemen.

The thesis that hostility toward middleman minorities is exacerbated by the importation of stereotypes and ideologies from abroad requires some documentation. This type of outside-agitator theory should be more fully tested by intellectual historians; it is certainly not self-evident. Many historians of anti-Semitism[11] favor what Bonacich has termed a "pure prejudice" or "universal ethnocentrism" approach, often combined with a modern variant of the "chosen people" or "suffering servant" concept, namely the Jew as eternal victim. This has the twist of absolving Jews of any responsibility for provoking hostility, since non-Jews are perceived as always hostile. Socioeconomic interpretations—especially cultural explanations—seem to blame the victim.

In exploring anti-Semitism and its relationships to other anti-middleman ideologies, we must make some distinctions. "Anti-Semitic," as used here, is equivalent to anti-Jewish. The fact that Arabs are speakers of a Semitic language and were supposed to be members of a Semitic race has created some spillover from anti-Jewish sentiment to anti-Arab stereotypes, but this is secondary.

While it is anachronistic to call pre-nineteenth-century anti-Jewish ideologies—especially those which were hostile to Jews as a religious group—anti-Semitic, it is done in this study for the sake of convenience. This is not as much a violation of one's historical sense as it may seem since, prior to the present century, the distinctions between genetic heritage, language, and culture were not refined at all. Modern racial anti-Semitism is, in fact, based on theories which did not clearly differentiate between race, language, and culture.

Anti-Semitic imagery must also be distinguished because this may be found even among those who are not ideologically anti-Semitic. Weber was not so much an ideological anti-Semite as a user of such imagery. Anti-Semitic imagery—for example the hooked nose—may be used in current contexts. Note the hooked noses of Arab oil sheiks in contemporary American cartoons or of Uncle Sam in Soviet caricatures.[12]

While there is a tradition of alleged Jewish misanthropy, going back to Greco-Roman days, the image of the Jews as usurer, sorcerer, and Christ-killer—a combination of the wandering Jews with Shylock—is medieval European. It was during that period that Jews became specialized as moneylenders. A permanent association was also made between the infidel Jews and the recurrence of Christ-killing.

In European folklore this took various forms, such as legends about wandering Jews who had rejected Christ, or Jews who had stolen the Virgin Mary's shroud at her death; and accusations that contemporary Jews recrucified the Host, the symbol of Christ's body, or that they killed Christian children and ritually used their blood.[13]

Many of these types of blood accusations were and are made elsewhere in Southwest Asia and Europe against other groups, but they became crystallized into anti-Semitic stereotypes.[14] Elements of this stereotype have persisted and diffused even in areas without Jews. The *judio* as devil and Christ-killer is a figure in the Eastern dramas of Indian-Hispanic America. Chaucer, Shakespeare, and Marlowe depicted Jews in their work at a time when Jews could not legally live in England. Shylock, the archetype of the mythical Jewish lender, was the product of a writer who could not have had much contact with real Jews. It is an example of what Leon Poliakov calls "anti-Semitism in the pure state."[15]

One of the best illustrations of anti-Semitism in the pure state comes from seventeenth-century Paris. In 1652, the guild of the *fripiers* were accused of the murder of a merchant's son. The *fripiers* of Paris were old-clothes merchants, a profession associated with Jews in neighboring countries, and their guildhall was therefore called "the synagogue." The campaign conducted against them used explicitly anti-Semitic imagery, including comparing the murder of the youth to the deicide of Jesus. The *fripiers*, who were Catholics of long standing, were portrayed as Jews, the descendants of the Christ-killers and usurers. It is obvious that the secondhand clothing trade was identified with Jews, and, thus, anyone so involved was identified as a "Jew" of sorts.[16]

The identification of certain commercial people with Jews, Mammon worshippers, or the devil was also applied by Europeans and Euro-Americans to others of their religion.[17] In Spain during the sixteenth and seventeenth centuries, Genoese financiers were seen as materialists undermining Spanish life, including using money to seduce women. One author noted the resemblance of Genoese to devils with their horns and tails.[18] As early as the 1680s, the Quakers were perceived as being shrewd and industrious business people by their adversaries. One author wrote of them:

> In a Word, they are singularly Industrious, sparing no Labour or Pains to increase their Wealth; and so subtle and inventive, that they would, if possible, extract Gold out of Ashes. I know none that excel them in their Characters but the *Jews* and the *Banians:* the former being the craftiest of all Men, and the latter so superlatively cunning they will overreach the Devil.[19]

The Christians of Lebanon also associate Jews with devils, as shown in a proverb in which Jews, devils, monkeys, or Gypsies are contrasted with clerics.

"To meet a Gypsy early in the morning is better than accompanying a priest."

Alternative proverbs substitute Jew, monkey, or Devil for the Gypsy, while the priest may be replaced by a bishop or a monk. These proverbs show ambivalent and even anticlerical attitudes in which even Jews or devils may be better than priests. In this proverb, there is no reference to money.[20]

Scottish peddlers in Germany and Poland were often lumped together with the Jews as unfair competitors in the sixteenth and seventeenth centuries. Sometimes even Scots who had settled in Germany viewed their newly arrived countrymen in this light. They were accused of selling goods regardless of guild rates, adulterating the goods, and undercutting urban retailers by hawking their wares in the countryside.

The famed Scottish attitude toward money evokes an image that their thrift is a kind of Mammon worship. The stereotype is shared by descendants of Scottish immigrants to North America, including John Kenneth Galbraith.[21] In the early United States, the Yankee peddler was a mythic figure larger than life. In James Fenimore Cooper's *The Spy*, the hero is a peddler who works clandestinely for Washington during the Revolutionary War. He is skillful and mysterious, as well as reprehensible, even though he sells attractive goods. He is perceived as having only one loyalty—to money—although he is a true idealist. Even though this peddler is not a Jew, the association of the peddler as a vagabond with the Devil is implicit in the story. It is also noteworthy that, while there were few Jews in the United States prior to 1840, early American literature carried over European stereotypes of Jews.[22]

The association of Yankees with Jews was present in German immigrant and antiemigration literature during the nineteenth century, with such comments as "There are three Christians in a Jew and three Jews in a Yankee," and "Jews find masters in the Yankees."

Southerners also made such references as "Yankees are too sharp for the children of Israel."

German immigrants often said that Yankees learned their business methods from Jews, and they compared Jews and Americans with regard to their haggling. Some even saw physical resemblances between Jews, Yankees, and Englishmen. One German emigrant guide calls Yankees "The Jews of the New World."[23]

Some of these proverbs and phrases are similar to observations made by Europeans in the Balkans and Levant to the effect that Greeks were superior to Jews in shrewdness, but Armenians were superior to Greeks. In Uzice, a Serbian city in Yugoslavia, there is a story that there had been the Jews doing business in the town, but the people were too clever, and forced the Jews out of business.[24]

In Germany and other parts of Europe, the association of Jewish and Anglo-Saxon commercialism is of more significance than folk proverbs. England, after all, was considered to be a nation of shopkeepers. During the nineteenth and twentieth centuries in Germany, antiliberal, anti-British and anti-Semitic strands were strongly linked. All criticized England (and later America) and the Jews for being materialistic, as opposed to the idealistic Germans. Many of these same themes are found in Sombart's work on the Jews and in his anti-British propaganda during World War I.[25]

The English, of course, have not been devoid of anti-

Semitism. During World War I, the German danger was associated with Jews. In the famous thriller, *The Thirty-Nine Steps,* the hero is told that behind all the Balkan intrigue which has led to the war is a Jew in a dark room somewhere. After the war, the anti-Semitic *Protocols of the Elders of Zion* were widely read and taken seriously in Britain and America, as well as in Germany.[26]

THE DIFFUSION OF ANTI-SEMITISM BEYOND CHRISTENDOM

The transfer of the concept of the Jew as moneyman and worshipper of Mammon from Christian Europe to the rest of the world began with the Age of Discovery. Edmund Scot, who was in Java in 1602, extended the Jewish stereotype of the Chinese traders whom he found there. He wrote about the Javans and the Chinese in the following manner:

> The Javans are generally exceeding proud, although extreame poore, by reason that not one amongst an hundred of them will worke... The Chinois, doe both plant, dresse, and gather the Pepper, and also sowe their Rice, living as slaves under them, but they sucke away all the wealth of the Land, by reason that the Javans are so idle...
>
> The Javans themselves are very dull and blockish to manage any affairs of a Commonwealth, whereby all strangers goe beyond them that come into their land: and many of the Country of Clyn, which come thither to dwell, doe grow very rich, and rise to great Offices and Dignitie amongst them... especially the Chinese who like Jewes live crooching under them, but rob them of their wealth, and send it to China.

> The Chinese are very crafty people in trading, using all kinds of counsoning and deceipt which may possibly be devised. They have no pride in them, nor will refuse any labour, except they turne Javans (as many of them doe when they have done a murther, or some other villanie). Then they are every whit as proud, as as lasie as the Javans. For their Religion they are of divers sects, but the most of them are Atheists.[27]

Scot, a contemporary of Shakespeare, here extended the European stereotype of the Jew to a far-off people and also encapsulated the dichotomy between the "hardworking, crafty migrant middleman" and the "lazy native," a distinction which persists in Southeast Asia and other parts of the world.

Sometimes the appellation "Jews of X" is the only reference we have to the comparison which has been made. In recent times, the Kwahu have been called the "Jews of Ghana," while during the slave trade, the Ijebu were called the "Jews of Yorubaland" (West Nigeria).[28] Often, other ways are found to make such analogies, such as referring to a group as being like the Scots or simply worshipping money. A British clergyman contrasted the European and mixed Eurasian population of Ceylon by contrasting the "bigotry" and "fanaticism" of the Catholic Portuguese with the "venality" of the Dutch. Of the latter he wrote:

> The Dutch did not bend down before the grim Moloch of religious bigotry, nor did they worship at the shrine of superstition, but cent, per cent, was their faith, gold was their object, and Mammon was their god....[29]

So far we have been considering European evaluations, even though they were made in non-European settings. As non-Europeans were given Western-style educations, they adopted Western stereotypes. This was especially true after the intensive missionary activity of the nineteenth century.

Tracing the rise of anti-Semitism is easiest in the Middle East. There was always a degree of anti-Jewish sentiment present in Christian and Muslim cultures in that area. The rivalry of Christians and Jews in particular kept the old religious hatreds alive, especially in the form of blaming Jews for the killing of Christ and extensions of this in the ritual murder charge.

The stereotype of Jew as moneyman, however, was not omnipresent. In fact, as late as the 1950s, the Christian Arab proverbs collected by Frayha show an association of Jews with poverty and meanness, not wealth.[30] Beginning with the 1880s, however, some Arab authors began to adopt European anti-Semitic views. The images which appear in this literature are those of Jews as swindlers, "sons of clinking gold," and as controlling the finances of Europe. One of the first pieces in this literature is an adaptation of Shakespeare's *The Merchant of Venice.* The Arab focus on the Jews was, of course, associated with their realistic opposition to Zionism. What concerns us in this context is the fact that they, like others, acquired much of their knowledge from European literature.[31]

In the Middle East, Jews were present, but elsewhere in the Third World, we are concerned with something close to anti-Semitism in the pure state. Tracing the connection between antiminority prejudice and anti-Semitic imagery and ideology becomes exceedingly difficult. In Thailand, however, we have a clear instance, because of a pamphlet attributed to a King of Thailand, called "The Jews of the East."

The appellation of the Chinese as the "Jews of Siam" appears in the work of H. Warrington Smythe, British Director of the Royal (Thai) Department who served during the 1890s. Smythe saw the Chinese as advancing socially and economically at the expense of the Thais. They were in control of the economy of Bangkok. He wrote:

> Considering the money they make out of the country and the freedom of action they enjoy when compared with the native Siamese, it is no wonder that the children of mixed marriages adopt the pigtail when they can. They are the Jews of Siam; and though they have been subject to a little fleecing by the local Siamese authorities, they have on the whole enjoyed an immunity from official interference which they have neither merited nor appreciated . . . The (Chinese secret) societies are nearly as powerful as the King himself. By judicious use of their business faculties and their powers of combination, they hold the Siamese in the palm of their hand. The toleration accorded them by the Government is put down to fear; they bow and scrape before the authorities, but laugh behind their backs; and they could sack Bangkok in a day.[32]

When Smythe was in Thailand he was an advisor to a Westernizing Thai government. Members of the royal family in particular were being given European-style educations, even being sent to Europe itself. Chulalongkorn was king when Smythe was in Thailand. Chulalongkorn's son, Wachirawut (also spelled Vajiravudh), was sent to Oxford and Sandhurst in this period. In Britain at that time, there was a large Jewish immigration which was viewed as being a mixed blessing, and anti-Semitic expressions were quite common. In addition, fear of the "Yellow Peril," a new threat from the Far East, was also felt. His son, Wachirawut, succeeded his father to the throne, ruling from 1910 to 1925.

In 1914, a pamphlet authored by one Asavabahu, a pen name of Wachirawut's, appeared, entitled "The Jews of the East." It combined themes of European anti-Semitism with the fear of the "Yellow Peril." In the pamphlet, he accuses the Chinese of excessive "racial loyalty" and astuteness in financial matters, and wrote:

> If it is to their advantage to do so, Chinese are glad to adopt Buddhism, or Christianity or Mohammedanism or Hinduism. They will worship any god or any madness at all if only in so doing they will derive a profit. To sum up: the Chinese have only one god more precious to them than all other gods together, and that is the GOD MONEY . . . Where money is involved there is no method of acquiring it which they consider dishonest or wrong. They revere and practice the ethic which says that "The end justifies the means."
>
> All manner of sacrifices, no matter how bitter the wasting of men's lives, no matter to what extent, the enduring the privations and sorrow, like beasts of hell, no matter how severe—leave the GOD MONEY still unsatisfied, still demanding more and greater payments. All the conscienceless Chinese continue to serve him with tireless perseverance with an energy which should be directed to better ends than these . . .
>
> To my mind, there is little room for choice that, if one were obliged to have either the Jews or the Chinese, selection would be difficult. Further, I do not believe there is any doubt that at some time in the future we shall see violence and disorder in countries where "Jews of the East" reside.[33]

This pamphlet was written during a period when the Thais and other non-Westerners were undergoing extensive Westernization, including the beginning of studies abroad and mission-school education.

Wachirawut is considered to be the propagator of modern Thai nationalism, who sought to mobilize the symbols of national development and to put Thailand in the vanguard of modern nations.[34] His pamphlet is the clearest evidence of a link between the stereotype of the Jew in Europe and antiminority sentiment elsewhere.[35] The rhetoric of "The Jews of the East" is obviously derivative. Compare some of the following statements:

> Money is their God. Life itself is of little value compared with the leanest bank account.[36]

> Money is the jealous god of Israel, besides which no other god may exist. Money abases all the gods of mankind and changes them into commodities.[37]

The importation of anti-Semitic attitudes results in a variety of attitudes to both the local "Jews"—such as Chinese and others—and the Jews themselves. Thailand, despite its officially sanctioned anti-Chinese propaganda, has been a country in which many Chinese have successfully assimilated, while other Southeast Asian countries have been the scenes of expulsions and pogroms. Thais, however, have learned to fear Jews. One anthropologist reported an incident in which a Thai, visiting in the United States, became afraid when some Jewish house guests began to light their Sabbath candles.

On the other hand, the secondary anti-Semitism of the Japanese was mild. Even when the Japanese Army interned the European Jews of Shanghai in a ghetto at the behest of their Nazi allies during World War II, their treatment of the Jews was relatively mild and humanitarian. This was true even of the "Jewish experts" of the Army who had become learned in anti-Semitic lore.[38]

Obviously, an imported ideology is not enough to produce genocide without the right conditions. In recent years, several best-selling books have been published in Japan which assert that "America is a Jewish nation" and is dominated by Jewish interests. In one public opinion poll, Japanese displayed negative attitudes toward Jews, although there is very little contact between Japanese and Jews.

It is hard to find direct links between anti-Chinese ideology and anti-Semitism among the other peoples of Southeast Asia, but a few clues are available. Certainly the stereotypes have features in common. One scholar describes the Chinese in Vietnam, especially the south, as being the businessmen, merchants, and moneylenders of Indochina. They were said to control most international trade, rice mills, sugar refineries, and sawmills, as well as holding much urban property. Under the French, only mines, rubber plantations, and rice-growing lands escaped their grasp. They were said to send most of their wealth out of the country and did not create any wealth within it. At the same time, anti-Chinese riots in Haiphong during the period between the two World Wars were blamed on French provocation or Vietnamese intellectuals and not on unpopularity with the Vietnamese.[39]

In Malaysia, we find some tenuous association between the Jewish stereotype and that of the Chinese. British educators introduced their colonial charges to the New Testament, Shakespeare, and Dickens. Ishak bin Haji Mohammed, a Malay nationalist, read Shakespeare's *The Merchant of Venice,* as "an anticapitalist tract and regretted the lack of similar humanity and wisdom in the English in Malaya." Ishak saw the British in Malay as avaricious and unprincipled, and we have no evidence that he applied the same stereotype to the Chinese. Yet, since the British so frequently called the Chinese the "Jews of the East," that he and others might make such a connection is likely.[40]

In 1957, after a series of anti-Chinese moves in various Southeast Asian countries, the Chinese Nationalist Foreign Minister George Yeh was quoted as saying, "We Chinese are being looked on as the Jews of Asia."[41]

The pervasiveness of such stereotypes emerged in a short book, *The Malay Dilemma,* published in Singapore by Mahathir bin Mohammed, a Malaysian politician who subsequently became premier of his country. In it he discusses the problem for Malays of regaining control of their own country and reducing the economic power of the Chinese. In one passage, he discusses the racial characteristics of Jews, Europeans, Malays, and Chinese. Jews are seen as "not merely hooked-nosed, but understand money instinctively," while Chinese are described as "almond-eyed" and "good businessmen." The Malays are seen as easygoing and tolerant. Yet, in the next paragraph, he points to Jewish stinginess and financial wizardry as provoking European anti-Semitism, while the tolerance of the Malays led to the British conquest and the influx of the Chinese and Indians. He sees the Chinese role as universal middlemen of Southeast Asia as the outcome of their business acumen. While he avoids the old cliche of the Chinese as the "Jews of Asia," the connection is clear. He accepts the image of the Malay as the indolent native which is found in works by Edmund Scot and H. Warrington Smythe.[42]

The association of local middlemen with Jews is also found in Africa. There is little direct reference in scholarly writing connecting anti-Semitism with the anti-middleman sentiment in East Africa on the part of both European residents and Africans. Yet the novelist, Paul Theroux, who was in East Africa during the expulsion of many Asians from Kenya in 1967–68, cites comments on the part of the residents of East Africa, such as "They're just like the Jews," "They're the Jews of East Africa," and "There is a pathetic Jewishness about the Asians in East Africa."[43]

During the same period—which preceded Idi Amin's expulsion of Asians from Uganda—a Kampala Sikh showed how the Asians themselves began to identify with the stereotypes by publishing a poem in which he sees the Asians as "brown Jews." Jagit Singh wrote, "My subordinate Asian smile of friendship—That proclaims the Jew also as a citizen..." Here he completes the contrast between Jew (or stranger) with citizen.[44] Idi Amin, who expelled the Asians from Uganda, was both anti-Zionist and anti-Asian. The connection he made was oblique. He saw the Zionist as controlling America, much as he saw the Asians controlling the Ugandan economy. While he viewed the Asians as servants of imperialism and Zionism, he did not accuse them directly of being Jews, anymore than he claimed that all Jews are Zionists in his public statements.[45]

While anti-Semitism has entered into the imagery applied to middleman minorities throughout the world, it is not the only strain in the vilification process. If a plot by the Elders of Zion is not plausible, there are other conspiracy theories which can be used as explanations. Populist agitators in Brazil during the late nineteenth century accused Portuguese small businessmen of having monarchist and Papist-clericalist connections,[46] while the Chinese have always been perceived in terms of a "Yellow Peril," sometimes tied to international communism as well.

METAPHORS AND INTERETHNIC TENSION

Social scientists from Becker on have taken the "Jews-of" metaphor as a verification of the similarities present among middleman minorities. Others like Paul Theroux see the use of such an analogy as a sign of prejudiced, antidemocratic personality. No one has seriously examined the connection between the group to whom the metaphor is applied and the words used to evoke the image. "Jews" and "worshipper of Mammon" are powerful images in Western Christian culture. While in some instances, the terms may be used teasingly, referring only to the business acumen of an ethnic group or individual, in other instances images of venal traitor (such as Judas Iscariot), Christ-killer, blood-sucker, usurer, or all-powerful financier can be invoked. The same is true of the imagery of the "Yellow Peril," which calls to mind Genghis Khan's Mongol hordes, the vermin of the Great Plague, the overpopulation of Asia, and the robotlike behavior often attributed to the Chinese and Japanese by Westerners. All of these caricatures contribute to making one view shopkeepers and businessmen—be they honest or shady—as representatives of some dangerous conspiracy or bearers of some disease which must be uprooted.[47]

In this book, only the surface of material relating to intergroup imagery has been scratched. Much more research must be done, not only into the stereotype of the middleman but also into other cliches applied to peoples around the world, such as the "proud nomad" or the "indolent native." The historical and functional aspects of these recurrent portraits in different parts of the world continue to play an important role in interethnic behavior. Such stereotypes and labels are used by opponents as well as friends of these minorities in the struggle for political and economic power.

Chapter 4

ETHNIC SOLIDARITY IN THREE MIDDLEMAN MINORITIES

A high degree of ethnic solidarity and ethnocentrism has been attributed to middleman minorities. Generally, theorists have seen these groups as having a "separatist complex" often expressed in terms of ritual segregation, familism, ethnocentric attitudes, and the maintenance of separate religious, educational and political institutions. The similarity of the different minorities and their unity have been stressed. Various theorists have usually been vague about the locus of ethnic solidarity which makes for economic success. It is assumed that *inordinate* group loyalty, the perception of unity, and seeming influence bring hostility down upon the heads of minority members. In fact, the political organs of such ethnic groups often exhibit political impotence even though outsiders perceive a high degree of political cohesion. The solidarity which does exist may arise out of cultural norms of the minority, but unity may also be imposed by powerful outsiders.

In this chapter, three classic middleman groups will be compared in a wholesale and uncontrolled fashion, with particular attention to ethnocentric cultural attributes, the locus of ethnic solidarity, communal organization, and reactions to outside threats. The three groups compared are Ashkenazic Jews (particularly in nineteenth- and twentieth-century Europe), overseas Indians (especially the trader groups), and overseas Chinese. For this type of comparison, I will rely on secondary and tertiary sources, as well as case-studies of individual communities.[1]

The comparison of three aggregates will show the inherent differences between Jews, Chinese, and Indians.[2] It will also show the force of a similar social position in bringing about convergence. By examining these three aggregates in some detail, we will also be able to examine what is meant by such rubrics as "the separatist complex" and "ethnic solidarity" by which social scientists have papered over complex phenomena.

Ashkenazic Jewry

Introduction

Ashkenaz,[3] or the main body of European Jewry in the past four hundred years, was a cultural diaspora which extended from Alsace-Lorraine to the Ukraine. At the beginning of the nineteenth century, this entity was still united by language (Yiddish) and a religious great tradition. By the end of the century, large numbers of Jews in this area had ceased to speak Yiddish and substituted standard High German, Polish, and Magyar, as well as ceasing to observe or even pay lip service to the religious customs of their fathers. This large entity had always lived dispersed among peoples who spoke different languages and who practiced different religions.

Occupational Structure

By 1800, the Ashkenazim of Central and Eastern Europe had adapted themselves to a wide variety of socioeconomic niches, most of which could be seen as middleman roles. In all countries, a disproportionate number of Jews were in trade, particularly international commerce and peddling. Artisans tended to be concentrated in cities and were in particular trades. The artisans of this period were not the majority. There were also large numbers of beggars and other unemployed people.

During the next century and a half, large numbers of Jews from this section of Europe emigrated and formed the vast majority of Jews in Western Europe, the Americas, South Africa, and, for about three decades, in Palestine. They helped enlarge much smaller communities and founded new ones.[4]

The large-scale migrations of these Jews were more to the metropolitan or core areas of North America and Europe than to the colonial peripheries of the tropics, although there were significant migrations to Argentina, rural parts of North America, and to South Africa. In this way, the pattern of Jewish migrations differs from that of the Chinese and Indians. Even the descendants of many Jews who had lived in rural areas in the beginning of the period moved to cities by its end.

The period from 1800 to the present was an era of intense secularization and modernization. It was a period when many Jewish communities suffered expulsion and ultimately large-scale genocide, as well as economic dislocations and transformations. The socioeconomic transformations include the growth of the learned professions and industrial enterprise and employment. During the nineteenth century, there was a shift from rural trade—sometimes forced by governmental policies—to involvement in industry. At the higher levels of society, this took the form of entrepreneurship, while many of the poor became unskilled and skilled workers in certain industries.[5]

In the Austro-Hungarian empire during the nineteenth century, for example, one still could find traditional rural middlemen, such as estate agents in Hungary, peddlers in Bohemia, and innkeepers in Polish Galicia. Jews were also capitalistic entrepreneurs, by creating a textile industry in Bohemia and Moravia, produce trade in Hungary, the lumber industry in the Carpathians, and dominating the real estate markets and newspapers of Vienna. They included petty lenders, speculators, and big bankers who helped finance the new railroads and coal mining. They seemed to be the very incarnation of the dreaded new capitalistic system. What was true of the Hapsburg domain could be found in Germany and in Eastern Europe as well.[6]

While the enterpreneurs were suceeding at the top, Jews in the older niches of the rural and urban economies were displaced by a combination of capitalistic preemption, social reform measures, and nationalism. For instance, in the post-Napoleonic era, the Jews of the Duchy of Posen (Prussian Poland) were cut off from their traditional markets in Russian Poland. Craftsmen who had exported to those markets were unemployed and impoverished. Various reform measures in the Tsarist empire to decrease the consumption of liquor by peasants pushed many Jews out of rural areas. Napoleon issued several edicts aimed at forcing Alsatian Jews out of rural moneylending. In Russia and Poland, Jews suffered from organized boycotts, pogroms, and governmental edicts.[7]

The Jewish industrial proletariat in Central and Eastern Europe was concentrated in consumer-goods industries, rather than in basic heavy industry. The largest branch was clothing, in which workers ranged from thirty to fifty percent of all Jews in industrial employment, while only 10 percent of Gentiles were employed in those industries. Other branches in which the Jewish share of employment was larger than that of non-Jews were food, leather, and printing. The shares of textiles, metal, construction, and the like were below that.

Generally Jews were employed in the manufacture of finished consumer goods and in hand-trades and small-scale enterprises rather than in large factories. This trend was present in Eastern Europe and continued in the lands of immigration, particularly in Britain and the United States. Such industrial organization was adversely affected by mechanization and a tendency to hire even more lowly paid gentile workers, especially after Jewish workers organized unions.[8]

In the learned professions, too, there was a massive transformation. Prior to 1800, the Jewish communities in Europe had their own religiously oriented servants and professionals, primarily ritual slaughterers, rabbis serving as judges, and the like. There were a few Jewish physicians. As secular learning increased and legal restrictions dissolved, more and more Jews entered the learned professions. By 1931 in Poland, Jews accounted for 54 percent of all private physicians. In Hungary in 1920, 50.6 percent of all lawyers were Jews.[9]

Jews, however, suffered from legal restrictions. The low ratios of Jews in salaried and public employment were often the product of discrimination. While many Jews had been employed in many capacities—including working for the railways in Galicia under the Austrians—the number of Jewish public employees in this region declined drastically under the Polish Republic. After World War I in Romania, newly naturalized Jews found the professions open to them, but pro-Nazi and anti-Semitic regimes in the 1930s closed these professions off again. Persons of Jewish descent who had flourished in prewar Hungary under the Hapsburgs were forced to emigrate under reactionary regimes between the two World Wars. The racial anti-Semitism of this period affected both those who desired to maintain affiliation with Judaism and those who wished to renounce it.[10]

Cultural Attributes and the Separatist Complex

In medieval society, separation of the Jews from gentile society was largely by mutual consent. Jews—as well as burghers and peasants—were excluded from the aristocracy. In countries like Prussia, Poland, Hungary, and Romania, the tradition of a separate nobility and aristocracy persisted well into the twentieth century, even if the definition of who was truly noble was often blurred. The exclusion of Jews from the Prussian officer corps and the refusal to grant them reserve commissions was typical of this tendency.

Up to the nineteenth century, intermarriage between Jews and non-Jews was rare, if not nonexistent. It was forbidden by both Jewish law and Christian law. Well into modern times, orthodox Jews have forbidden intermarriage, and children who converted to Christianity and/or intermarried were mourned as if dead.

The Jewish dietary laws certainly can discourage social interaction between Jew and gentile. These rules go well beyond prohibiting foods permitted Christians by their religion—such as ham or pork—to considering wine touched by gentiles as improper for consumption. We must avoid, however, assuming that, because a prohibition exists, that it is followed.

For instance, the prohibition on gentile wine was not considered to be a serious offense so long as this wine was not used for pagan ritual purposes. This was especially true since Christians were not considered to be idolators.[11] One can imagine many situations in which Jewish courtiers, coachmen, itinerant peddlers, traveling merchants, and innkeepers would need to drink and eat with gentiles. During the Middle Ages, the Church forbade Jews to have Christian servants and gentile cooking was prohibited by Jewish law. Yet, there were rabbinic homes with Christian cooks, and rabbis stayed in Christian homes while at spas. In mideighteenth century Germany, many of these laws were observed in the breach; a century and a half later, in Eastern Europe, one could find both violators and strict adherents of these laws.[12]

By 1900, many Jews violated such Jewish religious regulations as the Sabbath, the dietary laws, and rules pertaining to menstrual prohibitions. Whole movements within the Jewish community permitted and even encouraged such trespass. The degree of observance and nonobservance, in fact, divided orthodox, traditional, reform, and nonreligious Jews from each other, as much as they marked the boundary between Jew and gentile.

On the other hand, some taste preferences derived from Jewish observances still could be used as boundaries. For instance, many nonobservant Jews continued to prefer cooking without adding bacon as a flavoring ingredient. In Poland and Germany, Jews were stereotyped as reeking of garlic, and Jewish food was seen as overspiced. Jewish patterns of drinking alcohol were different from those of neighboring populations for long periods of time.[13]

So far, ritual segregation has been considered negatively. We must not neglect the positive side; many Jews believed in the special destiny of the Jewish people as God's chosen people. All the rituals are given meaning by their connection with this belief, which was later secularized by Zionists and other nationalists. Jewish suffering was transformed through this belief. Personal guilt over transgression and a sense of redemption because of ancestral merit was also connected to it in Jewish memorialism.[14]

Efforts stemming from Weber's Protestant ethic thesis to seek a relationship between religious doctrine and economic behavior have not been particularly satisfying. With regard to Rabbinic Judaism, it is as plausible to argue that religio-legal authorities adjusted the law retroactively to fit appropriate adaptations as to identify Judaism with huckstering after Marx, or with rational capitalism in the manner of Sombart. Still, the fact that Jews in Europe were a commercial class—even if many were not traders—would help many Jews learn how to enter the marketplace, give them contacts, and provide them with role models and a self-image which would help them succeed. Jewish women were as involved in such dealings as men. In societies in which Jews are an important component of the mercantile sector, the association of Jewishness with trade is natural.[15]

The double standard of morality is an important component of Weber's pariah-people model. With regard to Jewry, this was expressed in the Jewish interpretation of Biblical laws forbidding interest-bearing loans to ingroup members, but permitting them to outgroupers. The actual situation in which this emerged is more complicated, because Jews, Christians, and Muslims have all practiced multiple standards of morality with regard to lending. While it is possible to point to particular laws which indicate such a dual morality for Jews, there were also ethical injunctions against taking advantage of gentiles on religious grounds. The full "behavioral mix" was complex and it is difficult to conclude that they were more ethnocentric than were their neighbors.[16]

The Locus of Ethnic Solidarity

In economic success, the importance of familial and kin ties cannot be underestimated. The family is the main welfare and employment agency for individuals who are not supported by the state. It is particularly helpful to the small businessman. The small shopkeeper needs reliable assistants who do not pilfer and who will work long hours, while wholesalers need partners in far-off places who are trustworhty. Kinsmen can serve this purpose quite well, although few after the first generation desire to work the long hours of the shop assistant.

The importance of kin is stressed in several histories of successful Ashkenazic enterprises. The old German Jewish banking families remained in the enterprises bearing their names for generations. The businesses of the House of Warburg, a Hamburg merchant banking family, can be traced from the eighteenth century to the twentieth century. Of course, members of the family often broke off and formed independent firms. The Warburgs had marital connections with other such families, including the Russian Guenzberg family.

The establishment of the Mosse advertising and publishing company in nineteenth century Central Europe shows how family ties aid businesses. Rudolf Mosse, the founder, started with the aid of his brother-in-law, Emil Cohn, who had the legal training which could be of use in such an endeavor. Cohn eventually left to start his own business, which was a common occurrence. He was replaced by Rudolf's younger brother, Emil Mosse. Through similar patterns of branching through brothers, brothers-in-law, and other kin, the establishment of familial dynasties and break-offs can be found among the furriers of Leipzig, who were of Polish origin and many of whom continued in the fur business from the beginning of the nineteenth century until the Nazi period.[17]

Katz characterizes the Ashkenazic family during the period of the sixteenth through eighteenth centuries as monogamous and patriarchal, with nuclear and small extended family households Such a reading of the record, even for his own data, is overly simple. There was extensive influence on the part of the women of the house in various affairs, although the view that East European women ran businesses is also a stereotype. It is hard to know how many women actually tended shops while their husbands studied the Talmud; their husbands certainly were not major enterpreneurs.[18]

The Jewish family, especially in Germany, was affected by governmental action. For instance, only a limited number of Jews were allowed to live in a community, and only limited numbers were able to obtain permission to marry. While women inherited only limited goods, their husbands were sometimes brought into the family business or received support from the family.[19]

Jewish families had their financial ups and downs. During stable periods, much of the wealth which accumulated might remain within the community because of charity and Jewish specialization. Even family firms , such as that of the Warburgs, show splits in every generation. Despite the weaknesses of the family, the conclusion of Katz for the period up to 1800 applies to the later period as well:

> The unit in the struggle for existence was the small family, with the larger kinship circle available at times of neccessity.[20]

Interpersonal ties in addition to kin ties must be taken into account. An extensive system of patronage existed within Jewish communities in the past. Jewish merchants and entrepreneurs were often the employers of Jewish craftsmen and the benefactors of religious functionaries. Often, court Jews in eighteenth-century Germany helped found Jewish communities by employing a large household in areas where Jews previously had not been permitted to reside.

The entry of Jewish workers into the manufacture of woolens in nineteenth-century Lodz, then "the Manchester of Poland" shows an extension of this process. Some Jewish mill owners built separate factories for Jewish workers which were closed on Saturdays, while mills employing gentile millhands were closed on Sundays. A wage differential was also maintained, which reputedly favored the Jews, although, in the long run, this may have caused even Jewish mill owners to prefer to hire gentile workers for the less skilled posts.[21]

In addition to providing employment, the wealthy in the Jewish community lent money to those less fortunate and set up charitable funds of various kinds. In the nineteenth century, certain Jewish philanthropists also attempted to improve the poor Jews by educating them in a modern form and resettling them on the land.[22] They also interceded for the poor Jews with governments. The leadership of the community by the wealthy points up both the strengths of common bonds within the community and their weaknesses. Of course, their own collaboration with the government often served their interests to the detriment of their less-fortunate coreligionists.

Personal dislikes between leaders can contribute to factionalism, while the very different circumstances of life between the wealthy prominent heads of the community and the masses are elements in class conflict.

Internal Cleavages

One of the key internal cleavages was between those from different places. In medieval times, Jewish communities, like their urban Christian counterparts, sought to restrict competition by not permitting Jews from elsewhere to settle in the local community.[23] Later, there was considerable mutual antagonism between different groups of Ashkenazim on the basis of region and dialect, as between Litvak and Galizianer or Polack, or between Poznan and Bavarian Jews. Such divisions could occur in old communities when Jews from another place immigrated or in new communities, whether in Europe, such as Vienna faced by a mass migration of Galician Jews during the nineteenth century or New York City in the 1880s. The *lantsmannschaften* or immigrant associations of Russian Jewish immigrants in New York were one response to such migration.[24]

Even within Poland, the "oldhand" versus "greenhorn" division existed. The Polonized Jewish intelligensia was descended, in part, from families which had long lived in Warsaw and the other cities and had thrived there. They were easily drawn to Polish nationalism, assimilation, and even conversion. During the late nineteenth century, the assimilationists led the communities, but their leadership became discredited.[25] Elsewhere similar divisions occurred.

The Magyar Jewish nobles, the Anglo-Jewish cousinhood, and the German Jewish "our crowd" in New York were such veteran groups which had assimilated to the elites in their respective countries. Language, education, and outlook often separated these Jews from the new immigrants. It was not only a question of education as some groups of new immigrants brought their intelligensia with them.[26]

Occupational and other socioeconomic differences often divided Jewish communities in connection with other factors. In all communities, there was a divergence of interest between the very wealthy who controlled the communities and those who were less well-to-do. Prior to the French Revolution, property qualifications restricted participation in communal affairs in many parts of Europe, including Germany and Poland.

These *kehillot* or corporate communities, prior to their dissolution and/or transformation, were as much agencies by which the state extracted taxes from the Jews and regulated Jewish populations, often preventing its growth, as they were agencies of an autonomous community. This was especially true under the absolutist regimes of the eighteenth century, as well as their revolutionary and reactionary successors. The wealthy—who often flourished through governmental connections—served these regimes and had little sympathy with the poor. Later, the wealthiest often became the leaders of the movement for assimilation and conversion, especially in Germany and the Hapsburg empire.[27]

With the beginnings of the Industrial Revolution in Poland, class conflict within the Jewish community became more open. The growth of a Jewish entrepreneurial class on the one hand, and a radical labor movement on the other, led to open conflict in Russia and Poland. Later, this conflict was exported to the United States and Britain.[28]

The class differences between Jews often took striking form, as in the division between the protected and tolerated Jews in many German communities in the eighteenth century and the large underclass of vagabonds who often associated with the underworld.[29] Later, the important social differences were between the rurally oriented, peasant-like *Vieh-juden* or cattle dealers and the more urban-oriented shopkeepers in South Germany. In urban areas of Germany, this division might be between the poor immigrants from the East and the established bourgeois German Jews.

The conflict of generations, often marked by different social and cultural experiences, was quite pronounced in European Jewry. Jewish novels, short stories, and the biographies of prominent Jews from 1750 to the present are punctuated by such storm and stress, with each new generation adopting new ideologies. First, one finds enlightenment versus orthodoxy, then rationalism versus romaticism, conversionism versus reform versus neo-orthodoxy, Germanism versus Hungarian, and Polish revivals versus Hebraism and Yiddishism, socialism versus assimilationism versus Zionism, and more.

Gershom Scholem, the great historiographer of Jewish mysticism, has traced his own path from a German assimilationist household to Zionism, involving a revolt against his father's conformity to German ways. One of Scholem's brothers was a founder of the German Communist party, while other brothers conformed to the parental pattern. Such struggle is not at all surprising in the homeland of the "Oedipus conflict."[30]

Another ideological cleavage was of a more traditional variety, although it took its present form only in the eighteenth century. This was the formation of groups of Hasidic Jews under the authority of their rabbis. For them, the rabbi or *Rebbe* or *Tsaddik* was much more significant than the other Jewish secular and religious authorities. Despite assimilationist attack and genocide, these groups have survived with remarkable vigor into the late twentieth century. They represent a significant subgroup within the Ashkenazic Jewish communities.[31]

All of these cleavages often prevented the Jewish community from exercising the power which it might have had, if it had been a unified force. The rifts often allowed powerful outsiders to manipulate the Jews. The divisions did sometimes serve useful purposes. One segment of the community, for instance, might open up new economic opportunities for Jews, while others maintained the old traditions and, thus, helped the whole group to preserve its separate identity. Still, these conflicts point to the locus of ethnic solidarity which is economically effective residing in the family. As generational strife suggests, even the family is not immune from such struggle. Cultural strategy is inherent in many of these cleavages. The issues of Jewish separatism versus integration, and Jewish outward visibility as opposed to maintenance of a low ethnic profile cut across many of these divisions.

Communal and Supracommunal Organizations

While Jewish unity may have been illusory throughout the modern period, communal organizations have existed which did provide a facade of Jewish solidarity. During this period, there were several Jewish communal types:

1. The state-recognized *kehilla,* a corporation able to enforce Jewish law and to tax the Jews on behalf of the state and for its own needs
2. State-recognized communities recognized by public law. In most cases these are limited to the religious sphere, for example, the German *Kultus-gemeinde*

3. Entirely voluntary communities including all or most Jews in a territory, but not recognized in law, such as the British Board of Jewish Deputies
4. Pluralistic communities, being entirely voluntary, but marked by a combination of competition and cooperation and lacking any "umbrella" structure, as does American Jewry

In the history of modern Jewry, one can see a movement from the compulsory, state-recognized corporate *kehilla* to the voluntary, *laissez faire* American pluralism with the German *Kultus-gemeinde* and the British Board of Deputies as intermediate types. Since the eighteenth century, governments have sought to break down many autonomous structures which impede state control or the free market. Elazar has called this process "decorporatization."[32]

The internal organization of the traditional *kehilla* repeated itself for many centuries. It consisted of a religious court (the *Bet Din*) which regulated internal affairs according to Talmudic law, and a secular leadership of wealthy notables, who generally ruled the community in an oligarchic manner. As noted later, these plutocrats often mediated between the community and the authorities. Some states had little interest in interfering in Jewish internal affairs. In such countries, Jewish communal leadership could become strong "states within states."

In absolutist Germany of the eighteenth century, Napoleonic France, and nineteenth-century Tsarist Russia, however, the state intervened actively in regulating the Jewish community and using the *kehilla* to regulate Jewish growth, tax the Jews, exclude unproductive members, and, in the case of Russia, conscript Jews for the army. The autonomy of Jewish officials was restricted, and they became accountable to the government. Ultimately, the authority of the community was undermined and destroyed. The state itself could not tolerate such a "state within the state."[33]

By the end of the nineteenth century, the claims which Jewish nationalists, both Zionist and Yiddishist, made for nationhood, and autonomy came to represent a similar threat to the unitary state in Eastern Europe. In Russia and Poland, Jewish claims for autonomy were never fully affirmed despite partial recognition by the USSR and interwar Poland.[34]

Even when this type of organization developed into a state-recognized religious body which was under governmental supervision and with rabbis who received salaries from special taxes, parallel voluntary organizations arose. The *Alliance Israelite Universelle,* the German *Zentralverein*, and the Russian Society for the Promotion of Culture among the Jews are examples of such voluntary efforts. The context in which each of these societies worked, both to acculturate Jews to modern European values and to defend Jewish rights both in Europe and elsewhere, differed. Many of these societies were based on a narrow core of rich burghers.[35]

The great plethora of Jewish philanthropic institutions which arose throughout Europe and America—such as a Burial Society and a society for visiting the sick—can be seen as the outgrowth of traditional charitable societies found in early modern Jewish communities. In institutions paralleling those of the general society, provision was made for specific Jewish needs, such as Jewish hospitals providing posts for Jewish doctors excluded by anti-Semitic policies in general hospitals and the provision of kosher food to orthopraxic patients. Jewish philanthropy was certainly an expression of identification with Jewry which went beyond the nuclear family for many individuals. If anyone wishes to argue for the existence of a strong sense of separateness, the many institutions which Jews built in the various countries of Central and Eastern Europe are proof of this.

Yet, there are paradoxes. Philanthropy itself became a substitute for actual religious participation and for nationalism. Philanthropic institutions were used by the assimilationists as instruments for acculturating Jews to the general society. Often, giving to a Jewish charity was the last tie which a well-to-do assimilationist had with the Jewish people.

In the nineteenth and twentieth centuries, supracommunal or countrywide organization of the Jews has taken various forms. A state-recognized, tax-supported, organization was under state supervision and was usually religiously oriented. In Germany and Hungary, such an organization was often embroiled in controversy between Orthodox and Reform elements, while nonreligious Jews withdrew entirely. Another type of association which developed was the defense organization, along the lines of the German *Zentralverein*, the American Jewish Committee, or the Russian Society for the Promotion of Culture among the Jews. These organizations acted as lobbies, pressure groups, and self-improvement societies. In some countries, such organizations as the Jewish Board of Deputies in Britain have succeeded in uniting otherwise opposed groups of Reform, Orthodox, and nonreligious Jews.[36]

Such unification has, however, been more the result of outside threats than of an internal desire for unity. Even where organizational activity is high, the "integral Jews" who exhibit the fundamental values of the group and the regular participants in the synagogues have often been a minority, while consumers of Jewish organizational services, contributors, peripheral members, repudiators, and quasi-Jews (half-Jews and the like) have often been the majority.[37]

Without outside threats that appear to involve all Jews, even integral Jews and regular participants in Jewish activities would have little reason to unite for political action and philanthropic activity. While such groups would continue to resist assimilation, they would have little reason to coordinate their efforts.

Overseas Chinese

Emigration and Occupational Structure

Most emigrants from China have come from certain parts of southeastern China, namely Fukien, Amoy, and Kwantung provinces and the island of Hainan. These provinces of China were close to various ports of trade between the Middle Kingdom and the outside world, and they also supplied the colonists in Taiwan. These Chinese were uncharacteristic, because most migrations of Chinese were only on the continental frontiers of mainland China. Relatively small numbers of non-Southeasterners emigrated before 1949 and, even today, they are a minority.[38]

The emigrant areas of China were regions which, by the nineteenth century, suffered from overpopulation and scarcity, and they encouraged frugality. It was a section oriented to maritime trade, even with other parts of the Empire, because mountains isolated it from the system of river traffic which connected the rest of China. Europeans had found Chinese-junk trade of great importance in the East Indies when the Europeans arrived in the sixteenth century. Trade between China and Southeast Asia was always of importance. Most of this travel to *Nanyang*, as the Chinese called this area, was through the southeastern ports. Commerce as a vocation and money making had greater prestige in the Southeast than in the rest of China. The growth of cities in this region made for a peasantry familiar with commerce and city life. While the emigration which is our concern included many who were already engaged in trade, it was largely a migration of peasants, albeit of farmers familiar with urban ways and motivated to make money for themselves. The Southeast, like other coastal areas, was greatly affected by the opening of China to trade with the West in the nineteenth century. It was soon to become a locale of labor recruitment for Western enterprises throughout the Pacific and the rest of the world.

Many of the places to which Chinese immigrated were the tropical frontiers of colonial expansion, where they supplied labor for plantations, tin mines, and railroads, such as Thailand, Malaysia, the Outer Islands of Indonesia. They also did this in California. In more settled areas, such as the port cities of Java and southern Vietnam, they came often as traders. In the highly developed metropolises of North America and Europe, the Chinese came to play highly specialized roles as laundrymen, restaurant owners, and sweatshop textile workers. In Mississippi, the Chinese became grocers and petty retailers.[39]

The situation in the Mississippi Black Belt can serve as an illustration of how Chinese enterprise grew in an area where the Chinese were relatively isolated. Chinese had been imported as farm laborers following the Civil War. After a time, they opened grocery stores, filling the status gap between whites and blacks. The Chinese in Mississippi were limited by their position as people of color, first classed as Negroes and later acquiring an anomalous position of their own. The United States' exclusion of Chinese immigrants affected their status.[40]

Elsewhere, the Chinese were also subject to restrictions on owning land, as in Java and California, and to outright expulsion, as in Sonora in the 1920s. After World War II, restrictions on Chinese immigration were eased in the United States, but anti-Sinitic legislation and nationalism increased in Southeast Asia. In Indonesia, there were outright pogroms against the Chinese in the 1950s and 1960s, as well as efforts to expel the Chinese from rural trade. The Chinese in Vietnam have been an important component of the boat people, while Sino-Cambodians suffered alongside the Khmer during the recent traumas of that land. Meanwhile, there was an increase in the numbers of Hong Kong and Taiwan Chinese in the United States and ex-Indonesian Chinese in the Netherlands. Many Hong Kong residents anticipating the annexation of that Crown Colony to China are emigrating and investing their capital elsewhere.[41]

In many ways, the Chinese went through economic transformations as radical as those of the Jews, from peasants to proletarians and to merchants. As with the Jews, the social ascent is more rapid, and the Chinese community is more uniformly a middleman minority where there are relatively few Chinese, such as in Peru, Mexico, Guyana, and Tahiti. This gereralization, however, must be qualified. The Oriental exclusion policies of the United States and other countries made many illegal Chinese immigrants escaping the poverty of China seek anonymity in humble laundries and restaurants. This prevented many from bringing over their wives and children, possibly reducing their motivation to increase their wealth. Much of the latest Chinese immigration to San Francisco and New York reproduces the sweatshops of earlier Jewish immigration, and this new population is proletarian in its occupations. Many American-born Chinese are turning to employment in the public sector, thus leaving the middleman niche.[42]

In the Netherland Indies, as in other European colonies, the Chinese had taken the role of intermediary between the colonial economy and the indigenous subsistence sector during the Dutch period. Although restricted by the colonial authorities, they became the small rural traders, shopkeepers, and moneylenders. The main connections between the Indonesian economy and the world market were through large Dutch and other European trading companies, but, even there, one found interstices in which the Chinese had gained control.[43]

The way in which the Chinese became a major factor is illustrated by their role in the South Sumatran rubber industry. The Chinese had been prohibited from owning lands in the Netherlands and East Indies after 1870, and they dealt mainly with the trading and processing of agricultural products. Rubber was introduced into Indonesia in the first part of the twentieth century. Since Indonesian smallholders had found the crop to be a valuable addition to their cash income, there was a need for someone to process and bring it to the world market. This mediation was provided by both the Chinese and natives. Rubber production increased between the two Wolrld Wars and, by 1940, had become the main agricultural export of the Netherland Indies. By this time, the Chinese dominated small-holder rubber trade and processing. The Chinese owned mills which were able to process the rubber for shipment abroad. The Chinese had connections through the Sumatran ports and also with the large Chinese firms in Singapore.

Despite post–World War II pressures—such as competition with synthetic rubber and nationalist efforts to replace Chinese aliens with native traders—the Chinese survived. Alien Chinese mills and enterprises were transferred to Chinese who carried

Indonesian citizenship, and Chinese capital and skills were needed to maintain the industry during the 1960s and 1970s. In fact, in the late 1970s, the marketing of natural rubber in Singapore and Sumatra was still controlled by four clans from the Hokkien-speech community. Collaboration developed between Indonesian Chinese and ethnic Indonesians, both in government and the rubber trade.[44]

Like the Jews, the Chinese had also undergone a cultural transformation. They were the objects of Christian missionary activity, both in Southeast Asia and in the Americas—as well as in China proper. This missionary activity encouraged the acquisition of Western-style education, and introduced the Chinese to new types of organization. In Mississippi, most Chinese became affiliated with Protestant churches. On the other hand, in Southeast Asia, Christian activity called forth imitation in the form of a neo-Confucian revival combined with a modern Chinese nationalism. Schools, a press, chambers of commerce, hospitals, churches, and entry into white-collar professions were all products of this transformation.[45]

In most of Southeast Asia—and indeed elsewhere—there were few Chinese professionals and white-collar workers prior to World War II. At that time, most of those occupations served the Chinese community itself as teachers, journalists in the Chinese press, traditional and modern doctors, and the like. In Thailand, there were royal officials of Chinese origin. There were almost no government servants of Chinese origin in Southeast Asian countries that were under European colonial rule. In both Asia and the Americas, white-collar occupations are seen as more desirable than starting life as a petty trader or artisan. Even in Southeast Asia, government service is more and more open to ethnic Chinese, especially in technical posts. In Singapore, a city-state with a Chinese majority, the government is dominated by the Chinese. The opening of opportunities in universities and government service is also apparent in the United States, which has attracted many exiles and immigrants with university training and including several Nobel Prize winners from the Mainland and Taiwan. In the 1950s, many of these individuals who had come as students were stranded when the Revolution took place and the Korean War broke out. Unlike the other immigrants, many of the scientists and professionals are not from Southeastern China. Undoubtedly, the Chinese are still affected by discrimination. Many recent immigrants to the United States are middle-class professionals. Some help finance other relatives who go into business.[46]

Cultural Attributes and the Separatist Complex

While there is no doubt that there is substantial Chinese ethnocentrism—including a belief in the superiority of Chinese culture—Chinese tradition lacks bans on sexual relations and marriage with outsiders, commensalism, and conversion to other religions. While all the Chinese speech groups who emigrated participated in the Chinese national cultural tradition which includes familism and ancestor worship (its Confucian component) and the various spirit cults of Chinese and Buddhist origins—all were pragmatic about participating in local religions, which is compatible with the Chinese tradition. Thus, it was fairly easy for many to adopt Theravada Buddhism in Thailand and Cambodia, as well as Christianity in North America and various European colonies.

Before independence, relatively few Chinese adopted Islam in Malaysia and Indonesia. Even the assimilationists in this Muslim region became Christians. Many Chinese in Malaysia continue to seek religious succor outside of Islam. In Java, however, the Indonesian-born and intermixed Peranakan Chinese conform to local custom by eating almost no pork.[47]

Still, pragmatism should not imply that the Chinese, even in Christian and Buddhist lands, easily give up all aspects of their culture. In Theravada-Buddhist Cambodia and Thailand, the Chinese preference for burial over the Theravada rite of cremation has continued to serve as a marker of ethnicity and assimilation. Tobias suggests that the Chinese and Thai have a kind of joking relationship, in which each does the other's dirty work, with the Chinese as traders. The Buddhist heritage gives them a common vocabulary for such a relationship.[48]

The failure to adopt the Muslim religion can be explained, in part, because Malaysia and Indonesia were under European rule until recently, and it was Christianity which was then the more attractive religion, being associated with the dominant Europeans. After independence, a combination of persistent institutionalized pluralism which survived the colonial period and outbreaks of anti-Sinitic violence made Islam less palatable for the Chinese. Even Chinese who convert to Islam may continue to be perceived as non-Malays and non-Indonesians, and thus not fully benefit from their change of identity.[49] Such explanations are not fully satisfactory and may require further study.

Chinese pragmatism with regard to intermarriage is shown by the acceptance of *mestizos* (*metis* in Cambodia, *lukjin* in Thailand, and some Peranakan in Indonesia) into the Chinese community, not the fact that they exist.[50] Intermarriages generally have been one way, between Chinese men and non-Chinese women. External forces are as important in determining these attitudes as are internal Chinese values.

Demographic patterns are crucial. The early Chinese immigrant society in Nanyang and in North America was a "bachelor society." First, this was because the Imperial government forbade emigration, and families were reluctant to permit women to emigrate. Most of those who did emigrate were destined for brothels. After the Chinese Exclusion Act and the very restrictive Immigration Act of 1924, immigration to the United States was not legally possible. In nineteenth-century Thailand and Malaysia, Chinese men had the choice of remaining single or marrying local women. Most laborers did not marry, but farmers, merchants, and artisans did—often several times. In the United States during the restricted immigration period, even marriage to local women was limited by laws against miscegenation. The dubious legal status of the illegal migrants made their whole situation precarious, and civil strife and war in China often made return impossible. The Chinatowns of the period between World War I and 1950—and even later—had a large bachelor population.[51]

After the fall of the Manchu Dynasty in 1911, when emigration was freer, there was large-scale immigration of families and the Chinese populations of Thailand, Malaysia, and Indonesia received a large influx of pure Chinese. The fact, however, that so many overseas Chinese communities have large components of those of mixed ancestry is, in itself, an indication that the separatist complex of the Chinese is either weak or substantially different from that of Jews and Hindus.[52]

The economic ethic of the Chinese is, of course, related to their attitudes toward family, ethnic group, and other factors. Willmott finds familism at the heart of the Chinese orientation. Chinese enterprises tend to be small enough so that there is no need to employ outsiders above the level of clerk. Expansion usually takes the form of sending a family member to open a branch and stops at a certain point. This also leads to diversity of lines and business, since one may expand in different ways in different cities or towns. There are also many business failures, a trait often ascribed to Chinese tendencies to speculate—which contrasts sharply with their other traits of hard work and frugality. Other characteristics which Chinese often attribute to themselves are extreme individualism, family loyalty, driving power, austerity, independence, and poor ability to cooperate.

While in Java, the newcomer or Totok Chinese have a reputation of being more hard-driving than the Indonesian-born Peranakan, both still are seen as more hard-driving than the Indonesians themselves. There is a similar dichotomy between the *lukjin* and China-born in Thailand. In the 1950s there was some doubt about the ability of the Chinese in Indonesia and Thailand to adapt to the new conditions. Beginning in Thailand and later in Indonesia, Chinese businessmen have succeeded in surviving severe blows through collaboration with the military elites of these states.[53]

The dual morality has been attributed to the Chinese. Merchants who are Chinese have been condemned as swindlers, yet praised for their high sense of business honor. Donald Willmott wrote: "There is an apparent morality, there was an implicit distinction between relatives and friends on the one hand and strangers on the other."[54]

Obligations to the former are strong, but not to the latter. One must take the time to build a relationship of trust, if one expects to be treated as a friend in this system. On the other hand, keeping the honor of the family name is a deeply felt responsibility.

In Indonesia, some of the violations of this high standard were a result of Chinese immigration to a new area where all were strangers. As time went on, they did adjust to the Indonesian form of trust-relationships, as well as learning the ways of European business. In the long pull, the behavior of Chinese commercial people is similar to those of other groups.

Licensed deviance appears among the Chinese, too. While the Chinese in Southeast Asia had legal monopolies for gambling and opium, these were primarily for sale to other Chinese, not to outsiders. In the Muslim countries of Malaysia and Indonesia, of course, the fact that the Chinese eat pork and drink alcohol can make their restaurants places where impious Muslims may indulge themselves. Golub found this to be the role played by the Thai minority in Malaysia, but the more numerous Chinese can also fill it. The Chinese part in moneylending makes them fill a niche similar in Islamic Southeast Asia to that filled by Jews in medieval Europe, since Islam also forbids interest on loans.[55]

In California, during the late nineteenth century, Chinatowns were often vice districts. Perception of wicked practices—such as opium addiction, white slaving, and gambling—were among the components of anti-Sinic agitation.[56]

The Locus of Ethnic Solidarity

With regard to the Chinese, it is clear that the original locus of ethnic solidarity is the family itself. The Chinese have a "big-house" or joint familial household ideal, even though few among the millions of Chinese lived in such a domestic menage. Certainly, it was the peasants who provided many of the emigrants. Still, the importance of family ties for Chinese businessmen has already been noted. One such leader is Mr. Shih, whose father has been an incense-maker in China. A paternal uncle had migrated to Thailand and become an import-export merchant in Thailand. After his classical schooling at home, Mr. Shih went to Bangkok to join his uncle when he was 14. When the uncle died, Mr. Shih became head of the firm with a cousin as partner. Then, he established a hardware firm on his own, but registered the two businesses under one corporate name with family members as chief stock-holders.[57]

One lineage, the Mans of San Tin Village in Hong Kong, has utilized familial ties in Western Europe. Members of this lineage of former farmers began emigrating as seamen. By the early 1960s, they had begun a chain of Chinese restaurants, first in London and later throughout Western Europe. The men of active working years now go to England to work and later manage restaurants and send remittances home. It is an extraordinary example of how traditional familism can adapt to modern economic specialization.[58]

As this example shows, the family is valuable as a resource which one can fall back on during hard times, but it is also vulnerable to other problems such as sibling rivalry, generational conflict, lack of heirs, and violation of trust. Immigration and citizenship laws, as well as wars, have also placed additional strains on Chinese immigrant families. The phenomena of the bachelor society of American Chinatowns in the early 1900s and the stranded students and intellectuals of the 1950s were products of such external forces. Relationships in such families after reunification were often strained. The strength of kinship ties, however, among the Chinese has been seen as an important component of Chinese success, as opposed to the failure of others such as Thais (in Thailand), Mauritius Creoles, and American blacks, who appear to have weaker kin ties.[59]

The business relationship, however, does not depend solely on familial ties. As indicated in the last example, ties beyond the family are used as well. The descendants of Tjan San Go, an entrepreneur in Java, maintained close relations for several generations with the family of the man who had given Tjan a job and helped him. One means of extending kin ties fictionally is the use of the surname. Chinese who share an ideogram or character for their surname assume a kin tie. This has become quite important among overseas Chinese.

Tien Ju-kang, a Yunnanese Chinese anthropologist, found himself included in the two Tien surname associations of the Fukienese and Hakka in Sarawak. All members of another surname association in one town had had pictures on the wall of the clan's ancestral hall in China, which their contributions had helped build. Surname and clan associations have existed in the Phillippines and United States as well. They are usually divided along dialect community lines and, if large enough, internal disputes may also divide them. These functions include settlement of internal disputes and aid to the less fortunate. Some associations include members bearing several family names.[60]

For both business and other reasons, Chinese communities were characterized by clientalistic relations. Businessmen extended credit to employees which helped them establish their own businesses. Networks of credit and other relations developed especially in such Chinese-controlled lines as the rubber trade.[61] In dealing with the governmental authorities, most overseas Chinese felt threatened and preferred to go through certain powerful Chinese intermediaries than through proper bureaucratic channels.

Such relationships were used in the communities of the United States in order to cope with the complexities of immigration. During the 1950s each immigrant had to have a sponsor, who bore ultimate financial responsibility for him or her. This, as well as the preceding and concurrent illegal immigration, contributed to forcing many immigrants into a dependent status relative to their powerful patrons.[62]

While credit relationships tend to be assymmetrical, the Chinese also utilize more egalitarian rotating credit associations. In this type of group, all contribute equally, and each gets an opportunity to borrow from the common till. As pointed out elsewhere in this book, rotating credit associations are particularly vulnerable to manipulation by unscrupulous individuals. This is, however, controlled by the same mechanisms of exclusion and ostracism within the community that prevail within the family.[63]

Internal Cleavages

An important component of the internal organization of Chinese communities overseas is the segmentation along the original dialect and regional lines which the immigrants brought with them from China. In most large- or medium-sized urban communities, one may find several origin-groups: Fukien (Hokkien), Tiochiu, Hakka, Hainanese, Cantonese, and sometimes others. In some areas, one group or another predominates, but certainly in large metropolises such as Singapore, Bangkok, and prerevolutionary Phnom Penh, there are representatives of several such groups. Even in a small city like Kuching in Sarawak, Malaysia, there were substantial numbers from all of these dialect groups.[64]

Just as the Chinese community as a whole may play a special role in the economy, so the various Chinese-speech communities may also be specialized. In Kuching, for example, most employees of coffeeshops are Hainanese, even though the owners come from other groups. At the top of the social hierarchy, one finds Cantonese, Foochow, and Hokkien domination, even though the Hakka have a numerical plurality in Sarawak. It is these groups who achieved prosperity early on, and who have connections with leading businessmen from their own speech communities in Singapore and elsewhere. In the United States, Cantonese are generally dominant in the older Chinatowns.[65]

Overlapping with speech community is the division between the veteran immigrants and their descendants on the one hand, and newcomers on the other. In Java, the Peranakan, or old-time, community is generally of Hokkien ancestry, while the Totok or new immigrant segment is much more diversified in its origins. In addition, the oldtimers are generally more acculturated into the indigenous culture. This is certainly true of the Peranakans. The Peranakans speak Indonesian, eat a Javanese-type of food, and resemble the surrounding population in many other ways. The old-time Chinese-Americans similarly differ from new arrivals after 1965. Sometimes, social and economic differences also appear, but not always in the direction of veteran superiority. For instance, many new immigrants to the United States come as members of an academic and technical elite.[66]

In Indonesia in particular, governmental policies since independence have aggravated the division between Totok and Peranakan. Those Chinese who are native to Indonesia and who opted for Indonesian citizenship were more likely to be Peranakans than are the children of Totoks. While citizenship, even for them, was not secure, the fact of their Indonesian nationality has made it possible for them to carry on their business in certain strategic parts of the economy, such as the rubber trade. A combination of laws and events gave the Chinese who were Indonesian nationals a much bigger role in the rubber industry and the economy in general than they had had prior to 1960, sometimes to the detriment of the alien Chinese.

For instance, in 1963, when the Malaysian Federation was formed, the Sukarno government of Indonesia instituted a confrontation with Malaysia, which then included Singapore. Firms which were owned by alien Chinese and connected to companies in Singapore were forced out of the rubber trade. They were replaced by Indonesian nationals of Chinese origin as well as other Indonesians. While these firms were permitted to re-enter the Indonesian market after 1967, they now faced competition from the Indonesian nationals who were ethnic Chinese and ethnic Indonesians. This was one instance where the interests of WNI Chinese opposed those of alien Chinese.[67]

Despite the Confucian tradition of filial piety and respect for elders, Chinese society at home and abroad has not been spared generational conflict, as the Cultural Revolution of the 1960s showed. In Java, Tan finds tensions between fathers and sons and a lack of understanding between the Chinese parents and the more Westernized and Indonesianized children. Despite this, children still tend to obey their parents, even when they have been trained in Christian or government schools which neglected the Confucian tradition. There are also tensions present between first-generation and second-generation Chinese in the United States.

In a study of second-generation Chinese in Thailand, it was found that those who used Chinese surnames and went to Chinese schools were more apt to identify as Chinese than those who were sent to Thai schools and those parents had adopted Thai family names. This suggests conformity with patterns imposed by the elders of these people.[68] Further studies of age and generational tension and harmony among overseas Chinese is warranted, since it is not clear as to how sharp such conflicts are, compared to what is found among others such as the Jews.

Since many overseas Chinese communities are internally stratified, economic class conflict may be present. In several of the societies where Chinese reside, the tension along ethnic lines cuts across class lines. So it is in Malaysia. There have been situations in which Malays and Chinese who are poor resent their own rich as much as those of the outgroup and see them as members of a broad class of exploiters. Still, such class-based solidarity has not been permanent and often class struggle may be confined to the ethnic group itself.[69]

Even in the United States where young Chinese-American militants and the International Ladies Garment Workers Union are attempting to organize the employees of Chinese sweat shops, it is likely that the badge of color and ethnic origin is still more important than that of class. The distance between the Chinese reality and their full incorporation into American life is amply documented in the works of Hsu, Nee and Nee, Lee, and Sung. Nevertheless, competing economic interests do divide the actions of Chinese communal leaders.

Ideological divisions also cause cleavages in the Chinese community, although they often intersect with other interests. Overseas Chinese in Singapore and Malaya gave refuge to and funds which supported nationalistic revolutionaries such as Sun Yat Sen in 1911, while Peranakan Chinese in Java, often reacting to the missions, began the foundation of Chinese schools.[70] In the period of the Japanese occupation (1942–1945) and later the post–World War II period, overseas Chinese communities became sharply divided between collaborationists and resisters and later, Nationalists and supporters of the Communists. Both the rival regimes in Peking and Taipei and the various host governments competed for the loyalties of the Chinese communities.[71]

In countries such as Thailand and Indonesia, the various school systems established by the Chinese communities, the Christian missions, and governmental authorities often became the instruments for attracting people to a particular ideology or national allegiance. The Thai and Indonesian governments, among others, eliminated separate Chinese language instruction.[72]

Terming such alliances as ideological may be misleading. While some Chinese clearly made ideological commitments to nationalism or communism, many others responded in terms of social pressures. One finds little evidence among the Chinese of tightly knit sectarian groups, such as the Jewish Hasidim or the South Asian Ismailis.[73]

Communal and Supracommunal Organizations

Both in Southeast Asia and in the rest of the diaspora, either formally or tacitly state-recognized mediators have arisen, with the exception of small and dispersed Chinese communities as in London or the new metropolitan areas of the United States. In much of colonial Southeast Asia, the Kapitan system—as found in the Dutch East Indies—was typical. Similar institutions developed in Thailand and Cambodia, prior to the latter's conquest by the French. The officer system began with Portuguese and Dutch rule shortly after European discovery and control.

The Kapitan, as he came to be known, was the communications link between the Dutch and the Chinese. They were not officials empowered to make administrative decisions, but they were the ones who carried the orders of the colonial rulers to the Chinese and informed the administrators of events in the Chinese quarter. They also acted as advisors, guarantors, and spokesmen for their compatriots. In nineteenth-century Thailand and the Spanish Philippines, tax farmers were among the most important officials of the Chinese community. In both cases, the ruling power was either weak or willing to leave the Chinese alone.

In some cities, however, the officials registered Chinese residents, controlled the finances of Chinese cemeteries and other institutions, and even headed councils dealing with divorce cases. In the Dutch East Indians, the institution broke down with the rise of Chinese nationalism, but a similar official called *chef de congregation* survived in Cambodia and Vietnam under the French until those countries became independent. These *chefs* could be autocratic in their regulation of the Chinese in Indochina.[74]

In Singapore, such an institution broke down in an earlier period than elsewhere, and there was apparently less regulation of the Chinese there than in other places. For a time, the various secret societies were strong, but late in the nineteenth century, they were suppressed. These were succeeded by the wide variety of origin groups and surname associations, Chambers of Commerce, political groups, and voluntary associations aiming to establish schools and hospitals. This also took place in other overseas communities, such as Indonesia, Thailand, and elsewhere. Political groups from 1900 to 1960 were often oriented to one or another of the China-based political factions—the reformists and revolutionaries early in the century and the Kuomintang and Communists in midcentury. This was reflected in such local institutions as school committees.[75]

In Indonesia and Malaysia, Chinese political parties which participated in local and national politics developed. In Indonesia, however, the main Chinese party, Baperki, was suppressed in the wake of the 1965 attempted coup and the resulting fall of the Sukarno regime. A new variety of patron-client relationship has emerged with entrepreneurs who had connections with the military as leaders. In Malaysia, the Malayan-Chinese Association, a major coalition partner in the first days of the Malaysian Federation, has been buffeted by Chinese extremists on the one side and Malay demands for greater control on the other.[76]

Despite the plethora of voluntary associations, umbrella bodies have developed to coordinate the communities internally and to represent the Chinese to the authorities. In Phnom Penh during the 1950s and 1960s, the Hospital Committee served this function. In some small Asian communities, the school boards took over this task. In San Francisco, an informal oligarchy called the Six Companies controlled many of the affairs of Chinatown. Often interlocking directorates, business associations, and the Chamber of Commerce have been important in coordination, even without an officially designated body. After the 1965 coup, the Indonesian military government abolished the Chinese umbrella organization, but was then forced to recreate it.[77]

The proliferation of organizations may be a mechanism for widening participation in community affairs, but it may also be a sign of alienation from the central bodies of the community. The tightly controlled Phnom Penh community under the French actually had fewer voluntary associations than did the much smaller Chinese community in Vancouver, Canada, which had more than 80 organizations.[78]

As among the Jews, membership in a community must be clearly distinguished analytically from participation in that community's organization. While membership is based on ascribed attributes of a common origin or identity, participation is optional. It involved payment of dues and formal activities. In Chinese communities, no more than one-third to one-half of those eligible bother to join.[79] Hsu has pointed out that in the United States, the old familial, kin and fictive kin, and locality-origin groups have been more important than organizations on the basis of interest. Chinese schools are relatively underfunded. The Chinese-Americans organize less on a religious basis than do Japanese, Jews, and other minorities. Hsu also deplores the lack of political activity on behalf of Chinese interests in the United States. He does, however, note the newly founded scientific and professional organizations of foreign-born "brain drainers" who are a significant segment of the Chinese-American society, albeit outside the old Chinatowns. Again the lack of solidarity and mobilization on the communal and supracommunal level is apparent.[80]

Overseas South Asians

Overseas South Asians are even more heterogenous than are overseas Chinese or European Jews. They are divided by language, by religion, by region, and by caste. The tendency toward self-employment was clearer among the overseas Chinese than among certain overseas-Indian communities. While some groups of Indians have become classic middleman minorities, such as the Gujeratis in East Africa and the Chettiars in Burma, other groups have had a different mode of adaptation.[81]

The way in which a group has entered the economy of a particular society has had long-term effects on how that South-Asian community develops. Those groups which entered as contract agricultural labor were generally at a disadvantage, often remaining laborers. For instance, in Guyana, the descendants of the former indentured servants have become sugar workers, rice farmers, and professionals, and comprise an important segment of the "penny capitalists" who own small shops. Some Indians there, as in Natal, have risen from laborers to small businessmen. "Passenger" Indians, who arrived on their own, have a different pattern, usually entering the business-sector immediately. In Guyana, where the majority of the Indians arrived as unskilled laborers, there is a small class of businessmen who are able to compete directly with the larger British and Portuguese firms. In East Africa, the "passenger Indians" have been the dominant group among the South Asians since the beginning of the century.

The socioeconomic situation of the immigrants has affected the retention of traditional patterns. Merchants, for instance, have greater resources for maintaining traditional institutions than have the laborers. The very ethnic solidarity which has aided their success in business has also provided them with means to recreate some aspects of the indigenous heritage in their new homes and insulate them from the outside culture. Such a recreation has been less feasible among the more proletarian communities of Guyana, Fiji, and Natal, than in East Africa.[82]

It should be noted that some groups which moved rapidly into middleman positions often came from rural backgrounds and were not originally from the mercantile castes. One of the most important commercial caste groups in East Africa—the Patidars—had been an agricultural caste in Gujerat and still include cultivaters to this day. In the seventeenth and eighteenth centuries, however, they began to climb into commercial statuses. The Sikhs in Malaysia often immigrated as military or police personnel. They then drifted into jobs as watchmen on plantations. In that type of employment, they lent money to the laborers, thus beginning careers as moneylenders.[83]

While most attention up to the 1960s was given to the Indians and Pakistanis in tropical countries under colonial and post-colonial rule, South Asians have, in increasing numbers, immigrated to temperate, metropolitan lands, such as Britain, Canada, and the United States. Some of these are overseas Indians, fleeing actual or feared persecution and instability in Uganda, Kenya, or Surinam. Some are poor peasants from the Punjab, Gujerat, and Bengal, seeking their fortunes abroad. Still others are brain drainers, highly skilled scientists, doctors, engineers, and other academicians whose skills are highly sought-after in the developed economies of the West. While the former two groups often rely on "penny capitalism" and commercial skills to make their way, the latter group—as do their Chinese and Jewish counterparts—work in highly bureaucratic corporations or governmental agencies. In the United States, the "brain drainers" are more significant than the other two varieties of South-Asian immigrants and the analysis of their situations follows a path which is different from that of the shopkeepers and migrant workers. They may, however, open small businesses on the side, such as Indian restaurants, and bring in relatives to run them.[84]

In South Africa, as well as some other countries, Indian professionals have been quite important. In Guyana, the leader of the Peoples' Progressive Party, which is a socialist party but which became associated with the Indian community, has been led by Cheddi Jagan, an American-trained dentist.[85]

Cultural Attributes and Ritual Segregation

Much of the discussion about solidarity and division within the overseas-Indian communities revolves around caste. Considerable variation exists in the degree to which caste persists, both structurally and ideationally. Among the old, often Creolized Caribbean Indian groups, caste is fairly weak. Guyana, which has one of the largest concentrations of Indians, intercaste and even interreligious marriages are tolerated and are not even considered to be remarkable, although the idiom of caste persists. It is used to denote low and high value, as well as relations between the Indians and such groups as the Afro-Creoles, the Europeans, and the Portuguese. In part, the change from arranged marriage to free choice of spouse—albeit with consent of the parents being sought—has accompanied the change from considering caste as highly salient to indifference to caste.[86]

Among Indian university students in Malaysia, the topic of caste is still highly sensitive, even though it is no longer relevant in day-to-day interaction. Consciousness in Malaysia of the connection between the higher-caste origins of the mercantile group in that country—as opposed to the origins of those who came as laborers—has probably influenced the persistence of caste.

The situation in Natal is similar. Former caste divisions are gradually giving way to pan-Asian solidarity and class division in the face of apartheid.[87]

In the commercially oriented East and Central African communities, caste has been salient, although there have been significant changes there, too. Up through the 1960s, caste remained significant with regard to marriage; and marriage across caste lines was rare. Prohibitions against eating with Asians of another caste and Europeans were dropped. On the other hand, Africans—in particular servants—were treated like lower-caste individuals in India.[88]

The very recently formed immigrant communities in Britain still retain close ties with their home communities in India and Pakistan. There, at least among Gujerati and Punjabi immigrants, marriage with Europeans is frowned upon. Marriage with English and other European women was not viewed as legitimate by the immigrants. This is probably not true among many of the professional and educated immigrants.[89]

Overseas South Asians differ sharply from overseas Chinese in their treatment of their "mixed-blood" offspring. Most disapprove of interracial marriage. This is more pronounced among Hindus than Muslims, and is more negative to marriages with blacks than with whites. Bharati wrote, with regard to the Indians in East Africa:

> Asians do not accept children of mixed parentage as their own; hence, these people identified with their mothers' kin in all matters.[90]

Muslims are somewhat more liberal in this regard than Hindus. In Malawi, some Muslims contracted marriages with African women, as did Gujerati Muslims with Swahili and upland tribes in East Africa. In Malaysia, too, there are some descendants of marriages between early Muslim traders and local women.[91]

The ideology of caste—connected as it is with purity, pollution, and marriage within a fairly constricted circle of families—can be seen as a "familistic" world view. Marriage is the central rite, as much as memorialism is with the Chinese. At least in its modern East African formulation, this view of the world is extremely puritanical with regard to sexual relations. Among the Gujeratis and Punjabis who predominate among the East African Asians, sex is viewed as dirty and polluting. It must be avoided whenever possible. The more sexually open Europeans and Africans are seen as being of a lower order and are bitterly resented.[92]

The frugality of the overseas Indians, especially the *dukawalla* (small shopkeeper), was proverbial. While this type of Indian has grown to be relatively rare, his image still forms an important part of the stereotype of the Indians in East and Central Africa, as well as their own self-image.

Of course, frugality must be defined. It might mean working the long hours which are demanded in running a small shop with no or few assistants. Factory workers must make choices of how to best fulfill their needs. Among South Asian immigrants in Great Britain, there is a preference for taking a job with lower wages but opportunities for much overtime work, which may make for a net gain in income, to the reverse. This makes sense for "sojourning" workers, seeking to return to their villages, rather than for immediate consumption. This is especially true where these workers are, at any rate, confined to low-paying jobs. Asian small shopkeepers in Britain work longer hours than do their white competitors.[93]

In addition to sexual puritanism, the Indians in Africa and elsewhere are affected by other ritual taboos. Many Hindu castes forbid the eating of beef, and some are strictly vegetarian, while the Muslims prohibit the eating of pork. Both the Hindu and Muslim religions prohibit drinking of alcohol. In East Africa, the women generally do not drink alcohol openly, but men may engage in social drinking. A measure of segregation in that area may be the fact that Indians did not mingle with Europeans in their ritual cocktail drinking, known as "sundowners." Indians, especially Hindus, often owned taverns for Africans in Central Africa, but the Europeans and Africans were the ones who let Indians drink openly.[94]

Differences in food tastes, quite apart from religious prohibitions, serve as boundaries. Indians often find European food bland, while Europeans dislike the highly spiced Indian food. In one

English factory, where workers had to work in close physical proximity, English workers refused to work in gangs with Indo-Pakistanis, because they claimed that they could not bear the smell of garlic.[95] The growing popularity of Indian and Pakistani food in Britain may change some of this in time.

The Asians in Africa—much like the other minorities—have been accused of unfair economic practices. This is particularly true of shopkeepers and other middlemen. Africans, for instance, accuse the Indians of exploiting and cheating them. The Africans charged the Indians of treating their African employees like lower-class people in India and of engaging in such practices as using short-weights, overcharging, and misleading advertisements, and haggling and bargaining were particualrly resented.

In bargaining, Asians—who are friends of the shopkeepers—have an advantage over all others, while upper-status whites and Africans have the edge over lower-class individuals. Asian businessmen were also accused of preventing Africans from competing with them and with holding back the economic progress of the country through such practices, a charge which has been made in comparable situations in other countries. Those who are favorable to the Indians see the characteristics of bargaining as arising from the particular circumstances of small shopkeeping, while the competitive advantages of the Indians arises from their greater experience in business and need for achievement.[96]

The Locus of Ethnic Solidarity

Alongside other factors, close-knit family life and reciprocal aid among related families have been seen as contributing to the economic success of Indians in East Africa. Among South Asians, family and kin ties are intertwined with sect, regional-linguistic loyalties, and caste. This is what one would expect, considering the fact that castes (at the *jati* subcaste level) are marriage circles which limit nuptial unions to a relatively small number of people.

Important economic links exist between members of what Desai calls the village-kin network. In Britain, the internal economy of Gujerati grocers and hawkers depends on such links, both for employees and for relations between grocers and their customers.

Valued workers in the small stores, and even in large concerns, are members of the family. In small shops, immediate members are often unpaid, unless they are partners. Houses are also bought and maintained by sets of partners who are often kinsmen among the immigrants. Asian shopkeepers in Britain utilize kin, family, and friends for information and for raising capital, as well as for labor. It should be stressed that white British shopkeepers also mobilize family and kin for their entrepreneurial success. The new Pakistani discount clothing manufacturers and traders are also known for their kin ties, although large Pakistani enterprises have multiethnic labor forces.

In large corporations, the family principle persists, even though laws outside of India do not give legal recognition to the joint family. Still, an effort is made to keep the firm under family control and to entrust only family members with corporate secrets. In one instance, the Indian head of an East African corporation sent his son with messages to shareholders before an important meeting, even though he had lower ranking employees for such purposes. He felt he could only trust his son. Indians went first to kin and then to their own communities for economic aid of all kinds.[97]

In extending relationships beyond the family, Indian businessmen think first in terms of their own sect, village-kin group, and caste. For instance, Allidina Visram who founded a chain of stores in British East Africa drew many of the managers of his stores from his own Ismaili community. The Ismailis, who are known as a fairly tightly knit Muslim sect, have both a regional and caste base in India.[98] Except where broader coalitions are necessitated by political conditions—as in Guyana or South Africa—Indians appear to be quite tied to the narrow regional caste and sect groups. This was also true of Indian labor contractors who recruited plantation workers in India for work in Malaya and Ceylon by utilizing members of their own kin and regional and ethnic groups.[99]

Internal Cleavages

The divisions within the Indian community have already been discussed. Within relatively small enclaves of Indians—especially in new immigrant communities—these divisions may be less important. First, the process of chain migration makes it likely that most or all members of a small community will be of one origin. Second, even where this is not the case, the common identity with the South Asian subcontinent imposed by outsiders makes all realize their common identity. When this changes, however, then cleavages come to the fore.

In larger communities—such as those of Britain or the cities of East and South Africa—there are important divisions along caste, sect, and speech-community lines, which may overlap. Castes and sects usually have a regional basis in India and belong to the same speech community. This kind of regional-sect-caste division affects fieldwork among Indians and even associations which bear names like the Indian association.

Desai, a Gujerati anthropologist, concentrated his fieldwork in Britain on Gujeratis, with some attention to Punjabis as well. He gave less attention to the Muslim Pakistanis than their numbers might have warranted. Desai also describes two British Indian associations which were predominantly Gujerati, although both had names which would seem to include all Indians.

Asian organizations in recent years have become stronger, both through organizing in favor of civil rights and through government suport for some cultural activity. The government may, in fact, have strengthened conservative religious groups, such as the Muslim organizations which organized rallies against publication of Rushdie's *Satanic Verses.*[100]

Isolation and political impotence of the East African-Asian community was caused, in part, by its own internal cleavages combined with the rigid colonial "colour bar." The caste system, in its indigenous form, could not operate in East and Central Africa. Still the occupational choices of an individual were limited by caste and religion. Each of the South Asian sectarian and caste groups tried to organize social and cultural institutions for its adherents, as the increase in its numbers permitted. Thus, East African-Asian society was essentially a conglomeration of a series of close-knit castes and sects.[101]

The economic separation of each group was paralleled by the development of separate hospitals, schools, social clubs, and burial societies. Even the small Roman Catholic Goan community of Nairobi—which numbered 5,000 prior to the Asian exodus of the mid 1960s—was divided in that manner. Each of the five castes had its own voluntary association or caste. Members of the highest caste—the Brahmins—earned the most. Goan umbrella organizations failed because of a rivalry between the Brahmins and the other upper caste, the Chaddoes. No single leader could speak for the whole community.[102]

Other types of divisions also appear among overseas-Indian communities. There are differences between "oldtimers" and "greenhorns." The oldtimers are more familiar with conditions in the new country, while greenhorn immigrants may bring with them political developments in the old country or else from a third country. The British-trained barrister, Mohandas Gandhi, began his political career as a leader of South African Indians. There were economic and political differences between the veteran Zanzibar Indians and the newer immigrants. Similar differences existed in Malaya between the merchants who had settled there during the eighteenth and nineteenth centuries and the new immigrants. Obviously, the merchants belonged to a different class than that of the plantation workers.[103]

In Malaya, South Africa, and Guyana, the differing interests of the merchants, moneylenders, farmers, and plantation workers all clash with each other. In Malaya, Indian trade-union leadership is visible, while Cheddi Jagan, a Marxist, has been the most notable Indian political leader in Guyana. This suggests that the power of the more numerous proletarians is greater than that of the traders. Among the disenfranchised South African Indians, there is also an internal class struggle—sometimes manifest and often latent—among businessmen, professionals, and poorer workers.[104] In Britain and Canada, one would expect similar divisions to prevent internal unity, unless the professionals feel that their fate is bound to that of poorer immigrant workers and shopkeepers.

Generational and ideological clashes also affect Indian communites. Some generational conflicts occur within the family, but on the basis of new ideas of romantic love and free choice of marital partner, which also challenge castist values. This has been well-documented among the Natal Indians.[105]

Even the more conservative East African-Asian communities were not immune to such influences. During the 1960s, the latest Western popular music and dances, including rock music and the twist, could be found among Asian adolescents, despite a rather prudish subculture. Still, it seems that the tightly knit caste communities of East Africa—which were highly specialized economically—were freer of intergenerational culture conflict than were other groups.[106]

As with the other groups, integrationist leaders have appeared in the East African-Indian communities, as have leaders espousing assimilation and accommodation elsewhere. In countries such as Guyana, the national interest is a concern—as well as the particular interest—of the Indian community.

Guyana and Malaysia, of course, are classic examples of ethnically dichotomized nations or states, based on colonial plural societies. Although the economic niches occupied by each group is different, the Indians in Guyana are comparable to the Chinese in Malaysia, in that both groups are immigrant groups threatening the older population's control of the country. However, the Africans in the former case—and the Malays in the latter—have, with the help of outside powers and coalitions with smaller groups, succeeded in retaining political control.

Integrationism has a different meaning for Indians in such states, or even in countries such as Trinidad and Malaysia, than it does for the small middleman minorities in East Africa or the new immigrant communities in the Western industrial societies.[107]

In East Africa, African and Indo-Pakistani leaders did suggest that, after independence, the Asians "should strive for full integration if they want to be accepted by their neighbors." This advice included intermarriage and making Africans their business partners. The latter counsel went utterly against what the various Hindus and Muslim groups had practiced, and Indians did not see the Africans as ready for business. As it turned out, time was against any gradual transition. Even the Ismailis—whose leader, the Aga Khan, had advocated acculturation—were unprepared for the changes required.

In general, the few Indian friends of African political leaders apparently were isolated within the communities. But they did participate in the independence movement in various ways.

Makhan Singh, for example, was an avowed communist and was detained for several years by the British. Another considered himself to be a disciple of Jomo Kenyatta, the African nationalist. In postindependence Kenya, however, these individuals were given token positions, high in status but without real power. At most, they might serve as intermediaries.[108] Among the Indians in East Africa, integration seems to have been a weak force, if not simply irrelevant.

It is fair to conclude that, in this context, one is dealing with conglomerates and aggregates of culturally related but socially divided communities. While each group maintains a high degree of cohesion, the Indian community as a whole never coalesced. Some communities, like Guyana, had the appearance of political unity, but these were not middleman communities.

Communal Organization and Reactions to Outside Threats

Given the deep division within the eastern and central African communities, it is not surprising that most supracommunal organizations, such as the East African-Indian Congress, arise only when danger to all Indians is present. There are some differences, however, between the different countries, but there are still certain commonalities.

In Central Africa, for instance, one could not talk about the community as an organized corporation under a legitimately recognized leadership, which could represent the group to outsiders. Instead, one found various factions based on a variety of cleavages, especially religion and caste, but also on generation and personal ambitions and loyalties. Despite this, as Floyd and Lillian Dotsan wrote: this was a population within which relatively intimate communication was possible.

The Central African communities were relatively small enclaves compared to those in East Africa. By 1960, some younger leaders representing a more pan-Asian viewpoint were emerging. But, in fact, there was little political activity on behalf of Indian rights in either preindependence or postindependence Zambia, Malawi, or Rhodesia. In any case, these small enclaves were politically impotent.[109]

In Uganda, there were several all-Indian bodies—such as the Central Council of Indian Associations and the Indian Merchants' Chamber of Kampala. The former was formed in 1921, at the height of tension between Europeans and Asians, which will be dealt with on later pages. Men of the upper class—for example, the richest—were responsible for the formation of the Council. The Council split after the Partition of British India in 1947. While they united briefly to provide self-defense for Asian shops after African riots in 1949, the new unity disappeared again and did not help the Indians through the Amin era.[110]

In Kenya, there was a rivalry between the British white settlers who sought to make that East African colony into a white dominion, and the Indians who feared that they would share the fate of their Natal brethren. While around the turn of the century, British East Africa had been tied to the (British) Indian government and Indian law, settlement was freely permitted. This policy was changed by World War I.

There was also an effort to exclude nonwhite representation in governmental councils. In the period after the First World War, there was no effective African political voice. New immigrants from India, aware of nationalist sentiment there, revitalized Indian associations in Kenya and organized an East African Indian National Congress, with representatives from the other British colonies. The main organizers were Hindus. They presented the Indian case, which opposed discrimination against nonwhites in general and Indians in particular. They demanded representation on govermental boards and other public bodies.

The Indian question was settled with adoption of a policy which abandoned the earlier concept of direct Indian participation in the development of East Africa. Instead, the Indians would be tolerated in subordinate civil service jobs and in commercial enterprise. The policy of ultimately reserving most of East Africa for the Africans was also promulgated at this time, particularly with regard to Uganda and Tanganyika. As a result of such moves, one could say that the Indian community, as a whole, achieved official recognition. At least it was recognized as having the right to representation, even if the government did not control it internally.[111]

After the 1920s, Indian political leadership was primarily defensive. Indians sought to prevent further discrimination and restrictions on immigration by the European administration and, later, to preserve Indian rights to trade when threatened by African nationalist movements.

Some Indians gave active support to the African nationalist movements, but such active supporters were in the minority within the community. In the long run, the mounting African criticism of the Asian socio-economic position in the countries far outweighted the importance of Asian political collaboration with the Africans.[112]

The weakness of the Asian position was emphasized by the partial expulsion from Kenya of Asians not holding Kenyan citizenship in 1968, and the nearly total expulsion of Asians from Uganda in 1972. The plight of East African Asians was accentuated by the peculiarities of citizenship.[113]

Many Asians who were native to Africa had opted for British citizenship, rather than Kenyan, Ugandan, or Tanzanian citizenship. Just at the time when the Kenyanization policy took effect, British agitation against "coloured commonwealth" immigration was at its height, and the British government restricted even those holding British passports from entering the United Kingdom.

In order to pressure the British Kenyans, the Indian and Pakistani governments also decided not to accept British citizens leaving Kenya. Thus the Kenyan Asians were in limbo by 1972.

While the British government tried to avoid leaving the Ugandan Asians with no place to go and other countries—such as Canada and the United States—accepted some Ugandan refugees, the situation was not altogether different. Families were often separated with one individual holding a British passport in the United Kingdom, while other family members, holding Ugandan and other passports were stranded in Canada or the United States.[114]

When faced with the type of anti-Asian public pressure with which even the more liberal East African governments had to deal, it is hard to guess whether a more cohesive Indian community in East Africa would have made much of a difference.[115]

A Comparison of the Three Minorities

The results of the foregoing case-studies are summarized in this manner.

- All three groups are drawn from limited and specialized populations. Most of the overseas Chinese come from one region of China. The mercantile overseas Indians are generally from certain castes of Gujerat and the Punjab, as well as members of mercantile castes from Madras. European Jews, of course, have been concentrated in certain occupations and appear to have been an inbred minority for centuries.
- While circumstances of recent migration forced many Chinese and South Asians into mercantile-middleman roles, the case of European Jews is somewhat different, as has been discussed in an earlier chapter.
- These three groups are disproportionately represented in trade and finance, and they are generally self-employed or work for coethnics, with the qualification that this is not the case for all South Asian enclaves.
- The search for common and persistent cultural attributes becomes less obvious when closely examined. The dual standard of ethics is particularly problematic. In the Weber view, it is limited to some groups, although I would argue that it is an concomitant of an almost universal ethnocentrism. The separatist complex—as manifested in various religious beliefs (for example, the Jewish "chosen people" axiom and the Hindu caste system), as well as ritual practices such as prohibitions on intermarriage—are, however, culture-specific. They are found most clearly among traditional Hindu and Orthodox Jewish groups and are more limited for nonorthopraxic Jews and for Chinese.

- All three groups show considerable family and extended-kin solidarity. Family organization is, at least formally, patrilineal. Family ritual is important in all three groups.
- In addition to family and extended kin, assistance may also be found on the basis of formerly local and/or regional groupings.
- Group leadership in most of these communities is plutocratic, but the previous cultural heritage also plays a role in internal organization. Caste and sect are important among Indians, while rabbis have played important roles in various Jewish communities.
- The internal organization of each group stems from both its adaptation to the world economic system and to the particular colonial or national government of which it is a part.[116] The supracommunal or umbrella organizations of each community must be seen as agencies created either to conform to the wishes of the local government or as reactions to outside threats.

THE MYTH OF SOLIDARITY

Another point in common between all three of these minorities is that they have been highly visible, and each has been viewed by its hosts as ethnically unified and almost conspiratorial in their control of certain sectors of the economy. When examined more closely, we find that most communities belonging to these middleman minorities are deeply rent along all sorts of lines: subethnic, factional, kinship, class, and generational.

An important issue around which such communities divided in modern times was that of cultural strategy. In each community, there were those who advocated traditionalism and/or an ethnic nationalism oriented toward the group's homeland, while others were proponents of greater or lesser integration with either the rulers or the surrounding population.

Among Ashkenazic Jews, such divisions followed the Jews from the period of the French Revolution to the gas chambers of Nazi period, with Christian converts, assimilationists, nationalists, and traditionalists alike subject to the same destinies. In Uganda, too, the Ismailis who had been urged to adopt Ugandan citizenship, as well as the Hindus who preferred to remain British subjects or Indian nationals, were all forced to flee in the wake of Idi Amin's decrees. Such divisions continue among the Chinese in Indonesia, while the Chinese in Thailand are following a course toward assimilation. In Vietnam, the scale has tipped toward expulsion of both integrated and separationist Chinese.[117]

The unity and disunity of various minority communities has been used and manipulated by various governments, as well as by different minority members. Indirect rule of minorities as of tribes lessens the costs of administration to the government. A unified community under a predictable leadership can also be controlled more easily. Such a form of government suited Central European feudal rulers, as well as French and Dutch colonial officials.

The modern state—including both the Absolutist monarchies of eighteenth-century Europe and contemporary independent states—are caught between contradictory motivations. On the one hand, they seek to monitor and control those living within their boundaries. On the other hand, they cannot tolerate a "state within a state," which an apparently autonomous but recognized community is. Thus, they remove more and more powers from the communal organization and undermine the authority of its leaders.

Similarly, the desire of the state to exploit the talents of minority members for purposes of national development combat the strong motivations of majority members to exclude the minority entirely and to take over its enterprises. The treatment of Jews in Europe, Chinese in Southeast Asia and even North America, and of Indians in East Africa shows these various trends. Policies of forcible assimilation are often followed by those of discrimination, explusion, and worse.[118]

In addition to this contradiction, policies toward the minority become entangled in the foreign relations of the nationalistic sovereign states. Attempts by outsiders to protect minority rights are perceived as limitations on independence and are resented. This was true of the Minority Treaties imposed on Poland after World War I and of efforts to protect the Chinese in Southeast Asia. In addition, the overseas Chinese, in particular, became pawns in the battle between the Chinese Communists and the Nationalists. After the fall of Saigon in 1975, the Chinese of Vietnam were enmeshed in the struggle for hegemony over Indochina between the Hanoi and Peking governments. The effort to impose socialism on South Vietnam, including its Chinese minority, was involved in border disputes and resulted in the virtual expulsion of many Chinese from all of Vietnam. The powerful Peking government could do little more to protect these Chinese than could the British with regard to the Indians of Kenya and Uganda. In fact, this has been true of the Peking government in dealing with other

Chinese minorities. To a large extent, outside efforts to protect minority rights have often exacerbated tensions rather than providing real protection.[119] Often the internal factionalism has been increased as has been the image of the minority as a potentially subversive element of the population.

One may wonder why, with all this factionalism and vulnerability, is the minority perceived as powerful and united. The answer is simple. The wealthy members of a community, who may have close relations with the ruling class, are the most visible. Outsiders rarely enter into the internal bickering of an apparently closed minority group. Outsiders do not distinguish between the small-group solidarity, which maintains family firms, from the large, but often weak, communal structures. Even if some of the internal factionalism is known, it is ignored.

In addition, outsiders may see the umbrella organizations which are imposed by the state—or which are formed to meet a particular threat—as internally motivated and as powerful as they would like them to appear. Attempts to protect the group from the outside only add to the conviction that the minority is part of a well-orchestrated conspiracy, such as that of the fictional "Elders of Zion" or the Chinese Communist party. It is, thus, the perception of ethnic solidarity which accounts for relations with the outside, not the actual lack of solidarity which may exist. After all, the minority is a convenient scapegoat, and this perception makes its use so such more plausible.

Arena or Federation

In discussing the image, even though one finds much disunity, one may also ask, "If the internal organization of such minorities is complex, how can we even use the term, 'community' or 'group'?"

Elazar, in studying the pluralistic American Jewish community and other modern communities, has suggested looking at them as a kind of federation. This implies that, under the force of circumstances, the disparate parts will somehow come together and form a unified whole, mobilized for an emergency.

Crissman, an anthropologist who has done research on overseas Chinese, suggests that overseas-Chinese communities have a "segmentary unity," much like that of some stateless tribal societies. The local units of a segmentary group may fight each other, but they will lay aside their disputes in order to fight an outside threat.

Both Elazar and Crissman appear to have similar forms of mobilization in mind. In fact, both admit that many members of the respective Jewish and Chinese communities are either never members of nor rarely do they participate in any formal minority voluntary organization. There are many who are identified as Jewish or Chinese who are nonmembers, or who are marginal, nonparticipating, or peripheral members. At any one time, even during emergencies, many will oppose the groups' leaders.[120]

One would propose that we use another term—namely, "arena"—in describing the communal interaction of such minorities. There are spheres of action which can be seen as clearly Chinese, Jewish, or South Asian. Some are fully encapsulated in such environments and act in minority families, kin groups, businesses, leisure-time, and religious activities. Others do so only on rare occasions. When a minority is economically specialized—as are the overseas Chinese, Indians, and Jews—the means of subsistence are included in this "arena" for the majority of the minority members, especially in familial and other primary group relations. Still, there are enough internal conflicts to prevent the group from ever acting with political solidarity. In speaking about ethnic solidarity, as in writing about a separatist complex, care must be taken to specify what we mean, for these terms can cover a wide variety of phenomena.

Chapter 5

PROTESTANT MIDDLEMEN

So far most of the examples used in this book have been groups which are conventionally considered to be middleman minorities. However, there are other ethnic groups noted for their success in business which have not been considered except as examples in the early chapters. An important category of such groups is the Protestants. These groups can serve as a "control group" in determining whether the relationship between different factors—such as occupation and cultural strategy—applies to all commercial groups or only to those usually labeled as "middleman minorities."

Weber, in his various studies, has raised interesting questions concerning the difference between "pariah capitalism" and modern "rational capitalism," the origin of which he attributes to Protestantism. As already noted, he associates the former with Jews, while Asian middlemen have also been called "pariah capitalists." The middleman literature has concentrated on Jews and Asians, although various Protestant groups have been included in several discussions of middleman minorities.[1]

In this chapter, a middleman minority perspective will be brought to bear on different Protestant groups. It will be seen that, while Weber's distinction between North European Protestants and Asian/Mediterranean pariah capitalists can be drawn, the economic success of the Protestants was due as much to the context in which they found themselves as to ideological factors stemming from their religious tradition.

After a review of the Weber model and related propositions, a number of cases will be examined. Particular attention will be paid to the roles of ethnic and sectarian solidarity, religiosity, and host-hostility in explaining the economic success and political position of each group. Finally, the assimilation of these groups into the elites of West European and North American societies will be considered.

Weber on Pariah and Protestant Capitalism

As was noted in the opening chapter, Weber contrasts Jewish or pariah capitalism with that which led to modern rational capitalist activity. A key to the latter is that it involves a single standard of ethics for all. The proprietor of a business follows the dictum of "honesty is the best policy," thus leading to one fixed price for all customers. By contrast, the traditional behavior of the pariah groups is marked by the differential treatment for ingroup and outgroup members. It is governed by a double ethical standard.

The Protestant, according to this view, is ascetic in sexuality and looks at his economic activity as a religious vocation in which he proves that he is "saved." The Jew, by contrast, has a frank respect for wealth and naturalistic attitudes toward sex; his economic activity is not religiously imbued. The Quakers and Baptists of the seventeenth century prided themselves on their legality, honesty, and frankness, rather than being false, overreaching, and unreliable.

Furthermore, Weber associates the pariah capitalism of the Jews with the politically oriented capitalisms of the past, such as the "booty capitalism" of robber barons and revolutionaries, tax farming, colonial monopolies, and trade closely tied to moneylending. In Weber's view, Jewish capital was "merchant's capital," rather than the organization of production. As he wrote:

> The Jews were relatively or altogether absent from the new and distinctive forms of modern capitalism, the rational organization of labor, especially production in an industrial enterprise of the factory type. The Jews evinced the ancient and medieval business temper which had been and remained typi-

> cal of all genuine traders, whether small businessmen or large-scale moneylenders . . . the will and the wit to employ mercilessly every chance of profit, "for the sake of profit to ride through Hell even if it singes the sails." But this temper is far from distinctive of modern capitalism.[3]

Although not directly derived from Weber, the ideal Protestant businessman may be viewed as universalistic and individualistic in upholding the same standards for all, rather than being particularistic. This would apply to the way in which he grants loans, sets prices and hires workers, while the pariah entrepreneur is particularistic and collectivistic (at least familistic) in all these regards.[2]

As noted in the earlier discussions of Weber, Sombart, and Becker, the latter two sociologists tended to pass over differences and stress similarities between Protestants and Jews. Others have seen differences in the Protestant and Jewish-pariah entrepreneurs as stemming from their different positions in the social structure. The Protestant was less of an alien in the European society, it is argued, and therefore, could serve as a model to others. In addition, the Protestant entrepreneur, for this reason, invested in basic heavy industries and did not keep his capital liquid, while the pariah entrepreneur sought liquidity.[3]

The work of Weber, Sombart, and the latter middleman minority theorists forces us to look at how acquired social and cultural patterns help a group of people to function in terms of a larger economic system. Although Weber focused our attention on the world view, this aspect of the culture is one of the most elusive. Therefore, more attention is paid here in this book than was paid by others to the social patterns of the groups discussed.

Problems in the Comparison of Protestant Middlemen

While, as we noted in the examination of anti-Semitic imagery, casual comparisons of Protestant businessmen with Jews are fairly easy to find, there are difficulties in comparing the Protestants with others. The fact that Jews in Europe and Asian immigrant groups in various parts of Southeast Asia, Africa, and elsewhere were clearly distinctive made it easier to find comparable studies which utilized the factors of ethnicity and occupational specialization. Of course, this apparent clarity is often misleading. Nevertheless, it is harder to locate studies about business-oriented European groups which use this kind of approach.

One reason for the difficulty in finding the material is that, while the problem of minority middlemen is alive with regard to the Asians and the Jews, hostility against the Huguenots or the Quakers is a thing of the past. Anti-Scot sentiment in northern Canada is at a low level of emotion. But this did produce a different type of writing.

There are two interests in these Protestant groups. One is sentimental and filiopietistic. Stories about institutions such as the Huguenot church in New York City, and books on where to find one's French Protestant ancestors or a Scottish firm's company history belong to this genre. Similar in kind is a book on the Yankee peddler, much of which is devoted to the goods he sold and thus appeals to antique dealers and customers.[4]

Most such works have valuable tidbits of information and occasional analysis, but they are inadequate for our purposes. Other works also have their problems. A history of Scottish immigration to Canada focused on the mass immigration of agricultural immigrants, not the fur traders.[5] The concentration on economic innovation is found in some studies.[6]

In this book, however, less attention will be given to matters of group cohesion or assimilation. Some of the works on the Quakers and Huguenots are, for our present purpose, the best because they contain useful data on both economic activity and ethnic group cohesion, as well as ideology and intergroup relations.[7] The examples used will be Reformation and Huguenot refugees, Quakers in England and in Philadelphia, Yankee peddlers in the early United States, and Scots in the north of Canada.

Reformation Refugees

The Reformation created divisions in what had been a single Christian entity. Among the urban populace, some who had once been merely Christians faced discrimination as Catholics or as Protestants and were prevented from continuing in their former roles. In Protestant countries, Catholics might not hold certain offices. The same was true of Protestants in Catholic countries which tolerated Protestants. In addition, the various persecutions and religious wars created a wave of refugees.[8]

The various waves of Protestant refugees were disproportionately represented by Calvinists, Anabaptists and other groups who were not part of established churches. Lutherans, after all, had successful establishments in a part of Germany and Scandinavia, while the reformed churches of Zwingli and Calvin were concentrated in Geneva and the Swiss cantons. Economic enterprise and the diffusion of technology in Western Europe are attributed to both the Reformation refugees and the Huguenot refugees.[9]

Many of the early Reformation refugees from the Low Countries met opposition from potential competitors in the countries where they sought refuge. The initial reception in English ports under Queen Elizabeth I was often hospitable. At first, the refugees received some welfare and temporary lodgings. Then, the municipal authorities would apply to the central government for permanent permission to settle the refugees. If they received permission, however, the government regulated aliens and often laid special levies upon them.[10]

In England, most of the refugees from such areas as Flanders and Brabant were craftsmen and merchants, and many worked in textiles and clothing. Still, there was an English woolen industry, and the guilds in these trades opposed the entry of the Low-Country refugees. They placed restrictions on them, such as not admitting them to masterhood. It was only with the help of wealthy patrons and gradual accommodation that they overcame such restrictions. Thus established the former immigrants also took English apprentices, and taught the "tricks of the trade" to their neighbors.[11]

The situation was much the same in northwest Germany, where cities like Frankfurt, Emden, and Hamburg received Protestant refugees from France and the Netherlands in the 1560s.[12]

Host-hostility took various forms. In Norwich and Southampton, refugee dyers were accused of using so much water that the rivers were polluted and the fish were poisoned. In one German community, the refugees' bake ovens were destroyed to prevent them from settling there. In Frankfurt, as in some other communities, the politics and sectarian affiliations of the refugees aroused some opposition.[13]

In their new homes, the refugees generally formed churches using their own languages and following their own sectarian viewpoints. In Elizabethan England—where the Church of England was seeking to maintain its dominance against Puritan and Catholic challenges—and in Lutheran German cities, the Calvinist immigrants were viewed with some suspicion, but, once they were accepted as residents, they were tolerated.

Through the church and kin, there was obviously a basis of ethnic cohesion. The fact that the refugees tended to enter similar trades and crafts reinforced this cohesion. Still, they were socially proximate to their German and English neighbors. In the long run, they were not outlandish. What we find here are all the elements of the middleman-minority model: immigration, filling specialized occupational niches, ethnic cohesion, visibility (if only short-term), and resistance by the local population. If these immigrants did succeed, however, in assimilating, the culture was not altogether alien, and they were religiously and racially similar to their neighbors.

The religious aspect of Reformation refugees is significant. One would guess that Reformation refugees—who became Protestants during the fervor of the Reformation itself—would be religiously motivated and would respond to the economic ethic through religious motives. This would be especially true of the Calvinist refugees. These refugees were zealous activists interested in spreading their revolutionary doctrine.[14] Still the doctrines of the Calvinist economic ethic had not fully crystallized during the Reformation period.

The refugees of this period certainly found niches for themselves in the host-economies. They also encountered short-term prejudice and hostility. Apparently, however, if they maintained their places in the host-societies, they assimilated fairly readily.

The Huguenots

Many of the same features reappear among Huguenot, or French Protestant, immigrants after the Revocation of the Edict of Nantes in 1686, when Louis XIV ended the formal toleration of the Reformed religion in France.[15] The original Edict of Nantes, promulgated in 1598, put an end to a civil war between Protestants and Catholics which had lasted for most of the last half of the sixteenth century. It secured the rights of Protestants in what was still a Catholic state. While not equal, they could hold office and practice their religion. Through much of the next century, these rights were eroded until in 1686, Louis XIV revoked the Edict. The next several decades were marked by an effort to suppress the Protestant religion in France entirely. Open Protestant worship was prohibited and many Protestants were forcibly coerced into becoming Catholics. In addition, "new Catholics" were suspect and discriminated against. As a result, many fled France and sought refuge abroad.

The Huguenots represent an interesting example of a group which, because of religious differentiation, became a minority in its own country and then a large portion of the group which emigrated and assimilated abroad. With the Huguenots, it is unclear whether they started as people in middle-class occupations who were attracted to Protestantism. In any case, by the end of the seventeenth century, the Huguenots were associated with commercial and manufacturing activities in France. In part, the French Protestant nobles assimilated into the Catholic aristocracy, beginning with Henry IV himself, leaving the religion to the middle and lower classes. The exclusion of Protestants from certain offices made that religion unattractive. The discrimination against Protestants in civic offices forced those who were ambitious to pursue commerce and crafts in order to make a better living.

Prior to the Revocation, Huguenots in public life tended to hire their coreligionists. Sully and other Protestant finance ministers employed the Huguenots. Later, Catholic ministers of finance continued to employ Protestants for certain tasks, "because of their honor and zeal" as well as their expertise in finance and trade.[16] Considerable numbers of Protestants had been employed as tax farmers, measurers of salt, and notaries, all offices which were related to the activities in commerce and trade.[17]

The involvement of the Huguenots in international trade reinforced their economic successes, both in France and prior to the Revocation. The Revocation made many seek refuge abroad, rather than undergo persecution or enforced conversion. Huguenots had an advantage in trade with such Protestant entrepots as London, Amsterdam, Hamburg, and Geneva. Catholics in various French Atlantic ports, such as Bordeaux and La Rochelle, felt excluded from foreign trade. Huguenot merchants might send their sons to Geneva or other Protestant countries to go to school, as well as to learn the ways of the traders and manufacturers there and to cultivate ties with them. Through such an apprenticeship, the young Huguenot would become familiar with new procedures and technology. Those Huguenots who had fled France during the upheavals of the sixteenth and seventeenth centuries remained in touch with their kin in the home country and served as their representatives abroad. In the eighteenth century, several Huguenots had family connections in the major commercial centers of Protestant Europe, which allowed them to build up small empires in international trade.[18]

In France, discrimination—both before and after the Revocation—had the effect of confining the Huguenots to a narrow range of economic opportunities. As entry to administrative positions was closed to them, they became eligible for new positions in the private sector. Even there, they were excluded from some crafts by guild restrictions. In fact, it was social discrimination by the Catholic majority as much as governmental action and law, which confined the Huguenots within France to certain economic roles. Still, there were Protestant gentry as late as 1685, the year of the Revocation.[19]

The Protestants within France, however, survived as a distinctive minority into the twentieth century, while those who fled abroad become assimilated after a few generations. Scoville suggests that the penalization which they suffered "helps explain why French Protestants in the twentieth century still maintain an importance in the economy which is more than proportionate to their numbers." He continued, "The degree of their penalization, however, has been greatly reduced since the eighteenth century, and concomitantly, their relative superiority in finance, trade, and industry has diminished."[20]

The Huguenots who left France in the late seventeenth century found a much more hospitable climate than the Reformation-era refugees, and they were quite successful in filling various economic niches. There was much sympathy for the Huguenots, crystallized by opposition to Louis XIV's decree. The countries which, a century earlier, had rejected refugees had now changed. England had become a more open economic field and believed itself to be underpopulated. In addition, it wanted to fill colonies like North America and Ireland with Protestant settlers. The Netherlands was still in a phase of economic expansion. Germany was slowly recovering from the devastating Thirty Years' War, and one of its leading states, Prussia-Brandenburg, was open to Protestant settlement.

Another change in the political climate was the acceptance of economic doctrines which favored the immigration of entrepreneurs and skilled foreigners. The Netherlands had prospered after gaining independence and permitting the immigration of Protestant refugees and Jews. England now permitted the practice of Judaism in its territories and encouraged both Dutch and French Protestant immigration.[21]

Still,there was some resistance to Huguenot immigration. Geneva and neighboring Swiss cantons received around 60,000 religious refugees from France between 1682 and 1720. About 25,000 were allowed to stay, while the others were forced to move.

Part of this was due to Louis XIV's military threats, but the refugees were also perceived as disruptive to the local economy. In Geneva, there were complaints that the French refugees drove up prices and engaged in unsavory business practices. Still, the Huguenots also helped the French Protestant cantons to consolidate their positions vis a vis other cantons.[22]

In England and its colonies, similar complaints were heard. There were charges of unfair competition. The French speech of the Huguenots gave rise to rumors from time to time that they were allied with the French monarchy and to the Jacobites who sought to overthrow the Protestant rulers of England. During the reign of William III, the Dutch prince who became king of England, there was much resentment directed at his Dutch and Huguenot soldiers and officials. Anglican clergy were also afraid that the Huguenots would strengthen Calvinism in Britain.[23]

The first wave of Huguenot refugees after the Revocation had some expectation of a quick return to France, hoping that victory of the anti-Bourbon allies under William of Orange in a war against France would put pressure on Louis to cancel his revocation. While this did not happen, as long as such hopes were alive, many Huguenots retained their French identity.

The maintenance of their Gallic culture, as well as their economic success and, at times, the special privileges which they enjoyed resulted in animosity against them. Except for some parts of Germany and Switzerland, however, such displeasure was low-keyed. It seems to have had little effect on their abilities to introduce new technical procedures into their host countries, although their own ethnocentrism and the resentment it bred may have interfered in this diffusion of innovation for a time.[24]

This cohesion, however, was dissipated in the dispersion within about two or three generations. For instance, by 1724, the French Reformed Church in New York was experiencing difficulties. The French language was falling into disuse. Few people studied it enough to understand a sermon in French, and there were no new Huguenot immigrants. Kinship connections between the refugees and those remaining in France were becoming lost.

The New York congregation has had much difficulty in surviving as a distinct French church into the present century. This church left the Reformed-fold for Anglican affiliation. Members included individuals of the New York upper class, many of whom did not have French surnames, even though many probably had some Huguenot ancestors. Nevertheless, efforts were made to retain French-speaking pastors and to service the French-speaking of New York City, many of whom were transient visitors to the city. The New-York-community assimilated quickly following that of many of their co-religionists in Britain as well.[25]

In certain areas, a definable Huguenot group—not just an institution of Huguenot origin—survived for a longer period. One such community was that of Friedrichsdorf near Frankfurt-am-Main. The community was founded by the French Protestants in 1687, right after the Revocation and Germans did not settle there until 1741. This town was known for its textiles and for the production of zwieback (a type of toasted bread). They developed their own dialect of French which was a fusion of several French dialects, and they survived into the nineteenth century.[26]

In Brandenburg-Prussia, the Huguenots were granted considerable autonomy, evidently to prevent their mingling with and corrupting, the Lutheran majority. In such parts of Germany, the Huguenot identity was salient for a longer period than in Britain.

In the first generation after the Revocation, the clannishness of the Huguenots may have assisted them in mutual aid to their economic recovery. Having already established branches of the family outside of France would make resettlement easier.

The alienation of the Huguenots from other West Europeans was relative. Within France, the Huguenots, like the Dissenters of Great Britain, were a penalized native minority. In most of Protestant Europe, the French language, which was the main defining characteristic of this group, was a familiar, if foreign, tongue. The fact that they shared Protestantism with their hosts would be perceived positively.

By the end of the seventeenth century the differences between the many Protestant sects were still taken seriously, but were of less importance than they had been at the height of Reformation fervor. The Calvinistic Huguenots were not members of a lunatic fringe. They could be role models for fellow Protestants and were potential members of a national bourgeoisie.

The mutual influences of religion and economic behavior with regard to the Huguenots was clear. Their religious beliefs resulted in their status as a "penalized minority," and their Calvinistic beliefs "predisposed their response" to this penalization by engaging in business.[27]

The Huguenots provide an interesting example of a commercial minority which retained many of its characteristics in its native land, where it had suffered persecution but assimilated after a few generations in dispersion. In fact, Stryker suggested that the dispersed Huguenots are an example of such assimilation by middleman minorities when they find themselves in countries demanding conformity without suffering, discrimination, and persecution.[28]

The Quakers

Weber, as we have seen, looked on the Quakers (Society of Friends) as among the first modern capitalists. They were the upholders of the Protestant ethic which gave rise to capitalist culture. Certainly they saw themselves as upholders of a universal ethic. Yet as noted above, their competitors saw some similarity between Quakers and Jews.

The Quakers were differentiated from their neighbors through their religious conviction, which led to deviation in manner from the ways of their neighbors. It led to persecution in the seventeenth century, and political discrimination continued into the eighteenth century, as well. Even in Pennsylvania, where Quakers were a charter group, they withdrew from politics during the Revolutionary War. Particularly galling to their neighbors was their refusal to swear oaths during a period when swearing an oath was a sign of commitment. Their refusal to pay the tithe and to doff their hats before authority was also interpreted as disrespect. Their maintenance of an internal equality by use of the familiar "thee" and "thine," the religious equality of men and women within the sect, and the "fixed price policy" can all be seen as part of a "separatist complex," reinforcing their sense of "chosenness" and separateness from the world.[29]

Most of the original Quakers shared a common social origin. They came from the middle levels of seventeenth-century English society, with heavy representation from among the craftsmen and artisans. Their strongholds were in the north of England, with some strength in other areas such as London, Bristol, and Ireland. Most were probably drawn from the already considerable body of religious dissenters in Britain at the time of the Puritan Revolution. Those who had property or were on the land in the early years had their lives disrupted by persecution which included imprisonment and confiscation of property. They traveled to spread the "truth" as part of the ministry in which many Quakers engaged. The disabilities which Friends suffered—and their refusal to swear oaths and go to war—barred them from government service.

The social cohesion of the Friends was strengthened by attendance at meetings and by communications which were maintained between the scattered communities in Britain and North America. For the first two centuries of the sect's existence, marriages were restricted, with parents often disowning children who chose spouses outside the Society of Friends.

Apprenticeship into various occupations was also kept within the group. There were several phases in the process which led to the successful Quaker entrepreneurs who were prominent in the British Industrial Revolution. While the majority of the early Friends who followed George Fox were small-scale farmers, either owning land or renting it, they were led to trade because of failure to pay tithes, as well as confiscation and imprisonment. This, plus the demands of the religion itself, made small-scale trade attractive.

Traders were less subject to confiscation, and long absences by men could be managed, since his wife and children could run a small shop. The practice of apprenticeship led still more Quaker youths away from the land into shopkeeping. The connections which many Quakers had with farmers in raising sheep made it easy to go into weaving, wool-combing, and the like, while others became ironmongers and tanners.

By 1760, more and more Friends in England were involved in operating small ironworks, usually run as family firms. Some invested in mining ventures. As time went on, these family firms became consolidated and formed the basis of large Quaker-started industrial concerns, such as the London Lead Company.

In connection with these industrial concerns, there was a number of important banks founded by Quakers, including Lloyd's of London and the Barclay Bank. The family connections of these industrialists and bankers—along with other Quakers—were tied to both business and sect during the seventeenth, eighteenth, and nineteenth centuries. Several Quaker entrepreneurs in nineteenth-century England started their careers within the dense networks of the Society of Friends, and with close family ties as an important resource. With affluence, however, many left the Society of Friends, while those who were more fervent in their faith restricted their business activities.

Many of the patterns found among the English Quakers can be seen in Philadelphia, too. Philadelphia was founded in 1681 and became a major Quaker center. In early Philadelphia, one-third of the Friends came from London and Bristol, with others from Dublin and other British cities. Most were of an urban background. In addition, "It is striking that the Quaker merchants in Philadelphia came to that city from the other colonies, not directly from England." Even prior to the founding of Penn's colony, they had found greater toleration for their religion and fewer restraints on their commercial activities in the New World than in Great Britain.[30]

The cohesion of the Society of Friends stood them in good stead even when they were scattered, and it helped them in carrying on long-distance trade. They had a sense of community that transcended geographical and political boundaries. There were bonds of trade between Friends in Philadelphia, New England, New York, Maryland, the Carolinas, Madeira, Nova Scotia, Curacao, Lisbon, Hamburg, and England itself. Religious, commercial, familial, and personal contacts overlapped. While they sought other Quakers in some cities, they obviously had extensive dealings with non-Quakers.[31]

In the eighteenth century, they preferred partnerships and single proprietorships to forming large corporations. Unlike the London Lead Company, one attempt to form a large Quaker corporation called "the Free Society of Traders," failed.[32] In the nineteenth century, Friends were bankers and executives of large insurance companies, as well as of small businesses. But by that period, the cutting edge of Pennsylvania entrepreneurial activity had passed from the Quakers to others.[33]

The Quakers were here limited by their economic ethic. Weber rightly perceived that, for the devout, there is a connection between their religion and their behavior in the counting house and marketplace. As part of their Puritan background, Quakers saw their economic activity as part of their calling. They attacked laziness and stressed frugality and scrupulous honesty. Of course, their competitors perceived them in a different light.

Quakers who took the religious ethic seriously, and were subject to the discipline of the meeting house, did practice a different mode of doing business. In the early period, they were loath to seek credit. They were cautious and prudent, limited by a desire to pay cash, and they expected others to do so as well. Some saw paper money as a form of credit and opposed its use, although others disagreed.[34]

After their retreat from public affairs in Pennsylvania at the time of the French and Indian War and into the nineteenth century, such tendencies were quite marked among Philadelphia Quakers, just as they were among British Quakers. In the post–Civil-War period, Quaker Meetings continued to bear witness to a cautious economic ethic.

Unlike other middle-class churches of the time, the two Quaker sects attacked the spirit of what has been called the "Gilded Age." They did not vie for the favor of worldly and affluent businessmen. The various disciplines issued by both the orthodox and Hicksite groups in the 1860s and 1870s continued to stress traditional Friends' values, including complete honesty in business, keeping strict account of financial transactions, and viewing speculation as evil. Both dire poverty and too much wealth were seen as demerits. Monthly Meetings would disown those who became bankrupt, especially if they favored some of the creditors over others.[35]

Such a religion is suited to small businessmen. It limits economic activity to a sphere in which close personal ties reinforces moral behavior. In an age when large corporations were forming and dominating the scene, it became more difficult to retain a sense of accountability and personal integrity. Of course, the loyal Friends could transform and reinterpret their faith, rather than abandon it. For various reasons—both in the Colonial era and in the Gilded Age—this course was used less than another—abandonment of the Quaker Meeting for the Episcopal Church or another Protestant denomination.

The attractions of Anglicanism were several. During the Colonial period and in Britain, it represented the power of the British state, while, later, it became identified with the American elite. It was latitudinarian in outlook, while the Friends' sectarianism required strict adherence to religious precepts in deed as well as words. The Episcopal Church interfered less in the weekday behavior of its members. Finally, the boundary separating Friends from other English-speaking Protestants was primarily based on religion, and, it did not last for many generations.

This point is quite significant. For the affluent Quaker, who was relatively indifferent to religion, a change to another Protestant demonimation was no major step. On the other hand, as Benjamin shows for Philadelphia, many did remain Quakers. In fact, "Weighty," or wealthy, Quakers tended to be the children of Quakers and not converts, indicating that the solid, prudent path was a good springboard to wealth, even if many were only nominal Quakers. Most of those who were wealthy in the late nineteenth century had urban roots and were not rural migrants. Despite the fact that a Quaker elite existed, some still defected to the Episcopal Church.

The Quakers in Philadelphia were, of course, a charter group, and hardly a new immigrant middleman minority, even if they were outnumbered. Yet, because of their backgrounds, they did have a minority psychology.

In the eighteenth century, part of their economic success could be attributed to traits reminiscent of middleman minorities. They were inclined to trade and crafts. Sectarian and familial cohesion were important in their businesses. Their frugality was famous. While their economic ethic could lead to the methodical side of rational capitalism, it resembled that of middleman minorities. While their self-image was one of integrity, others viewed them as middleman minorities, such as the traveler who compared London Quakers in the seventeenth century to Jews and Banias (a Indian merchant cast). Some nineteenth-century Americans viewed Quaker frugality and caution as tight-fisted shrewdness, while others regarded their very success as proof of deceitfulness.[36]

The sharp distinction drawn by Weber between Jew and Puritan/Quaker is an ideal type which did not exist in reality. Obviously, the economic ethic of the fervently religious did affect their behavior and may have stimulated certain aspects of modern capitalism. The middleman minority model does, however, fit the Quakers in good measure. The sectarian nature of their religion helps them to maintain a high degree of group cohesion. If they did not remain a middleman minority, it was because they could be easily drawn into the orbit of Anglo-American elites. They were, after all, white Anglo-Saxon Protestants. In Philadelphia, even more than in New England and Boston, they were among the "Founding Fathers."

Yankee Peddlers

The first three groups were defined by religion. In the case of Yankee peddlers, however, occupation and regional origin are mixed. Religious affiliation is inferred, since most New Englanders in the late eighteenth and early nineteenth centuries belonged to various Protestant denominations, including Congregationalists, Baptists, Methodists and Episcopalians. While many New Englanders emigrated to New York State and other colonies, states, and territories, many were farmers. Still, they, too, might be stereotyped in terms of an economic ethic imputed to New England Yankees.

One New England emigre was Benjamin Franklin, whose *Poor Richard's Almanac* is seen by some as the epitome of the spirit of capitalism.[37] The Calvinistic background of New England and the image of the New Englander as a prototypical businessman makes the Yankee peddlers a significant category.

The Yankee peddlers are important as an example of middleman behavior by people who are neither from an external immigrant group nor from a persecuted minority. Yet, there is a problem. The material about Yankee peddlers which is cited reports a stereotype, rather than actual data on behavior.

The reputation of the Yankee peddler is relevant, because Weber's distinction between pariah and Protestant capitalists relies heavily on values and images. The fact that the stereotype of the Yankee peddler could be so like that of a Jewish tradesman is noteworthy as was noted in chapter 3.

The late-eighteenth-century New Englanders were compelled to emigrate because of ecological and economic reasons. The soil was poor. Local communities gave few licenses for opening shops and businesses. At the same time, idleness and vagabondage were severely punished. Such laws limited peddlers, but did not suppress them. Finally, the various policies of the British government prior to the Revolutionary War did not allow for expansion of New England's economy, while the Jefferson Administration's Embargo Act, which temporarily destroyed New England's overseas trade, also worked against the region.

Thus, many New Englanders became settlers west of their home region, while others became itinerants.

The peddlers were itinerants who did business throughout the original thirteen states and, later, to the territories to the west. They sold supplies to farmers and served isolated settlers as repairmen. All sorts of occupations were represented among these travelers, including doctors, medicine men, preachers, and judges. Those who followed them were the founders of the department stores and investors in the railways. William Ogden, the first mayor of Chicago and a prime mover in the founding of the Chicago-Galena Railroad; the speculator Jim Fisk; the inventor, Cyrus McCormick; and Richard Sears of Sears, Roebuck and Company all started as peddlers. They were later renowned as captains of industry and cursed as robber barons.

The stereotype of the Yankee peddler is as negative as that of any other middleman. J. R. Dolan cites an English tourist's account:

> The whole race of Yankee peddlers in particular are proverbial from dishonesty. They go forth annually in thousands to lie, cog, cheat, swindle, in short to get possession of their neighbor's property in any manner it can be done with impunity. Their ingenuity in deception is confessedly very great.[38]

Similar opinions were voiced by Americans.

Nothing here suggests Weber's honest Calvinist who sees business as a holy vocation. Rather, the image is not far removed from Kant's characterization of the Jews as a nation of cheats or certain stereotypes of Gypsies and tinkers. Railways and land swindles, adulteration of cotton and other American commodities exported to Europe, the sale of shoddy goods to the Union Army during the Civil War, and the exchange of worthless trinkets for fur from the Indians were all laid at the door of shrewd Yankee traders, even when they were Boston merchants and deacons of the church. Yet the ordinary peddler at his worst was a pennysnatcher, while the great financiers could be seen as pirates.[39]

German immigrants and Southerners alike compared the New England Yankees to Jews and saw little to choose between them,[40] yet there were important differences. While business practices as perceived by clients may have been similar, there is no evidence that these peddlers were part of a solidaristic trading group.[41] They were an aggregate, not a minority. They could easily cross over into the elite since they were not really separated from them by ethnicity or religion. In fact, those who became peddlers or tradesmen were similar to other New Englanders who left the Northeast to become farmers in other parts of the United States. The evidence for this case is obviously inadequate, but if there is no commercial difference between the Yankee peddlers in their own country and ethnic middlemen, then differences in economic ethics cannot explain the rest of minority middlemen. Further research is needed.

The Scots

Becker in his original formulation of the trading or middleman-minority type included the Scots. His various descriptions of this group must have been colorful when he delivered lectures and put on his best burr, as when he would talk of the Scots' attitudes toward their clients:

> Trade with the worldly reprobate? Of course. Treat him as you would one of the elect, a fellow-Calvinist with the outward signs of inward grace? Doctrinally, "aye"; in terms of rank and file mentality, "pairhops."

In a footnote, Becker notes, "No Calvinist 'sure' of election would *consciously* hold a dual ethic."[42]

Becker utilizes the following characteristics of the Scots: (1) they are frugal, indeed proverbially so; (2) they have been traders in many places including Scandinavia and northern Canada; (3) they are shrewd and canny; and (4) they have strong ethnocentrism, expressed in Calvinism. He also contrasts the poverty of Scotland with the ingenuity and success of the emigrants. Becker tends to associate these characteristics with Lowlanders, a group not particularly involved in the fur trade.

The stereotypic of the Scots for stinginess and respect for money has already been mentioned. Galbraith, a Scot-Canadian by birth, makes several references to this in his nostalgic book on the Scots around Lake Erie. In one passage, he points out that in the churches of his hometown there was no collection plate. He sees this as a desire to reserve Sunday for God and money for weekdays. He also writes that men spoke more respectfully of money than of their wives. He feels that the Scotch did not want money for power, prestige or goods, but "for its own sake."[43]

In addition to frugality, the Scots had a tradition of seeking their fortunes abroad. They were mercenaries for the French kings and in the armies of German princes. In the sixteenth century, they were traders in Scandinavia and continued such trade into the eighteenth century in Germany and Poland.[44]

Of great importance in the eighteenth century were the Clearances which followed in the wake of the Jacobite defeat in 1746. The laws imposed on the Highlands broke the old feudal bond of lord and vassal. The aim of the British policy in the Highlands was to shatter the clan system which had been one of the bases of the Stuart armies. Lords and vassals were relieved of mutual obligations. Like landlords elsewhere in the British Isles, the Scottish landowners found it more profitable to replace men, whom they no longer needed for armies, with sheep which could be bought and sold. Later in the nineteenth century, when Australian ranches were more lucrative for wool, these areas were converted into deer forests, which resulted in further depopulation. Even the rise of tourism and the tweed industry after World War I did little to stem the tide of emigration.[45]

These conditions triggered emigration to North America, as well as to the industrial areas of Great Britain. Many became farmers in Canada, the United States, and even Argentina, while others were employed as industrial workers for the new industries. Scots played a prominent role, disproportionate for their numbers in the population, as entrepreneurs in England during the early Industrial Revolution.[46]

In other areas of the world, Scottish entreprise also made itself felt. On the Pacific coast of both Americas, the Balfour, Williamson Company, a firm founded by Scotsmen, was quite successful in commerce. At one point, it even owned Easter Island and used it as a sheep ranch.[47] In Central Africa, the Scots played a crucial role in providing market goods. In 1878, Scottish businessmen, at the behest of missionaries, organized the African Lakes Company. Such companies persisted into the 1920s and were organized along bureaucratic lines. There were stores at all district headquarters with a resident agent, usually a Scot. In 1930, the Scottish company sold out to Jews, who, in turn, were succeeded by Indians.[48]

The religious sources for such Scottish enterprise are often unclear, whether in the England of the Industrial Revolution or the Montreal of the Northwest Company. In Africa, the religious motivation did induce Scots to become missionaries—such as Dr. David Livingston—and later, the missionaries encouraged the businessmen. In the Canadian fur trade, there is little evidence of any religious motivation at all.

In Canada, Scots were prominent in the fur trade from the early eighteenth century, when the Hudson's Bay Company, a royal monopoly, began employing Orkneymen. In the late 1700s, an independent fur trade developed in Montreal—which was, by then, a British city. While this fur trade by the "Montreal pedlars" included Yankees, Englishmen, Irishmen, and Quebec French, the Scots were disproportionately represented. They were among the most prominent in this group which later formed a loosely organized coalition called the "Northwest Company."[49]

The Scottish "Nor'westers" were not all Presbyterian Calvinists. McGillivray, a leading Nor'wester himself, came from a Jacobite area of the Highlands, which had given support to the Young Pretender, "Bonnie Prince Charles," and where largely Catholic sympathies were strong. In the wilderness, these Scotsmen took native concubines, by whom they had offspring, and, in Montreal, several married French Catholic women.

In many ways the Nor'westers combined the qualities attributed to Scots in the conflicting stereotypes of the dour, sober, but shrewd businessmen with the impulsive, hard-drinking, roistering Highlanders. They were known for carousing at the winter camp and the Beaver Club of Montreal and the capability for waging war against their rival Britishers of the Hudson's Bay Company. For nearly ten years, these two companies fought a near war for control of the fur trade in what is now Canada. The Hudson's Bay

Company also had its Scottish component, including the Earl of Selkirk and George Simpson, longtime Governor of the Company.[50]

In 1821, the two companies merged and formed a reorganized Hudson's Bay Company. The newly reorganized monopoly continued some of the Nor'wester traditions. Many of the servants and partners continued to be Highland Scots. The religious ambience was apparently marked by indifference at the top, especially while Sir George Simpson was Overseas Governor of the Company.

The Hudson's Bay Company continued to recruit Scots for the next 150 years. For the period up to and a little beyond World War I, Scottish boys were taken directly from the Highlands and Orkneys to Canada. Scots were preferred for promotion.[51] The frugal, dour character often attributed to Scots justified their employment by the Company, many of whose top men were, likewise, Scots.

In addition to their other qualities, however, the Hudson's Bay Company may have viewed lads from the Highlands and the Hebrides and Orkneys as pliable instruments in the remote outposts of their fur trade and trading posts. They were accustomed to hardship, as they came from peripheral corners of the British Isles. Work within the Company and obedience to its orders gave them access to a ladder of achievement which could lead from a remote outpost in the tundra to governor-generalship of Canada. The Company still employs Scots, but it is increasingly an Anglo-Canadian corporation which has undergone several changes of ownership. Many of its employees are locally born and include Indians and Metis. However, the tradition of favoring Scots has left its mark.[52]

Characteristics associated with middleman minorities can be found on an individual level among the Scots who worked for Hudson's Bay or the African Lakes Companies. Toil and endurance were vehicles for advancement in the corporate trading companies, as was delayed gratification. The Scots were strangers in the Canadian north and west, as well as in Central Africa and elsewhere. Their capital consisted primarily of their own skills and talents. As the history of these companies show, Scots were members of a small cohesive ethnic group who preferred to hire their own.

While theoretically following an ethic of "universal otherhood," their actual behavior, as perceived by the natives, showed signs of a double standard of morality, such as selling shoddy merchandise to naive native clientele. If the Scots are compared with the overseas Indians and Chinese with regard to their behavior toward native women, they are closer to the Chinese. In Canada at least, they often acknowledged their offspring and sometimes married the native women. All of this shows that the highly competitive, achievement-oriented entrepreneur often makes a decision which goes against a universal ethic, and the rational elite capitalists of a large corporation are not all that different from pariah hucksters.

Still there are other features which distinguish the Scots of these companies from the middlemen minorities. The most significant divergence lies in the manner of employment.

Generally middleman minorities have been seen as composed of those who are either self-employed or employed in relatively small firms by their kin and former countrymen. The Hudson's Bay Company—which contended for and won political and economic control of most of Canada—or Balfour and Williamson—which traded between Britain and the two Americas—were hardly such minority enterprises.

The top executives of such companies were part of the ruling elite of the British empire in its heyday. Even now, although diminished in relative stature and stripped of its *de facto* political power and economic monopoly, the Hudson's Bay Company is a formidable body with its chain of department stores in Canada and currently significant role in the international fur trade. Men recruited to serve in such a corporation are part of a potential ruling class, however humble their origins might be.

The host-hostility which middleman minorities face was also directed against Scots, particularly in Canada. However, rather than massive violence against Scots per se, it was directed at the Company and the Canadian government. Even then, these powerful agencies could suppress it. Prejudice against the Scots remains but is relatively minor.[53] The possibility of acting upon the hostility against the Scots is thus diminished. The Scots have found it fairly easy to assimilate into the remainder of the population of European descent wherever they have emigrated.

Comparison of Protestant Middleman Minorities with Jews

Implicit in this presentation of what must appear to be a hodgepodge of groups and categories is the comparison of these European and Euro-American Protestants with classic middleman minorities. The minority with which these Protestant groups will be compared are European Jews. After all, this was Weber's basis of comparison when he presented the contrast between the Puritans and the pariah people. Both are defined by religion. Both share a common European background.

Of greatest importance in the comparison are "cultural attributes." The seriousness with which different groups took the precepts of their religion is chief among these. Among Jewish groups there continues to be some variations. Certainly the same is true of Protestants, who range from sectarian *religious virtuosi* to those who are nominally Protestant.

What, of course, made the Quakers unusual was that economic activity was a focal interest in following religious teachings. Ethical behavior was what counted. This was less true of other groups, but Weber's choice of the Quakers as a group which fits his ideal type was correct. Still Weber's view of the dual ethic, as we noted previously, was more restricted than that of contemporary sociologists. Weber was concerned with a dual ethic insofar as it dealt with lending and borrowing, not with regard to hiring. Employment of fellow group members—whether on the basis of a common religion or ethnic/national origin—was apparently true of all of the groups mentioned. Preference for relatives was a trait common to all until modern corporations restricted such practices.

While today, one may contrast groups in terms of collectivist strategies—stressing aid from relatives and coethnics or coreligionists versus individualist strategies and utilizing impersonal institutions such as banks and government agencies—such options were not open to a businessman in the past. Until the nineteenth century, links with the government or banks involved personal ties. For instance, William Penn, the Quaker, used his father's services to the Crown in getting a proprietary grant to Pennsylvania.

The degree of cross-sect and interethnic personal ties, were, of course, explored in previous chapters. If the Yankee peddlers seem to have used fewer ethnoreligious bonds than did other groups, that was a matter of appearance. After all, one sees the peddler as a lone individual in a community, not in terms of his ties to the town which supplies him with his merchandise. Thus, there seems to be few differences between these groups until well into the nineteenth century.

Concerning other cultural attributes relative to entrepreneurship, the information is mixed. There are no test scores used to indicate achievement need in the various groups. Both Protestant and Jewish groups suffered some types of political or economic deprivation, which might have motivated them to seek new opportunities for making money and building new lives. Some of the nineteenth-century "Weighty" Quakers—such as the very wealthy Jewish families of the same period—are exceptions in this regard, but both the prosperous Jews and Quakers were tempted to leave their respective groups.

Quaker beliefs in the nineteenth century inculcated a methodical, honest business ethic which would be suitable for today's organization men as well as small businesses. Here again Weber's point is well taken. But one must be able to be hired by a large corporation to take advantage of such skills.

In sum, with regard to cultural attributes, there were differences between the Quakers and others with regard to stress on business honesty. Ethnic solidarity in general, however, was common to all. The entry into small business was also common to all, although the Reformation refugees and the Huguenots in particular were known for their activity in crafts. Jews were, in many places, excluded from many handicrafts and manufacturing by guild rules and other forms of legal discrimination.

Several of the Protestant groups considered—the Reformation refugees, the Huguenots and, to some extent, the Scots in northern Canada—were international migrants. In the first two cases, the immigration involved moving from one speech community to another and from one urban context to another. Thus, the Reformation refugees and Huguenots were competing with their hosts.

In the case of the Scots, the situation was a frontier-colonial context. They, like the Yankee peddlers, were filling a real "status gap." The Huguenots in France were natives, as were the Quakers in Philadelphia, except that no adult in that city in 1700 could be a native. The status of the Huguenots in post–Revocation France was most comparable to that of Jews—especially those Jews who had been forcibly converted to Catholicism in Portugal and Spain in the fifteenth and sixteenth centuries and who were discriminated against as "New Christians."

What is striking about the sixteenth century refugees is that they faced the same discrimination as immigrants that Jews, native or immigrant, faced in that period when they tried to enter new crafts. This was especially true in the city of Frankfurt-am-Main, which had a substantial ghetto, but where the Jews were restricted occupationally. The discrimination against dissenting Christians was immediately acute, but short-term, while Jews faced chronic disabilities. Even in modern times, such prejudice faced Jews working for the large corporations which employed the Scots. Obviously, the Quakers in Philadelphia in the eighteenth and even the nineteenth centuries did not face these types of entry problems. There, their own self-imposed discipline played an important role in determining occupation.

SUMMARY

The hostility and prejudice which the various Protestant groups faced has been shown. There were similarities between the imagery used against them and that used against the Jews. Even the Quakers were compared in this fashion. Still, with the exception of the Huguenots in France, the hostility was short-term and did not last much beyond the first generation.

Of the various groups considered, most of those who were immigrants assimilated into the host population within a few generations. With regard to sectarian groups such as Quakers, extraordinary measures had to be taken to maintain group cohesion. This situation is different from that of Jews in general, although the internal discipline of the Society of Friends could be seen as comparable to the internal organization of traditional orthodox Jewish communities.

The Scots are also special in this regard. Since the Scots dealt with in this presentation have entered a frontier situation, they did so with certain qualities of a ruling group. The continued connections which they have to a transnational corporation is of importance, too. What they show is that North European Protestants have the potential of rising to the top in a way which has not been open to Jews or to Asian middlemen. This is the opposite side of the same coin as the role-model issue. Unlike the Jew in feudal Poland, a Scot in Canada could be both role model and governor-general.

The comparisons made in this chapter were obviously exploratory. The information was too fragmentary for it to be much more than that. The effort to refute Weber was partially successful. He drew the ideal type of a special Protestant capitalism much too sharply. Yet, at the same time, there was a measure of truth in his delineation.

The Protestant groups can be seen as short-term small-business-oriented middlemen minorities. Many of the same characteristics applied to them as to the Asians and the Jews. They differed primarily in context. They had the ability to transcend the small-business sector because, as Protestant Europeans, they were acceptable to the ruling elites. It was only the more religious fraction of the Quakers who sought to remain modest and not rise to the top.

These instances of Protestant middlemen serve to highlight the fact that context and ethnicity, rather than economic behavior per se, can account for many, if not all, differences between middleman minorities and the economic elites.

Chapter 6

THE TRANSFORMATION OF A MIDDLEMAN MINORITY: JEWS IN THE UNITED STATES

In the preceding chapters, fruitful comparisons were made between the Jews and other groups classed as *middleman minorities.*[1] There is much overlap between the roles of trader, moneylender, and civilian retainer in traditional agrarian and colonial societies. In comparing European Jews with the Indian and Chinese diasporas, attention was given to their various roles in the world and local economies, as well as to their ethnic solidarity and impression management. This comparison revealed important differences between the various middleman minorities, both in terms of different settings and cultural heritages. While that chapter and chapter 5 on Protestant middlemen were synchronic in form, both contained hints about process, as well as making suggestions about the destinies of middleman minorities in modern industrial societies.

While social scientists rarely say it boldly, there is an expectation that all ethnic groups will assimilate into the majority, but that the middleman minorities are unassimilable and are often expelled or exterminated. Yet data in both of these chapters reminds us that individuals do change their occupational roles and that extensive assimilation has occurred. Again emphasis was given to the management of group and individual images.

This chapter is a consideration of American Jewry. Americans in general and American Jews have always argued about the degree to which America is "different." They have addressed the question of whether the passage across the Atlantic Ocean has removed the stigma of the "original sin" of European anti-Semitism.

Obviously, a "yes" or "no" answer to this question and the related one about the applicability of middleman minority theories to American Jewry are no more possible than is an answer as to whether baptism by salt water has transformed the old European sinners into the new American people. But processes, other than those which stem from host-hostility, can be examined in the North American context. These include the origins and transformation of the American Jewish occupational distribution, the relationship of the occupational structure to the American Jewish image as "stranger," "sojourner," and "citizen," the nature of Jewish cohesion and visibility in the United States, the participation of Jews in American politics, and a consideration of the present latency of anti-Semitism.

Since volumes have been and can be written on this topic, this chapter will only sketch some aspects of the relationships between the occupational structure of the Jews and the visibility and perception of that Jewry. It will be seen that American Jews are less and less embedded in traditional middleman roles than they were in the past, and they appear to have achieved a recognition as an integral part of the American population.

THE ORIGINS OF THE OCCUPATIONAL STRUCTURE

The origins of the occupational structure of American Jews can be explained by the existence of status gaps and the needs of the labor market in this country at the time of immigration. When Jews immigrated to the United States, they generally moved into niches which were either being abandoned by previous residents or which were newly created. Such entry was generally at the lower levels because most immigrants were poor. Agents of the Warburg and Rothschild banks who established branches in America were an important exception.

While several theories stress the important roles—such as filling status gaps—which these groups play in agrarian societies, this is not an appropriate model for a complex society as the United States. These groups do, however, fill necessary positions in the economy, either in newly expanding sectors or in older economic interstices which the native or veteran population has abandoned because of their onerous nature.[2]

The pioneering role which Jews have played in certain sectors of the North American and European economy is too well-known to repeat here. It includes the ready-to-wear garment trade, department stores, and mass communications. Filling the slots that have been abandoned by the veteran population can be seen in the behavior of Jewish immigrants in the United States and Britain, who, as peddlers, competed with and replaced native traders. As workers Jewish immigrants chose jobs in the needle trades, and, as slum shopkeepers, took over a niche which others found to be unworthy and unprofitable.[3] In some of these sectors, the Jews themselves have been succeeded by members of other ethnic groups. In urban areas, slum businesses which, in the past, tended to be Jewish now are passing to more recent immigrants such as Koreans and Iraqi Chaldeans. The garment industry is now increasingly in the hands of Chinese and Hispanic entrepreneurs and workers. As with the Jews at the beginning of the century, workers, of course, outnumber factory owners.[4]

In some occupations, the onus is not simply the fact that, as in agricultural labor, one works hard and becomes physically dirty, but that a moral onus is attached to the work. Pawnbroking, the sale of liquor, professional gambling, prostitution, and businesses serving the poor have such qualities. Such enterprises may be quite lucrative and serve important societal needs, but they do not carry prestige. The sale of liquor is still associated with ethnic minorities, including Jews. Some Jewish businessmen were involved in illegal and corrupt activities including the Murder, Inc., syndicate of New York in the 1930s, nursing home scandals in the 1970s, and insider trading on the stock market in the 1980s. All of these enterprises represent a type of "moral brokerage" for activities which are in demand, but for which the society, as a whole, disclaims active responsibility.

Previous residues of experience also give the minority some advantages in certain lines of work. After all, it is not a big jump for a Jew to go from innkeeping in Russia to owning an American tavern. In the nineteenth and twentieth centuries, many unskilled Jewish immigrants became peddlers, while Polish Jewish craftsmen, such as tailors, practiced their former lines of trade. Similarly, international connections with the centers of a particular trade have given members of a minority an advantage within certain businesses, such as Jews have demonstrated in the diamond trade.[5]

Of course, when others have a competitive advantage for reasons of priority or for political reasons, members of a minority which in other places were well-represented in certain lines of trade may be excluded here. Jews in Europe were quite important in banking and in the development of the petroleum industry, but not in the United States. In any case, while a simple yawning status gap has not existed in North American society, many economic niches have opened and closed for minorities entering different sectors of the system. In general, Jews have taken advantage of opportunities as they appeared.

THE TRANSFORMATION IN THE OCCUPATIONAL STRUCTURE

Changes have taken place in the economic structure of American Jewry since World War II. This transformation certainly makes some aspects of the characterization of middleman minority (in terms of trade, finance, and even self-employment) inapplicable to large segments of American Jewry.

Jews have found positions in large multinational corporations which formerly excluded them. They are employed as scientists, engineers, and even managers. The fact that individuals with obvious Jewish names and ethnic backgrounds can rise to head corporations like DuPont and Bendix is symbolic of this transformation. Jewish entrepreneurs such as Carl Icahn, have also been prominent in conspicuous corporate takeovers, as well as those who were involved in financial scandals resulting from the wheeling and dealing on Wall Street, such as Ivan Boesky. Such individuals have gone well beyond the petty-bourgeois small-commodity sectors to that of corporate capitalism. Important pockets of discrimination remained in the post–World War II period. Still Jews are concentrated in specific—albeit often high-level segments—of the economy.[6] Many Jews, of course, have become self-employed professionals, especially doctors and lawyers, but, even in these professions, one finds increasing employment by universities, governments, and corporations.

The entry of the Jews into the academic world in which they formerly suffered severe discrimination is part of this alteration in status. For those fields such as chemistry and economics which offer governmental, commercial and university employment, one finds many who have held positions in several sectors. For others, employment has been primarily in academia. Despite lingering remnants of discrimination, the academic world has opened its doors to Jews.[7] The surge into academia can be seen as a syncretism between the traditional Jewish value placed on learning with that of modern scholarship and science. While being distant from the commercialism of the classic middleman, the professor can be viewed as a broker of knowledge in the marketplace of ideas.

There has also been a dramatic increase in the number of Jews employed in governmental bureaucracy, which is a far cry from commercial self-employment. Jews in certain European countries, such as Austrian Poland, did work in the public sector despite discrimination. Under the Polish Republic, however, most of them lost their jobs as a result of anti-Semitic pressure in the 1920s and 1930s. In this country, the universalistic ideology of bureaucracy is especially important to Jews as many entered public employment through civil service rather than through the patronage of bosses.

With New York City's intense concentration of Jews, large numbers of Jews sought public employment there in the early 1900s. Because they represent such a large proportion of the state and metropolitan population, Jews in New York can be seen as a majority group, both in influence and psychology. The increase in numbers of Jews in federal service grew during the Depression, especially as a result of the New Deal. The large numbers of Jews now employed by such bureaucracies represent a radical shift away from the middleman heritage and its *petit-bourgeois* mentality toward a meritocratic ideology.[8]

Despite this trend, those who are self-employed are not small in number. In addition to the old-type of small businessmen and self-employed professionals, one finds a new variety of individuals, including those who serve as consultants to business and government. Other individual entrepreneurs in "high-tech" industries are dependent on government grants, and still others are subcontractors. Jews are well-represented in such small firms, and Jewish women are also among these newly self-employed enterprisers.

What also becomes clear from these studies of occupational structure is that the Jewish path of social mobility remains exceptional. Jews have not dispersed throughout the economy, but remain concentrated in a narrow range of professions. This may contribute to the continued pattern of relatively high, although diminished, ethnic consciousness and the separation of Jewish social networks, when compared with Protestants and Catholics.[9]

The fact that, as a body, American Jews can no longer be characterized as being primarily a middleman minority does not mean that American Jews now have achieved power and full integration. American Jews are disproportionately represented in various sectors of the economy where the relationships between power, income, and high status is notoriously tenuous.

SOJOURNER/STRANGER/CITIZEN

As already noted, the classic model of the middleman minority implies that these groups are estranged from the remainder of the population by race, religion, or language, as well as other cultural characteristics. Generally, these groups maintain this estrangement through the establishment of separate institutions, and show a lack of commitment to the local population through the economic action. They generally invest in liquid capital, rather than in industries or types of agriculture which would tie them to the place where they reside. These characteristics have been considered to be attributes of sojourners, yet it can be said unequivocally that the vast bulk of Jewish immigrants to North America intended to settle on this continent. The circular migration common to many other immigrants to the United States was not typical of North American Jews, and Jews had lower repatriation rates than many others.[10] Still, some small groups of Jews do display the psychology of sojourners.

Nevertheless, the heritage of small business and insecure existence was borne by the Jews to the New World. The ability to start a business on a shoestring, perhaps with savings borrowed from others, and success followed by bankruptcy and renewed success is a familiar pattern. While many of those who succeed take up an opulent way of life, Sir Isaac Wolfson, the British department store magnate, is not alone in maintaining the frugality of his youth.[11]

The convolutions of Jewish history have given rise to contradictory cultural trends within the Jewish community. While most Jews who arrived in the United States have intended to settle here, small—but often conspicuous—groups have maintained passionate interest in foreign politics. For instance, East European political exiles, such as Trotsky who lived in New York for a short time, were often more interested in Russian events than in their American setting. The various threats to Jewish life in Europe and elsewhere aroused extreme distress among the Jews of North America. The often strident expressions of support for Israel and Soviet Jewry must be seen against the background of failure to aid the Jews of Europe when they faced the Nazi Holocaust.

On the cultural level, Jews have taken great, although often merely ritualistic, pains to maintain loyalty to their religious tradition and their various languages, especially Hebrew and Yiddish.[12] The fact that large number of Jewish children continue to go to Hebrew school in the late afternoon or that Jews may send their children to day school has been an inspiration to others, including Greeks, Asian-Americans, and Native Americans who also wish to maintain their language and culture on this continent. In truth, this effort is often a brief episode in the lives of most Jewish Americans. Few know more than enough Yiddish to understand some Jewish jokes or enough Hebrew to do more than recite a few prayers.

On the other side, Jews have been avid in their desire to become Americans. Many learned English quickly enough to qualify for colleges and universities which were reluctant to accept them. The Jewish contribution to literature in the English language in the past half-century has been substantial. This includes writers from Great Britain and Canada, as well as the United States. Many of these Jewish writers—and the equally popular Jewish comedians—have often been notable in their negative attitudes toward Jewishness.

Jews have also been outspoken American patriots, as well as critics of America. Jews have been accepted as elected senators and representatives in regions where few Jews reside, such as Oregon, Nebraska, and Iowa. Several interpretations of American life by Jews have been accepted as authentically American, including the "melting pot" metaphor popularized by Israel Zangwill, a British Jewish author, and cultural pluralism. Both the melting-pot and cultural-pluralistic interpretations allow for a syncretism between the Anglo-American culture and that of the non–Anglo-Saxon immigrants.

The insecurity which lingers among American Jews stems from internal sources as well as external events, such as the Holocaust. There are several causes for this. America remains a predominantly Christian country. Anti-Jewish sentiment has its ups and downs, but has always been present in a culture with roots in

European Christendom. During much of the nineteenth century, American Jews were able to penetrate into the local national political elite, despite such prejudice, without facing social exclusion. After 1870, however, the position of even veteran Jewish Americans deteriorated. Fewer Jews were selected for visible positions, even in regions such as Southern California. The sons of those who had been members of upper-class social clubs were often excluded. Whether this was due to host-hostility aroused by the Civil War, the mass immigration of East-European Jews, European anti-Semitic literature, or to a combination of these, even the elite of American Jewry faced exclusion.[13]

The events which led to the Holocaust, the establishment of the State of Israel, and a continuing Arab-Israeli conflict have been sufficiently recent and so traumatic as to leave a lasting impression on any American Jew older than the age of 50. This, plus the fact that few American Jews can trace more than three or four antecedent generations on this continent, makes their sense of roots in this country a bit tenuous.

While the sojourner motivation does not apply to the majority of American Jews of German or East-European ancestry, it does fit small groups of Jews. The various wings of Hasidim have a quality of enclavement which is only accidentally American. They maintain an attachment to cultural patterns developed elsewhere and have not become rooted with any depth in American society. The Hasidim do participate in local and national politics, primarily to protect their own and Jewish interests. They are certainly deeply rooted in a traditional East-European Jewish culture. An important motivation for occupational choice among Hasidim is to support their religious way of life, not merely accumulate wealth. Some groups of Hasidim have, therefore, specialized in capitalizing on their religious virtuosity in providing religious services and products to other Jews.

Other Hasidim have entered occupations and lines of trade which permit the observance of the Sabbath and other Jewish ways. The diamond trade which has been connected to Jews for centuries, is one example of such a line. While Hasidim in particular and Jews in general do not monopolize the diamond trade entirely, their importance in its various operations is paramount. The diamond trade is international and relies on mutual trust in the manufacture and transport of a highly precious commodity. Kin, ethnic, and religious ties are, thus, highly important.[14]

While the motivation for occupational choice among Hasidim

is often religious, this is not the case with regard to Syrian Jews in the United States and Latin America. Thier familial and local ties have provided the trust and confidentiality needed to maintain far-flung small-business connections which sometimes bypass regulations imposed by a series of governmental jurisdictions.

For a long time after their arrival in the United States, Syrian Jews remained in certain limited commercial specialties. They began selling linen and lace, and later moved into the sale of imported infants' wear. By the late 1950s, they became the principal owners of stores in central business districts which specialize in selling a wide variety of imported goods, including cameras, tape recorders and bric-a-brac. More recently, discount department stores have been opened by Syrian Jews. These types of business require little formal education, but involve dependence on ethnic- and kin-based networks.

The connections of Syrian Jews in these businesses are international. There are branches of Syrian families overseas who supply Syrian wholesalers in New York. The retailers are connected to the wholesalers through the various Syrian congregations as well as through kin ties. Around 1960, the tendency to marry within the community was high, as was the tendency to go into the family businesses in partnership with a brother or a cousin. Up to the 1960s, most were politically uninvolved, although this has changed in recent years.[15]

However, the Syrian Jews, who were part of the pre–World War I wave of immigration, and the Hasidim, who represent the later wave in immigration, are atypical in their sojourning. They stand in sharp contrast to such groups as the German Jewish refugees in the 1930s, and the European displaced persons of the post–World War II era who saw themselves as immigrants, not sojourners, in America. The Americanization, in both cultural and political terms, of these groups was quite rapid. Those who were reared in America, whether born abroad or American-born, have quickly acculturated.[16]

Syrian Jews offer an interesting contrast to the German refugees and Polish displaced persons before and after World War II. The former remained indifferent to politics in the second generation. The latter—who came to this country much more recently—quickly became voters, and younger members of the immigrant generation have become active in public affairs. Two refugees, Henry Kissinger and Michael Blumenthal, have risen to Cabinet positions.

For Syrian Jews, the occupational structure is again important. Syrian Jews have been concentrated in certain lines of trade which require little formal education. They are, however, dependent on ethnically based networks. The general society was of little concern. The refugees who became prominent have done so on the basis of presumably universalistic criteria of formal education—which socialized them into the general culture—and proven talent.

The sojourner hypothesis, whatever its validity for certain small Jewish groups, does not apply easily to the majority of American Jews. Simmel's analysis of the "stranger," however, cannot be discounted in terms of its applicability. The paradoxical relationship of nearness and distance, of fixation in space and wandering, of intimate confidences given to the outsider, is not absent from the relationship of Jews and gentiles in America. We find that many of the promulgators of Hollywood's version of America's self-image were first-generation Russian Jews. In the 1970s, we have witnessed Richard Nixon's strange relationship with Jews.[17] While this was idiosyncratic, we are reminded of subterranean levels of the imagery and position of the Jew in American society. The psychology of Jewish-Gentile relationships may well outweigh the specific economic and political adaptations which individuals have made.

Ethnic Solidarity

As we have seen in previous chapters, unusually high degrees of ethnic solidarity are attributed to middleman minorities. The actual solidarity shown by such ethnic groups is real, but is often limited to kin and formerly local coethnics, with the total ethnic community taking second place. This is especially true in the economic realm in which it is presumed that ethnic cohesion gives middleman minorities an advantage in competing with others. It is this aspect which will be stressed in the section on Ethnic Solidarity.

The occupational structure is related to the maintenance of group ties. As previously noted, the desire for maintenance of the group—especially on the part of the pious—and fear of discrimination by others have been important features of occupational choice. The family, one's personal network of other Jews, and, finally, the Jewish community have all played a role in assisting the individual in making these choices, either by providing a job or by supplying one with contacts.

The family and its extensions have been at the base of such an employment system. It is likely that this is tied to the family business and will break down as more and more Jews go into the corporate bureaucracies, academia and government all areas in which the assistance of the families is less available. While several studies of Jewish kinship in North America support the tie to independent enterprise, they also demonstrate the tensions which spill over from business to family life when the two are connected. Under modern corporate capitalism, small businesses of a family-kin type often have short lives. Individualistic strategies which involve credit from banks and partnerships with strangers are becoming more and more important in business.[18]

The family firm is only one aspect of ties between Jews. Especially in a semisegregated community—such as the immigrant ghettos of early twentieth-century American cities or even the isolated Jews of small towns—there were many informal ties which bound Jews together. These links obviously reinforced the ethnic occupational specialization and, at times, may have helped regulate competition among Jews. Such ties, including one's own friends and acquaintances, were especially useful in finding employment. Even when one is answering want ads, such contacts are useful.[19]

The Jewish community has operated agencies to prepare Jewish immigrants for jobs in their new communities, as well as trying to steer Jews away from areas of Jewish concentration. This was particularly true of the fairly ambitious, but largely unsuccessful, efforts by groups like Am Olam and the Baron de Hirsch Fund to train and settle Jews in agriculture in Argentina, Russia, and the United States. Even if these efforts at making farmers of them did not succeed in the long run, they assisted some Jewish immigrants in getting out of the often depressed and overly competitive urban areas, and introduced Jews to new economic sectors, including chicken farming and running resort hotels. In addition to these efforts, there have been vocational services provided by local Jewish federations and B'nai Brith. Much of the fight against anti-Semitism was waged against economic discrimination.

The community also assisted its professionals by providing them with employment. For instance, the Sick Funds of *Lantsmanshaften* (immigrant aid societies) often gave Jewish doctors a place in which to begin their practices. Jewish hospitals not only provided religious patients with a kosher hospital, but Jewish physicians and surgeons—otherwise excluded from many hospitals—with a hospital practice.

Informal networks operate in the new corporate- bureaucratic sectors as well as in the older sectors, but without some of the reinforcement supplied by kinship ties. Whereas old business and banking elites, as well as middle-class family firms, often use a combination of kin and friendship ties such as the Anglo-Jewish "cousinhood" or the American German-Jewish "our crowd," academic professionals rely more on informal "old boy networks," such as the often-intermarried Jewish psychoanalysts of New Haven. These may have an ethnic base, but often have a fragile single-generational existence. They are associated with a high degree of mobility, and friendship ties have few strands, whereas the older "cousinhoods" and family firms combined kinship, friendship, and ongoing business. In such situations, finding and recognizing fellow Jews, who may or may not be helpful, requires subtle strategies.

As identity with the occupational group increases, involvement with the religious-ethnic community will decrease. This may well be related to the declining economic importance of familial ties. For instance, in the initial entry of professionals working for New York State, few had contacts through their families and, even when they got information about a job from the family, this rarely guaranteed getting the job or being promoted.[20]

The invisible organization on which Jewish communal solidarity is based—and which has been an important component of such activities as fund raising—may well have an economic foundation. If the trend toward professional or bureaucratic employment continues, the ties which have bound the community may well be weakened. Geographical mobility, intermarriage, failure to provide a Jewish education for the children, and failure to affiliate formally with Jewish groups are all part of the disintegration of the Jewish ethnic solidarity. They are related, not only to a breakdown of the family firm, but also to increasing competition between individuals, whether Jewish or Christian. In any case, this whole area deserves further study.

Visibility Strategy

Ethnic solidarity is important in terms of how it is perceived by the gentiles, as much as its actual occurrence, for this is part of the visibility of the Jews. Non-Jews often perceive Jews as a group and do not always distinguish between active participants and those who assimilate. A group which is as economically successful as American

Jews have been is noticeable. Yet, this recognition makes the Jews vulnerable to envy and hatred. Thus, one finds a dynamic—albeit contradictory—process in modern Jewish life between efforts to decrease visibility in order to reduce hostility to the group and the need for public perpetuation and legitimation of the Jewish religion and community, pressure on the powerful to aid Jewish interests, and the desire for a good image of the Jews. In some instances, there is a denial of the special character of Jewish culture and, in others, the effort is aimed at making Jewishness and Judaism less foreign in appearance so that Jews become 100-percent Americans.

Much of the content of American Jewish culture can be seen as an outcome of different strategies of image management. In speaking about management and strategy, it must be stressed that these terms include unconscious ways of coping with situations, as well as deliberate planning. Unconscious motives—such as guilt over betraying one's parental heritage or anger at the society for forcing one to act deviously—may enter into certain strategies and contradict them. For instance, an individual may seek to deny his Jewishness, but may draw attention to himself in seeking power, which also places the spotlight on his ancestry. Merton long ago pointed out that while anti-Semites have magnified the existence of Jewish prominence in America, Jewish defense organizations have stressed the discrimination against Jews and Jewish powerlessness and insignificance. This was certainly characteristic of the pre–World War II period. Later, in the more affluent 1950s, the emphasis changed. Jews called attention to their success as an example of the American dream and as a model for others.[21]

One can see the efforts to reduce the visible foreignness of Jews in a modern post-Christian society in such practices as the Americanization of personal and family names, the businessmen's observance of Christmas at the office, and the westernizing reforms in the synagogue services of the Reform and Conservative movements. Many American Jews have, at least partially, observed such Christian holidays as Christmas, Easter, and certainly commercial holidays of Christian origin such as Halloween and Valentine's Day. The festival of Hanukkah has acquired characteristics associated with Christmas, such as gift exchange and the sending of greeting cards. This is accompanied by the diffusion of Jewish traits such as eating bagels, rye bread, and matzo. In the 1960s, there was a billboard in New York City which read: "You don't have to be Jewish to love Levy's rye bread."

Part of this naturalization is the inclusion of Judaism in the list of the major religions of America and the presence of a rabbi at political conventions and at the inauguration of a President, as well as calling attention to the participation of Jews in the founding of the United States and an interpretation of economic competition as individualistic rather than ethnic.

This desire to reduce or tame the visibility of Jews as a distinct group has been a burden on the psyches of Jews. The inconspicuous behavior expected by members of a minority seeking to "pass" is what has been called the "ordeal of civility."[22] The present openness in North America to expression of ethnicity may only be a fad and can be replaced by another wave of assimilationist sentiment. It has not, in any case, wiped out the ambivalence which many Jews feel toward their heritage.[23]

On the other hand, the present assertiveness of contemporary Jews in America—including public, political, and cultural expressions of Jewishness-stands in sharp contrast with other modern nations. A young French Jewish sociologist once said to me that such expression is still discouraged in France. It is unheard-of in such countries as Argentina where Jews face anti-Semitic outbursts.[24]

It is difficult to relate the new assertiveness of American Jewry directly to a change in its occupational structure. One would, in fact, expect that those who work in the public sector would be even more "assimilationist" than would be businessmen who are dependent on fellow Jews. That this is not the case is more the product of the general political and cultural environment than of the economic structure of the Jewish community. Still the concentration of Jews in certain sectors of the economy and their relatively high status may contribute to this.

Jewish Political Participation and Leadership in the United States

The most visible indications of Jewish preeminence in both the past and the present have been wealthy and powerful individuals of Jewish ancestry.[25] Jewish courtiers and retainers in the past often became scapegoats and, when they were overthrown, the entire Jewish community might suffer. Even in modern times, the fate of such leaders and the Jewish community was often connected. The manner in which Jews in many places were blamed for the leadership of Trotsky and other Jews in Communist Russia in the early 1930s and Stalin's similar scapegoating of Jews shows that such linkage does occur in this century. All of this is consonant with the middleman minority's dilemma of apparent affluence combined with vulnerability.

An examination of Jewish participation in American politics—especially the role of elected and appointed officials—can show whether Jews, for the present at least, have shed the retainer roles which marked their political participation in the past. Implicit in this consideration of Jewish political participation and leadership is the old question: "Is it good for the Jews?" In dealing with the Jewish retainers, One can conclude that while Jews may have benefited from the patronage accorded by the powerful Jewish courtiers, they were often damaged severely if and when he or she fell from favor. Then, too, most premodern officials were retainers and not leaders of political parties. They were often physicians, merchants, or financiers. Their roles were rather loosely defined. The dependence on the favor of the ruler is still present today for certain appointed officials.

Some have seen a continuity between the role of the court Jew and the functions performed by Jews in American politics. These tasks include political contributions, serving on politicians' staffs, and holding appointive offices. Each of these roles, however, are much more specialized than that of retainers in the past. American Jewish political contributors are generally independent entrepreneurs, who often contribute through an ideological commitment, as well as personal gain.[26] Those who serve on the staffs of candidates and elective officials have highly specialized functions, unlike the fuzziness of earlier retainers' roles. This includes those who serve as liaisons between politician "X" and the Jewish community. Of course, meeting with staff members when one is lobbying for a Jewish cause is not so different from a community approaching a court Jew for a favor in the past. Still, such staff members operate in a different context.

Those who hold appointive offices generally have backgrounds in the area to which they are appointed or have acquired some political clout. Their roles are, again, more specialized than those of the earlier retainers. The most prominent Jews appointed to high office have often had only tenuous connections with the Jewish community itself, unlike the court Jews of an earlier period. This was certainly the case with Henry Kissinger. Still, depending on the post, the Jewish appointee may have to manage the Jewishness of his personal identity. Henry Kissinger, when he was Secretary of State, had to deal with the way in which various parties to the Middle East conflict perceived his fairness toward them.[27]

The base of power of elected officials is different from that of appointed officials, since their position is somewhat independent of patron-client relations. The way in which their ties to the Jewish community are managed may vary. Some, of course, have been elected from areas where few Jews reside. In some instances, this may have helped them bridge a gap within the gentile population itself. The first non-Mormon and Democratic governor of Utah, for example, was a Jew. If the elected official has a large Jewish constituency, he can, of course, use his post to plead for Jewish interests in a direct way, Jewish senators such as Herbert Lehman and Jacob Javits competed with their non-Jewish counterparts for the Jewish vote. They need not "bend over backward" to proclaim their patriotism or neglect Jewish interests as many prominent Jewish political leaders have in the past.[28] None of this obviates the fact that, if anti-Semitism would again become prominent in this country, Jewish officeholders would be highly visible targets.

The political participation of Jews in the United States has deviated from the retainer model. If a contemporary Jewish advisor is called a court Jew, this should be seen as a metaphor and not as an accurate description of that person's position. Patron-client relations and ethnic representation in the United States today are quite different from the medieval pattern, although remnants of the traditional pattern may be found in other countries. The merchant-banker of the past has been replaced by the reform politician, the professional specialist, and the administrative lawyer. They represent a different type of Jew than were the leaders of the medieval trading diaspora.

The participation of Jews in American political life—whether as voters, politicians, or elected officials—is an indication of their changed self-image. Through this participation, they assert their Americanism. They do not accept a status as tolerated strangers, but as full-fledged citizens. While retentions of past roles persist—such as in the importance of financial contributions—the variety of positions held by Jews in politics and government is an indication of their acceptance in American society.

LATENT ANTI-SEMITISM

The various theories which explain the economic position of middleman minorities are also explanations of hostility toward these groups. As minorities of all sorts in the world go, American Jews have faced little direct violence and only moderate discrimination. The lynching of Leo Frank in Georgia in 1914, the looting of Jewish stores during race riots, and recent Ku Klux Klan and other extremist violent acts are notable exceptions.[29] Conventional stereotypes of Jews, including anti-Semitic images, do persist, but have not had the results which they had elsewhere.

The middleman-minority theories have been useful in explaining the association of economic anti-Semitism and occupational roles in the many countries where Jews have suffered from violent persecution. Generally, the discussion of why anti-Semitism in the English-speaking world and the United States in particular has been relatively mild has been permeated with the ideology of American exceptionalism.[30] In accounting for the mildness of animosity toward Jews in America, it is useful to look at factors which have been used to explain extreme anti-Semitism in Central and Eastern Europe on the eve of World War II, and to examine the differences.

1. In Eastern Europe, Jews were highly distinguishable in terms of culture, language, and religion. As already noted, the visibility of Jews in America has been obfuscated, just as some Jewish cultural traits such as foods have been Americanized. In Eastern Europe, the boundaries between Jews and gentiles were sharp, and culture, religion, and physical features coincided. Most Jews in America are part of a larger white color-caste. The existence of widespread intermarriage, conversion in both directions, even interreligious and interracial adoption has made for many cross-cutting ties, rather than a congruence of cultural, racial, and religious dividing lines, especially among whites, but even with other groups.
2. In Eastern Europe and, to a large extent, in Germany during the interwar period, there was much general poverty and impoverishment. Since World War II and until the last few years, the American economy has been marked by economic growth and an expectation of general affluence.
3. As in other parts of the world, the Jewish proportion of higher income individuals and probably of overall wealth has been larger than the proportion of Jews to the general population. Still, for most of the period since World War II, there has been economic growth. In addition, the American emphasis on individualism, rather than on ethnic achievement, has made this factor less crucial.

4. In large parts of Eastern Europe, the Jews filled a status gap and, thus, were not in competition with the majority of the population. This broke down during the nineteenth century and, during the interwar period in Poland, there was increasing competition between Jews and Poles, which was interpreted ethnically. In Germany, the situation was similarly viewed. Such competition certainly exists in the United States, but it is not always perceived as group conflict. In fact, Jewish opposition to ethnic quotas, whether negative quotas or affirmative action, has always appealed to the American value of individual achievement.
5. A final factor which should be stressed is that, in the context of early twentieth-century Central and Eastern Europe, Jews were perceived as foreigners. Even the thoroughly Germanized Jews of Germany and Austria were seen as belonging to a foreign race and biologically distinct. Jewish converts and atheists were seen as "strangers," too. In the past thirty years, and even before that, American Jews have made a good case for their acceptance as Americans. Such acceptance was always challenged in parts of Europe.

While there have been some possible conditions for a high degree of anti-Semitism in the United States—including interethnic competition for jobs and a relatively high degree of success by Jews as compared to others—this has been mitigated by the acceptance of American culture by the Jews and an ideal of individual achievement and religious ethnical toleration by other Americans against the background of an expanding economy. This provides a plausible refutation to efforts at judgment in terms of group memberships. It accompanies a view that one may *become* an American, even if not born one. A change in circumstances, as in ideology, could change the equation and bring out the prejudice which is latent in American culture.

Conclusion

The analysis of American Jewry shows the development of a Jewish community away from the middleman pattern. While the occupational structure still shows traces of middleman and small-business concentration and self-employment, the increasing employment of Jews by government and large corporations is a step in another direction.

While some may consider the concentration of Jews in communications, including education, to be a form of mediation, calling this a *middleman phenomenon* is a figure of speech. The use of ethnic solidarity in corporate settings is quite different from past uses of such solidarity. A transformation in the situation of employment has occurred in a liberal political climate and an expanding economy.

One would expect, if some middleman minority theorists are correct, that behavioral and structural assimilation of the Jews in America will proceed. It does not, however, appear to be a straight line toward assimilation, as many have previously imagined.

Despite these conclusions which include a view that anti-Semitism in this country has been mild, one must be cautious. Anti-Semitism in the United States is latent, not absent. Anti-Jewish elements remain in the culture. In addition, many Jews, while no longer middlemen, remain in vulnerable positions within the society. Middleman-minority theories are helpful in isolating certain factors, such as occupation, competition, and complementarity. They are most helpful when used in conjunction with a consideration of the culture and symbolism of Jews and gentiles in America.

CONCLUSION

The inherent paradox of middlemanishness lies in the possibilities of a high degree of economic influence by a group which is able to survive and even flourish in commerce but which is also politically vulnerable. This phenomenon, as we have seen, has been linked, on the one hand, to structural and situational factors, and to cultural and historical causes on the other. Among the ingredients for economic success, many scholars have stressed the importance of ethnic cohesion, ethnocentrism, and similar traits. While some of these tendencies were found particularly at the level of primary group relations, they were often highly exaggerated when discussing the minority community as a whole.

Nevertheless, the image of middleman minorities as unified bodies was an important factor in creation of hostility toward such groups. This led to the conclusion which has appeared throughout this book and elsewhere that perception of group qualities may be mediated through a process of image manipulation. Image manipulation is seen in this work as a normal social process, and not necessarily as a sinister one. The middleman minorities would like to appear as good neighbors and good citizens, while, at the same time, their competitors or others view them in a quite different light. Priests may view Lombards and Jews as usurers, while the Filipinos, Indonesians, and Malays look at the Chinese merchants as moneygrubbing merchants who make profits at their expense and send the cash out of the country.

In nineteenth-century Syria, the competition between Jewish and Christian merchants and bankers for certain positions saw Christians making murder accusations against Jews, while Jews might collaborate with Muslims to best their Christian rivals.[1] In Java, Muslim traders joined others in using Islam as a way to make the pagan and Christian Chinese appear to be people with whom patriotic Indonesians shouldn't trade.[2] There is a constant effort to stigmatize one group as disloyal or to make another group of traders appear as upholders of the national cause.

In Morocco, Jews were obviously outside the fold of Muslim Moroccans and, since a large-scale Jewish emigration took place during and shortly after the struggle for independence, a large-scale campaign against the latter was unnecessary. Two major groups of indigenous Muslim traders—the Arab Fassis, from the city of Fez, and the Berber Sousis, from the Sous region, could, however, claim that they were patriotic Moroccans and good Muslims. [3]

These processes are comparable to those associated with viewing Protestants in the British Empire as people fit to rule colonies, such as the Scots who participated in the Hudson's Bay Company. On the other hand, Jews and other minority members holding positions of authority over members of the majority may be seen as insolent and dangerous. In the medieval and early modern periods of both Christian Europe and Islamic lands, when Jewish—and in the Middle East, Christian—courtiers were removed from office, not only were they often executed and their estates confiscated, but there were attacks on all minority members. The wealthy and powerful few symbolized the whole group.[4]

In dealing with antimiddleman hostility, violence, expulsion, mass killing, and image manipulation play a key role. Rational economic factors—such as competition between merchants or conflict between employers and employees, buyers and sellers, or creditors and debtors—may set the stage. But cases of expulsion and genocide are usually associated with political and ideological conflicts of a more intense nature. The exodus of many Chinese from Vietnam in 1979 was associated with the war between Vietnam and China, as well as with economic measures. Even North Vietnamese veterans of Chinese background were forced to leave Vietnam at that time.

The mass killings of Armenians in the Ottoman empire in the 1890s, and again, the deportations and massacres in 1915 came when the Ottoman empire was threatened with partition. There was an active Armenian nationalist movement, which at times, resorted to violence. Some Armenian nationalists sought assistance from the Allies, including Tsarist Russia. As in the case of Court Jews—whose roles symbolized that of all Jews for the majority populations—so the politically active minority symbolized all Armenians to the insecure Muslim majority.

In early twentieth-century Europe, anti-Semitic ideology tried to explain the appearance of inequality, class conflict, and revolutionary unrest through a conspiracy of Jewish capitalists and radicals against Christian Europe. The existence of Rothschilds and other wealthy plutocrats, as well as Trotsky and many other radicals of Jewish origin, lent credence to this theory, because people saw the Jews as having much more solidarity than they, in fact, had.

In all of these cases, the whole group was tarred with a brush which derived from part of the group. In most of these cases, the societies faced a number of critical pressures. Still, it should also be said that middleman minorities have been one set—but not the only set—of victims of such violence. Indigenous peoples, such as the Plains Indians, the Indian peoples of the Amazon, and Australian aborigines have been victims of genocide, while in sub-Saharan Africa, labor migrants from neighboring countries, as well as trading minorities, have been subject to expulsion on several occasions.[5] Dominant minorities, of course, may also face expulsion and massacre. Obviously, the stories and myths used against middleman minorities will have a different character, as was noted in chapter 3 and elsewhere, than those directed at other groups.

The relationships which I have noted may come to the fore today. When I began my research on middleman minorities, I paid very little attention to countries under Communist rule. In this I was not alone. Who would have thought that ethnicity, let alone trading groups, would have much of a role to play in a command economy where everyone worked for the government, where the government commanded all strategic resources, and employment was by merit. Closer observation of the Soviet Union, the Peoples Republic of China, and other socialist regimes, however, revealed that one could "pull strings" in the bureaucracy through the use of kin, friends, and bribes just as one could in capitalist societies—maybe even more so, since ruling elites also controlled access to information without the need to be accountable to an open press.

Then, just as the advanced-capitalist economies have informal sectors in which "penny capitalism" and the barter economy survive, the Communist countries had a "black market," an illegal sector, which was generally tolerated. While most economists and sociologists did not discuss ethnic factors, the existence of specialization on the basis of some type of primordial ties is not surprising. Similar to an African long-distance trading network, those in the Soviet informal sector had to maintain trust without the ability to use state agencies to police each other, as their activities were illegal. In fact, they needed to appropriate state resources in order to perform tasks such as manufacturing.

Bribery was also necessary to prevent arrest. Members of certain ethnic groups were particularly important. Konstantin Simis noted that Jews played an important role in this sector, seeing this as a reaction to their exclusion from prominent positions in the state and Communist party hierarchy after many were purged by Stalin. Simis and Hedrick Smith noted the importance in this endeavor of Georgians, as well as Armenians and Azerbaijanis in regions outside of the Slavic Republics.[6]

In the contemporary Soviet Union, an attempt was made to revive a legal private sector through the licensing of cooperatives. There are indications that Jews and people of southern Soviet origin are believed to play a disproportionate role in such enterprises and, in fact, do play such a role, although perhaps not to the degree that others believe them to do so. In an American study of Soviet cooperativists in Leningrad in the late 1980s, out of eighteen, nine were Jews by nationality, seven in this Russian city were "Russian," and two were Latvian. Generally Soviets believed that private enterprise was stronger among Baltic and Caucasian peoples than among the Slavs. People also believed that Russians did not work as hard as Jews, Caucasians, Muslims, and people from the Baltic.[7]

The filling of niches in the economy by particular ethnic groups continues in many societies. As was noted previously, American Jews, for the most part, appear to be leaving traditional middleman positions in the American economy. It is true that certain groups—particularly new Jewish immigrants from the Soviet Union and Israelis—continue to enter small business in the United States. For instance, in the center-city area of Philadelphia, one can find Israeli-owned electronics shops, restaurants, and food stores.

Other groups are conspicuously represented in small business in the United States. In New York City and Philadelphia, the Korean shopkeepers who sell fruits and vegetables as well as run other small businesses are ever-present. On the streets of New York, one can find Senegalese peddlers selling gold jewelry.

What is the relationship of ethnic specialization in the informal and small businesses and ethnic conflict? So far, whatever resentment exists against immigrant small business in the United States has been rather muted. There is prejudice against Asians in the United States today, just as there was a century ago. Some violence against Asians appears from time to time, such as the murder of a Chinese-American in Detroit. Some of this violence is linked to black resentment against nonblack businesses in their neighborhoods, and some of it is linked to feelings about growing East Asian, especially Japanese, industrial production while American production is declining. Although a potential for violence exists, the degree of deprivation, organized anti-Asian organizations on a large-scale, and the like have not tapped this hostility. In the spring of 1990, however, a boycott of Korean grocieries in Brooklyn received nationwide coverage.[8]

In the Soviet Union, the situation is very different. There have been several pogroms, especially directed against Armenians in Baku and Dushanbe. In Baku and elsewhere in Azerbaijan, the national conflict between Armenians and Azerbaijanis over the disputed territory of Karabakh has played a key role. Whether the Armenians also have played a prominent part in the informal and private sectors of the economy in these areas and how that may have contributed to the violence has not been reported.

There is also conspicuous anti-Semitism in the Soviet Union of the sort promulgated by the Tsarist regime and the Nazis. It is an ideology using religious, racial, and economic arguments. Apparently it includes the role of Jews as middlemen. Certainly, many Jews in the Soviet Union are afraid of violent actions against them.[9]

In other parts of the world where there are political upheavals and interethnic violence, we continue to hear about small businessmen belonging to a variety of ethnic groups and nationalities. In April and May of 1989, Mauretanian-owned cornershops in Dakar were attacked. This was followed by attacks against Senegalese fishermen and herders in Mauritania, and many citizens of each country were forced to return home. When the government of the "tribal homeland" of Ciskei in South Africa was overthrown in March 1990, there was looting. An estimated fifty or more stores and factories owned by Israelis and Taiwanese were destroyed.[10]

The founders of the social sciences saw modern society as shedding many of the characteristics of its predecessors. Marx foresaw a classless society in which huckstering would no longer predominate. Weber saw a rational universalistic ethic in which the particularism of earlier forms of capitalism would cease to play an important role. No one can make such predictions today. Rather than prophesying the demise of middlemanishness, we must try to understand what causes it to persist and to often be accompanied by conflict.

We cannot banish social friction or inequality from this less-than-perfect world. But through the use of scholarship, we can hope to understand, control, and resolve conflicts which threaten to destroy us.

NOTES

INTRODUCTION

1. Edna Bonacich and John Modell, *The Economic Basis of Ethnic Solidarity: The Case of the Japanese-Americans* (Berkeley: University of California Press, 1981), 13–36.

2. Walter P. Zenner, "American Jewry in the Light of Middleman Minority Theory," *Contemporary Jewry* 5 (1980): 11–30.

3. Hubert Blalock, *Toward a Theory of Minority Group Relations* (New York: John Wiley, 1967), 79–84; and Irwin Rinder, "Strangers in the Land," *Social Problem 6 (1958): 253–260.*

4. Bonacich and Modell, *Economic Basis of Ethnic Solidarity,* 13–36; and Edna Bonacich, "Middleman Minorities and Advanced Capitalism," *Ethnic Groups* 2 (1980): 311–320.

5. Igor Kopytoff, "Types of Religious Movements," in *Symposium of New Approaches in the Study of Religion,* M. E. Spiro, ed. (Seattle: University of Washington Press, 1964).

6. Bonacich and Modell, *Economic Basis of Ethnic Solidarity,* 13–36. They make the same argument.

7. Max Weber, *Ancient Judaism* [translation of *Das antike Judentum*] (Glencoe: The Free Press, 1952); and Bonacich and Modell, *Economic Basis.* op cit. The most commonly cited article by Bonacich is E. Bonacich "Theory of Middleman Minorities," *American Sociological Review* 38 (1973):583–594. Many critics have identified this article with "middleman-minority theory," ignoring both Bonacich's later work and the prior and subsequent work of others. For use of Gypsies as a prototype,

see Marlene Sway, *Familiar Strangers: Gypsy Life in America* (Urbana, University of Illinois Press, 1988).

8. See Maurice Freedman, "An Epicycle of Cathay: or the Southward Expansion of the Sinologists," in *Social Organization and the Applications of Anthropology,* R. J. Smith, ed. (Ithaca: Cornell University Press, 1975) 302–332.

9. The nominalist argument is made forcefully by Jacob Neusner, "Why Does Judaism Have an Economics?" (Saul Reinfeld Lecture in Judaic Studies, Connecticut College, New London, April 13, 1988). In this lecture, he criticizes Salo W. Baron, the noted Jewish historian, among others. Neusner's argument in favor of greater particularism is well taken, but continuities and common patterns do exist. See Walter P. Zenner, "The Jewish Diaspora and the Middleman Adaptation," in *Diaspora: Exile and the Jewish Condition,* E. Levine, ed. (New York: Jason Aronson, 1983):141–156.

CHAPTER 1

1. For another historical assessment, see Walter P. Zenner, "Jewish Communities as Cultural Units," in *Community, Self, and Identity,* S. Preston and S. Misra, eds. (The Hague: Mouton, 1978). *See also* Edna Bonacich and John Modell, *The Economic Basis of Ethnic Solidarity: The Case of Japanese-Americans* (Berkeley: University of California Press, 1981), 13–36, for a survey of theories.

2. F. M. A. de Voltaire, *Essai sur les moeurs et l'esprit des nations,* 2 (Paris: Garnier Freres, 1963): 1, 66–77. *See also* Immanuel Kant, *Anthropology from a Pragmatic View (The Hague: Nijhoff, 1974), 19, 22.* See also H. D. Schmidt, "Anti-Western and Anti-Jewish Tradition in German Historical Thought," *Leo Baeck Yearbook* 4 (1959): 37–60, who points to the use of the term "nation of traders" for both Jews and Englishmen. Marx's 1843 essay on the Jews is an important source for both Marxist attitudes toward Jews and discussions of anti-Semitism. *See* Karl Marx, *Karl Marx: Early Writings* (New York: Random House, 1975), 211–241; *Collected Works of Karl Marx and Friedrich Engels* (Moscow: Progress Publishers, 1975), 3, 146–174. For references to the related topics of Jews and merchants' capital, *see* Karl Marx, *Capital* (Moscow, Foreign Languages Publishing House, 1967), in vol. 1, pt. 1, sec. 4, 79; pt. 2, ch. 4, 154; and in vol. 3, pt. 4, ch. 20, 323–337.

3. W. Roscher, *"Die Stellung der Juden in Mittelalter vom Standpunkt fur die allgemeine Handelspolitik," Zeitschrift fue gesamte Staatswirtschaft* 31 (1875): 503–526; and "The Status of Jews in the Middle Ages from the Standpoint of Commercial Policy," *Historica Judaica* 6

(1944). For an application of Roscher's thesis to the Chinese in Java, *see* W. F. Wertheim, *East-West Parallels* (Chicago: Quadrangle, 1964); and for a criticism of Roscher's view of the Jewish role in the medieval economy, *see* Toni Oelsner, "The Place of the Jews in Economic History as Viewed by German Scholars," *Leo Baeck Yearbook* 7 (1962): 183–212.

4. F. Toennies, *Community and Society* (East Lansing: Michigan State University Press, 1957); R. Heberle and W. Cahnman, eds., *On Sociology: Pure, Applied and Empirical* (Chicago: University of Chicago Press, 1971), 308–310; and K. H. Wolff, ed., *The Sociology of Georg Simmel* (Glencoe, Ill.: The Free Press, 1950). For discussion on the interaction between migrants and the rise of capitalism, together with racial and cultural factors, *see* Werner Sombart, *The Quintessence of Capitalism: A Study of the History and Psychology of the Modern Businessman* (New York: Howard Fertig, 1967), 292–307.

5. For the influence of Simmel's stranger concept on middleman minority theory see Werner Cahnman, "Pariahs, Strangers and Court Jews—A Conceptual Classification." *Sociological Analysis* 35 (1974): 155–166; C. R. Hallpike, "Some Problems in Cross-Culturral Comparison," in *The Translation of Culture,* T. Beidelman, ed. (London: Tavistock, 1971), 123–140; Hilda Kuper, "Strangers" in Plural Societies:Asians in South Africa and Uganda," in *Pluralism in Africa,* Leo Kuper and M. G. Smith eds., (Berkeley: Univ. of California Press, 1971), 247–282; Jack H. Porter, "The Urban Middleman: A Comparative Analysis," *Comparative Social Research* 4 (1981), 199–215; R. A. Reminick, The Evil Eye Belief among the Amhara of Ethiopia, *Ethnology* 13 (1974): 270–292; William Shack and Elliott P. Skinner, *Strangers in African Societies* (Berkeley: University of California Press, 1979) *passim;* Paul C. P. Siu, The Sojourner, American *Journal of Sociology* 58 (1952), 34–44.

6. Benjamin Braude, "Jewish Economic History—Review Essay," *Association for Jewish Studies Newsletter* 19 (February 1977): 25–28. For a complimentary analysis of Sombart's evaluation of the Jewish economic role, *see* Marcus Arkin, *Aspects of Jewish Economic History* (Philadelphia: Jewish Publication Society, 1975), 143–148. A less favorable assessment of Sombart's work can be found in Paul R. Mendes-Flohr, "Werner Sombart's the Jews and Modern Capitalism—An Analysis of its Ideological Premises," *Leo Baeck Yearbook* 221 (1976): 87–108. For the intellectual context of Sombart's thinking and that of other German sociologists, *see* Arthur Mitzman, *Sociology and Estrangement: Three Sociologists of Imperial Germany* (New York: Knopf, 1973). The book-length works are Max Weber, *Ancient Judaism* and Werner Sombart, *The Jews and Modern Capitalism* (Glencoe, Ill.: Free Press, 1952). Their attitudes, however, are evident throughout their writings.

7. Sombart, *Jews and Modern Capitalism,* 177–183; and Sombart,

Quintessence of Capitalism, 232–235, 242–307. His attitudes about capitalistic peoples are summarized in *Quintessence of Capitalism,* 100–101. After citing examples of Florentine and Lowland Scottish commercial attitudes, which are dominated by a lack of adventurousness and a calculating attitude toward making profits as well as opportunistic hard work and submission to superiors, he wrote: "Put Florentine in place of Scotchman, and does not the statement hold good? It would hold good also if, in place of Scotchman, you put Jew . . . They derive it *by means of* war, murder or assassination, while other peoples seek an army, the Jews work their way up to being the mighty ones of the earth, using as their weapons those of the Florentines—money, treaties (i.e., contracts) and knowledge."

8. Weber, *Ancient Judaism,* 336–355. *See also* G. Roth and C. Wittich, eds., *Economy and Society* (New York: Bedminster Press, 1968), 164–166; and T. Parsons, ed., *Theory of Social and Economic Organization* (New York: Oxford University Press, 1974), 276–278.

9. Max Weber, *Sociology of Religion,* trans. by E. Fischoff (Boston: Beacon Press, 1963), 108–109; and Roth and Wittich, eds., *Economy and Society,* 493.

10. Roth and Wittich, eds., *Economy and Society,* 934; and Christian Sigrist, "The Problem of Pariahs," in *Max Weber and Sociology Today,* O. Stammer, ed. (Oxford: Blackwell, 1971), 240–250.

11. Roth and Wittich, eds., *Economy and Society,* 611–623, 1204, and Weber, *Ancient Judaism,* 343–345. While Weber saw the "ethnocentrism" of the pariah people as inhibiting their development of modern capitalism with regard to usury and ritual segregation, he did not see discrimination in employment as part of this, unlike Bonacich and other recent theorists. On the contrary, he saw the Quakers as helping poorer members of their sects by employing them in their enterprises more than Jews did. *See* Roth and Wittich, ed., *Economy and Society* 613. Weber obviously saw that there were differences between the Hindu outcastes and the Jews, but he often used words in a peculiar fashion, distorting the original meaning, such as Kadi justice (patriarchal justice), with only partial reference to actual Islamic legal practices. Jewish critics have objected to Weber's usage of the term, "pariah," with reference to the Jews on a wide variety of grounds. One is the inappropriateness of the term. Some of these critics saw an underlying anti-Jewish bias in his interpretation of both ancient and modern Judaism. *See* S. W. Baron, *Social and Religious History of the Jews,* 1 (New York: Columbia University Press, 1951): 23–24; H. Liebeschuetz, "Max Weber's Historical Interpretation of Judaism," *Leo Baeck Yearbook* 9 (1974): 41–69; and E. Shmueli, "The Pariah People and its Charismatic Leadership," *Proceedings of the American Academy for Jewish Research* 36 (1968): 167–247. *See also* Cahnman, "Pariahs, Strangers and Court Jews," who suggests that postenlighten-

ment Jews who began to internalize gentile attitudes saw themselves as pariahs more than did traditional Jews. For Weber's remarks on Jews in modern society and their possible assimilation, *see* Roth and Wittich, eds., *Economy and Society,* 40, 623, and 934; and Weber, *Ancient Judaism,* 353. While his vocabulary may seem cool to Jews, it reflects a mood of liberal assimilationism, not racism.

12. On the usage of "marginal trading minorities," *see* Howard P. Becker, *Through Values to Social Interpretation* (Durham, N.C.: Duke University Press, 1950); and *Man in Reciprocity* (New York: Praeger, 1956). "Out-caste traders" is a concept used extensively by G. Sjoberg, *The Pre-Industrial City* (Glencoe, Ill.: The Free Press, 1960). On "pariah capitalism," *see* J. P. L. Jiang, "Toward a Theory of Pariah Entrepreneurship," in *Leadership and Authority,* G. Wijeyewardene, ed. (Singapore: University of Malaya Press, 1968), 147–162; and on "guest peoples," *see* Don Martindale, "The Guest Community," *Journal of Asian Affairs* 1 (1976): 1–8.

13. Howard P. Becker, "Constructive Typology in the Social Sciences," in *Contemporary Social Theory,* H. Barnes, H. Becker, and F. Becker, eds. (New York: Appleton, Century, 1940), 17–46; *Through Values to Social Interpretation,* 110; and *Man in Reciprocity,* 225–237.

14. W. Cahnman, "Social-Economic Causes of Anti-Semitism," *Social Problems* 5 (1957): 21–29; Irwin Rinder, "Strangers in the Land," *Social Problems* 6 (1958): 253–260; Sheldon Stryker, "Social Structure and Prejudice," *Social Problems* 6 (1958): 340–354. *See also* B. Weinryb, "Prolegomena to an Economic History of Jews in Germany," *Leo Baeck Yearbook* 1 (1956): 279–306; Simon Kuznets, "The Economic Structure and Life of the Jews," in *The Jews: Their History, Culture and Religion,* L. Finkelstein, ed. (Philadelphia: Jewish Publication Society, 1960), 1597–1666; S. Andreski, "An Economic Interpretation of Anti-Semitism," *Jewish Journal of Sociology* 5 (1963): 201–213; "Methods and Substantive Theory in Max Weber," in S. N. Eisenstadt, ed., *The Protestant Ethic and Modernization* (New York: Basic Books, 1968); S. W. Baron, *History and Jewish Historians* (Philadelphia: Jewish Publication Society, 1964), 31–35; and Ellis Rivkin, *The Shaping of Jewish History* (New York: Scribners, 1971).

15. T. Shibutani and K. Kwan, *Ethnic Stratification* (New York: Macmillan, 1965), 168–198; Hubert Blalock, *Toward a Theory of Minority Group Relations* (New York: John Wiley, 1967), 82–83; and R. A. Schermerhorn, *Comparative Ethnic Relations* (New York: Random House, 1970), 55, 72, 74, 77, 99, 106, 111–112, 147, and 151, reflect the "race relations" view in middleman minority theory. David C. McClelland, *The Achievement Motive* (New York: Appleton-Century-Crofts, 1953) deals with the motives for entrepreneurship, although this

approach was not often applied to middleman minorities. For critiques of this approach, *see* Abner Cohen, *Custom and Politics in Urban Africa* (Berkeley: University of California Press, 1972); and John Waterbury, *North for the Trade* (Berkeley: University of California Press, 1969), 103–115. For a review of the literature regarding the needs for achievement and affiliation, *see* Ronald Gallimore, "Affiliation, Social Context, Industriousness, and Achievement," in *Handbook of Cross-Cultural Human Development,* Robert Munroe, Ruth Monroe, and Beatrice B. Whiting, eds. (New York: Garland, 1981), 689–715. *See* Everett E. Hagen, *On the Theory of Social Change* (Homewood, Ill.: Dorsey, 1962), 123–236, 247–250, for a theory on the psychic motives for entrepreneurship as well as the ability of entrepreneurs to serve as role models for others in the society. For additional discussion of this conceptualization, *see* Andreski, "An Economic Interpretation of Anti-Semitism." Examples of the Third-World studies of this period include Skinner, "Strangers in Plural Societies"; and Lloyd Fallers, ed., *Immigrants and Associations* (The Hague: Mouton, 1967). Other examples can be found in the notes of chapters 3, 4, and 6.

16. Edna Bonacich, "A Theory of Middleman Minorities," *American Sociological Review* 38 (1973): 583–594; "Class Approaches to Ethnicity and Race," *Insurgent Sociologist* 10 (1980): 9–23; "Middleman Minorities and Advanced Capitalism," *Ethnic Groups* 2 (1980): 311–320; Bonacich and Modell, *Economic Basis of Ethnic Solidarity;* Jonathan H. Turner and Edna Bonacich, "Toward a Composite Theory of Middleman Minorities," *Ethnicity* 7 (1980): 144–158; and Edna Bonacich, Ivan Light, and Charles Choy Wong, "Korean Immigrant Small Business in Los Angeles," in *Sourcebook on the New Immigration,* R. B. Bryce-Laporte, D. Mortimer, and S. Couch, eds. (New Brunswick, N.J.: Transaction Books, 1980), 167–184. For a review of Ivan Light's work on ethnic enterprise in America which is closely related to Bonacich's, *see* Ivan Light, *Ethnic Enterprise in America* (Berkeley: University of California Press, 1972): "Disadvantaged Minorities in Self-Employment," *International Journal of Comparative Sociology* 20 (1979): 31–45; "Asian Enterprise in America," in *Self-Help in Urban America,* S. Cummings, ed. (Port Washington, N.Y.: Kennikat, 1980), 33–57. For criticisms of Bonacich's "A Theory of Middleman Minorities," *see* Zenner, "Middleman Minority Theories: A Critical Review," in *Sourcebook on the New Immigration,* R. B. Bryce-Laporte, D. Mortimer and S. Couch, eds., (New Brunswick, N.J.: Transaction Books, 1980), 413–426. For critiques which argue that the "middleman" phenomenon in modern capitalistic societies is structurally unlike premodern and colonial contexts, *see* Gary Hamilton, "Pariah Capitalism: A Paradox of Power and Dependence," *Ethnic Groups* 2 (1978): 1–15; Pierre van den Berghe, "Asian Africans before and after Independence," *Kroniek van Afrika* N.S. 3 (1975): 197–205; Frank Bovenkerk, "Shylock or Horatio Alger: On the Theory of Middleman Minorities," in *Hevel Ya'akov:*

Jubilee Volume Presented to Jaan Meijer, L. Dasberg and J. N. Cohen, eds. (Assen: Van Gorcum, 1982), 147–164 [in Dutch]; and Robert Cherry, "Middleman Minority Theories: Their Implications for Black-Jewish Relations, *Journal of Ethnic Studies* 17 (1989), 117–138. *Also see* n. 24.

17. On the split-labor hypothesis, *see* Edna Bonacich, "A Theory of Ethnic Antagonism: The Split-Labor Market," *American Sociological Review* 37 (1972): 547–559; "The Past, Present and Future of Split-Labor Market Theory," in *Research in Race and Ethnic Relations: A Research Annual* (Greenwich, Conn.: JAI Press, 1979), 17–64; and "Class Approaches to Ethnicity and Race," 9–23.

18. Abram Leon, *The Jewish Question—A Marxist Interpretation* (New York: Pathfinder Press, 1970). For a criticism of Leon's work, see Cahnman, "Socio-Economic Causes of Anti-Semitism," 21–29; Zenner, "Jewish Communities as Cultural Units," 161–174; "Middleman Minorities and Advanced Capitalism," 311–320; David McElroy, "Middleman Minorities: A Comparative Analysis" (Ph.D. thesis: University of California at Riverside, 1977); and Bonacich and Modell, *Economic Basis of Ethnic Solidarity.* Other Marxist approaches to the "Jewish question" can be found in Mordecai Lahav, *Sotziologia shel Toldot HaGolah HaYehudit Le'Or HaMarxism* (Merhavia: Sifriat Poalim, 1951) [in Hebrew]; and Ber Borochov, *Nationalism and the Class Struggle* (New York: Young Poale Zion Alliance of America, 1937).

19. I. Wallerstein, *The Modern World System,* 1 (New York: Academic Press, 1974): 147–151; and *The Modern World System,* 2 (New York: Academic Press, 1980): 145. The "world systems" approach is implicitly applied in chapter 7.

20. Abner Cohen, *Two Dimensional Man* (Berkeley: University of California Press, 1974). The symbolic side of the dialectical relationship between symbols and power is best presented in his study of the Creoles of Sierra Leone. *See* Abner Cohen, *Politics of Elite Culture* (Berkeley: University of California Press, 1981). Incidentally, while the Creoles today are specialized as civil servants, they were a middleman group during the late nineteenth century.

21. Abner Cohen, "Cultural Strategies in the Organization of Trading Diasporas," in *The Development of Indigenous Trade and Markets in West Africa,* C. Meillassoux, ed. (London: Oxford University Press, 1971): 266–284. His analysis of trading diasporas is based on his study of Hausa cattle traders. *See* Cohen, *Custom and Politics in Urban Africa.*

22. *See* Philip Curtin, *Cross-Cultural Trade in World History* (Cambridge: Cambridge University Press, 1984), 1–14.

23. On ethnic enclaves, *see* Kenneth L. Wilson and Alejandro Portes,

"Immigrant Enclaves: An Analysis of Labor Market Experiences of Cubans in Miami," *American Journal of Sociology* 87 (1980): 295–319; Kenneth L. Wilson and W. Allen Martin, "Ethnic Enclaves: A Comparison of Cuban and Black Economies in Miami," *American Journal of Sociology* 88 (1982):125–160; Alejandro Portes, "The Social Origins of the Cuban Enclave Economy of Miami," *Sociological Perspectives* 30(1987):340–372. On the garment industry and ethnicity, *see* I. Howe, *The World of Our Fathers* (New York: Harcourt, Brace, Jovanovich). For a more recent account, *see* Robert Waldinger, *Through the Eye of the Needle* (New York: New York University Press, 1986). For a comparison of the middleman and enclave models as applied to Cuban immigrants in San Juan, Puerto Rico, *see* Jose Cobas, "Ethnic Enclaves and Middleman Minorities—Alternative Strategies of Immigrant Adaptation?," *Sociological Perspectives* 29 (1987):101–120.

24. S. W. Baron, "The Modern Age," in *Great Ages and Ideas of the Jewish People* L. Schwarz, ed. (New York: Random House, 1956), 315–484; and Alex Bein, "The Jewish Parasite—Notes on the Semantics of the Jewish Problem, with Special Reference to Germany," *Leo Baeck Yearbook* 9 (1964): 3–40.

25. *See* Milton Friedman, "Capitalism and the Jews: Confronting a Paradox," in *The Essence of Friedman,* Kurt R. Luebe, ed. (Stanford: Hoover Institution Press, 1987), 43–56.

26. *See* E. Bonacich "A Social Evaluation of the Ethics of Immigrant Entrepreneurship," *Sociological Perspectives* 30 (1987): 446–466.

27. Bonacich, "A Theory of Middleman Minorities," 583–594; and Bonacich and Modell, *The Economic Basis of Ethnic Solidarity.*

28. For a classification of theories, see Bonacich and Modell, *Economic Basis of Ethnic Solidarity,* 24–30.

29. Donald Horowitz, *Ethnic Groups in Conflict* (Berkeley and Los Angeles: University of California Press, 1985), 16–51; 105–125, and 141–228. His views on group-worth parallel those of E. E. Hagen, *Theory of Social Change,* 123–236.

30. Rinder, "Strangers in the Land," 253–260.

31. Roscher, *"Die Stellung der Juden in Mittelalter vom Standpunkt fur due allgemeine Handelspolitik"*; Leon, *Jewish Question;* Becker, *Through Value to Social Interpretation;* Andreski, "An Economic Interpretation of Anti-Semitism"; Shibutani and Kwan, *Ethnic Stratification,* 189–198; Schermerhorn, *Comparative Ethnic Relations,* 150–52; and Blalock "Toward a Theory of Minority Group Relations," 82. Bonacich objects to the inevitability of a status gap in explaining the middleman phenomenon, especially in advanced industrial societies, although her own theories point to "gaps" or "holes" in the socioeconomic structure.

See Bonacich, "Class Approaches to Ethnicity and Race."

32. Roscher, "*Die Stellung der Juden in Mittelalter.*"

33. Andreski, "Economic Interpretation of Anti-Semitism."

34. Wallerstein, *Modern World System,* 1: 151. S. W. Baron, *Social and Religious History of the Jews,* Vol. XVI: 211–312, gives a much more variegated picture of the situation of Jews in that era. For an application of this approach, *see* Richard Williams, "'Ethnicity' and 'Race' in the Small Business Literature: Some Lessons from the World-Systems Literature," in *Racism, Sexism and the World System* (Westport, Conn.: Greenwood Press, 1988), 153–168. Williams uses this approach to criticize conventional comparisons of blacks with Asian and white immigrants in the United States. He suggests that the background of the former as slaves while the latter came as free immigrants from semiperipheral and core nations is well taken. His critique, however, is weakened by his concentration on recent US-based comparison.

35. On the "black/gray market" in the Soviet Union, *see* Hedrick Smith, *The Russians* (New York: Quadrangle, 1976), 125–131; and Konstantin Simis, "Russia's Underground Millionaires," *Fortune* (June 1981), 36–50. Certain regions and ethnic groups continue to be disproportionately represented in the private sector in the *perestroika* era. *See* Elizabeth Schillinger and Joel Jenswald, "Cooperative Business Ventures in the Soviet Union", *Sociology and Social Research* 73 (1988):22–30.

36. *See* Bonacich, "A Theory of Middleman Minorities"; "Class Approaches to Ethnicity and Race"; "Middleman Minorities and Advanced Capitalism"; and Bovenkerk, "Shylock or Horatio Alger?"

37. At this point, Bonacich's discussion of middleman minorities overlaps with her split-labor market theory. *See* Bonacich, "A Theory of Ethnic Antagonism," and "Past, Present, and Future of Split-Labor Market Theory." For the distinction between adopting skills by training indigenous skillholders or importing skillholders, *see* Abraham Hirsch, "Importing and Adopting Skills," *Human Organization* 24 (1965): 124–127.

38. Wertheim, *East-West Parallels,* 80. *See* Horowitz, *Ethnic Groups in Conflict,* 226–228.

39. Simmel, *Soziologie;* Weber, *Ancient Judaism;* Jiang, "Towards a Theory of Pariah Entrepreneurship"; Skinner, "Strangers in West African Societies" *Africa* 33 (1963): 307–320; Shack and Skinner, *Strangers in African Societies;* Kuper, "Strangers in Plural Societies"; and Bonacich, "A Theory of Middleman Minorities." For a more complete discussion of pariah and stranger as opposing concepts, *see* Cahnman, "Pariahs, Strangers, and Court Jews."

40. Simmel, *Soziologie;* and Leon, *Jewish Question,* 134–135. For a discussion of itinerant craftsmen as landless strangers, see Hallpike, "Some Problems in Cross-Cultural Comparison," and Reminick, "Evil Eye Belief among the Amhara of Ethiopia." The literature is written in terms of a male stranger. It is worth investigating the effects of gender, but this has not been done yet. There might be important differences in how male outsiders are allowed to have dealings with female members of the resident ingroup, and how same-gender relations go on between natives and strangers. This also would depend on the strength of value-systems, such as the honor/shame dichotomy.

41. Brian Foster, "Ethnicity and Commerce," *American Ethnologist* 1 (1974): 437–448; Simmel, *Soziologie;* and Shibutani and Kwan, *Ethnic Stratification,* 191. *See* Horowitz, *Ethnic Groups in Conflict,* 141–143, who suggests the importance of different moral evaluations on interethnic contrasts.

42. Simmel, *Soziologie;* Cahnman, "Socioeconomic Causes of Anti-Semitism"; "Pariahs, Strangers, and Court Jews"; L. Rosen, "Muslim-Jewish Relations in a Moroccan City," *International Journal of Middle Eastern Studies* 3 (1972): 435–449; and Foster, "Ethnicity and Commerce."

43. Simmel, *Soziologie.*

44. Foster, "Ethnicity and Commerce."

45. Stryker, "Social Structure and Prejudice"; Leon, *Jewish Question,* 93, 133; Skinner, "Strangers in West African Societies"; Cohen, *Custom and Politics in Urban Africa,* 9, 141–150; Bonacich, "A Theory of Middleman Minorities"; and van den Berghe, "Asian Africans before and after Independence.

46. Blalock, *Toward a Theory of Minority Group Relations;* Cahnman, "Pariahs, Strangers, and Court Jews"; Foster, "Ethnicity and Commerce"; and Horowitz, *Ethnic Groups in Conflict,* 187–189.

47. Hagen, *On the Theory of Social Change,* 246–247; Bonacich, "A Theory of Middleman Minorities"; and van den Berghe, "Asian Africans before and after Independence."

48. Examples of "middleman groups" who were quasi-natives include Scots and Dissenters in England, Old Believers in Russia, and Antioqueños in Colombia. *See* Hagen, *On the Theory of Social Change,* 248–250; Andreski, "An Economic Interpretation of Anti-Semitism"; and S. N. Eisenstadt, *The Protestant Ethic and Modernism* (New York: Basic Books, 1968), 15. In Poland, Jews were "native strangers," born in Poland, but speaking a different language.

49. Certain culture areas such as the Mediterranean and Asia may

be spawning groups for middlemen, but this needs further study. The nature of peasant villages giving rise to middlemen deserves study. *See* Bonacich, "A Theory of Middleman Minorities."

50. Weber, *Ancient Judaism,* 344, 353; Becker, *Through Values to Social Interpretation,* 110; Cahnman, "Socioeconomic Causes of Anti-Semitism," and Stryker, "Social Structure and Prejudice"; and Bonacich, "A Theory of Middleman Minorities," and "Middleman Minorities and Advanced Capitalism."

51. E. A. Alport, "The Mzab," *Journal of the Royal Anthropological Society* 84 (1954): 34–54; and Russell Stone, "Religious Ethic and the Spirit of Capitalism," *International Journal of Middle East Studies* 5 (1974): 260–273.

52. Cahnman, "Socio-Economic Causes of Anti-Semitism"; Leon, *Jewish Question,* 139–140; Bonacich, "A Theory of Middleman Minorities," "Class Approaches to Ethnicity and Race," and "Middleman Minorities and Advanced Capitalism"; Weber, *Ancient Judaism,* 403–404; and Becker, *Through Values to Social Interpretation,* 110.

53. Burton Benedict, "Family Firms and Firm Families," in *Entrepreneurship in Cross-Cultural Contexts* S. Greenfield, A. Strickon, and R. Aubey, eds. (Albuquerque: University of New Mexico Press, 1979), 305–328. On women's roles in moneylending see chapter 2, notes 10 and 36, but the studies mentioned there do not relate this to family structure.

54. Sombart, *The Jews and Modern Capitalism,* 148, 206–207.

55. Bonacich, "A Theory of Middleman Minorities"; McClelland, *Achievement Motive;* and van den Berghe, "Asian Africans before and after Independence."

56. Implicit in Weber's and Sombart's views of Protestants.

57. Sombart, *Jews and Modern Capitalism,* 222–238.

58. Weber, *Ancient Judaism,* 345. This partly contradicts Sombart.

59. Studies of achievement have neglected overseas middlemen minorities. More basic research in this area on all levels is needed. *See* chapter 4 for some hints of cultural similarities and differences in three such groups.

60. With some additions, this list is derived from Bonacich, "A Theory of Middleman Minorities."

61. For a description of voluntary self-segregation among Ibadi Muslim Jerbans in northern Tunisia, *see* Stone, "Religious Ethic and the Spirit of Capitalism."

62. Nathaniel Leff, "Industrial Organization and Entrepreneurship in the Developing Countries: The Economic Groups," *Economic Development and Cultural Change* 26 (1978): 661–675, who has defined a looser type of structure—the "economic group" which draws managers from a number of different wealthy families. *See* Janet T. Landa, *The Economics of the Ethnically Homogeneous Middleman Group* (Toronto: University of Toronto Institute for Policy Analysis, 1979). Landa describes Chinese rubber traders in Malaysia as an "ethnically homogeneous middleman group," and seems to be describing this type of structure. *See also* Cohen, *Custom and Politics in Urban Africa;* "Cultural Strategies in the Organization of Trading Diasporas"; and *Two Dimensional Man.*

63. A. Cohen, *Two Dimensional Man,* 98–100. *See* Louis Auchincloss, *The Embezzler* (Boston: Houghton Mifflin, 1966), 10–15, for a dialogue between a Wall Street broker and an aggressive investigator in which the former defends friendship over patriotism. The men described in the novel are old friends from school and relatives as well as business partners and associates. For a description of ethnonational favoritism in hiring practices of multinational corporations in Brazil, *see* Pierre Michel Fontaine, "Multinational Corporations and Relations of Race and Color in Brazil: The Case of Sao Paulo," *International Studies Notes* 2 (1975): 1–10. This indicates that modern corporate elites still use a large measure of particularism in certain aspects of their business, despite adherence to a universalistic code.

64. Bonacich and Modell, *Economic Basis of Ethnic Solidarity;* Orlando Patterson, "Context and Choice in Ethnic Allegiance: A Theoretical Framework and Caribbean Case Study," in *Ethnicity: Theory and Experience,* N. Glazer and D. P. Moynihan, eds. (Cambridge, Mass.: Harvard University Press, 1975), 305–349.

65. During the Turkish massacres of World War I, Jews would describe how they were forced to show their distinctive undergarment, the *zizit,* and the sign of their circumcision to save their lives, so they would not be mistaken for Armenians or Christians. *See also* Andreski, "An Economic Interpretation of Anti-Semitism"; Stryker, "Social Structure and Prejudice"; and L. Poliakov, *The History of Anti-Semitism* (New York: Schocken, 1965). Geneticists point out that some gene flow is always present, even with minorities who seek to remain isolated or, to phrase it another way, interaction always leads to intercourse. *See* L. L. Cavalli-Sforza and W. F. Bodmer, *The Genetics of Human Populations* (San Francisco: W. H. Freemen, 1971).

66. Martindale, "Guest Community," *A propos* the example of the Armenian massacres, Jews in that period were not a prime target.

67. Baron, "Modern Age," 363–384.

68. Shibutani and Kwan, *Ethnic Stratification* 196. Horowitz, of course, would dissent on this point as noted.

69. Rinder, "Strangers in the Land"; Stryker, "Social Structure and Prejudice"; Ellis Rivkin, *The Shaping of Jewish History* (New York: Scribners, 1971); and Leon, *Jewish Question,* 195–256. *See also* Andreski, "Economic Interpretation of Anti-Semitism," which provides an excellent model for dealing with a move from complementarity to conflict in explaining open antimiddleman violence. I have also used points made by Horowitz, as cited in note 29.

70. See also Blalock, *Toward a Theory of Minority Group Relations.*

71. Andreski, "Economic Interpretation of Anti-Semitism"; and Stryker, "Social Structure and Prejudice."

72. Abraham G. Duker, "Acculturation and Integration—A Jewish Survivalist View," in *Acculturation and Integration—A Symposium,* J. L. Teller, ed. (New York: American Histadrut Cultural Exchange, 1965); and Wertheim, *East-West Parallels.*

73. *See* chapter 5 on Protestant middlemen, and Stryker, "Social Structure and Prejudice."

74. Stryker, "Social Structure and Prejudice"; Sheldon Stryker, "A Theory of Middleman Minorities—A Comment," *American Sociological Review* 39 (1974): 281; Bonacich, "A Theory of Middleman Minorities"; and R. A. Schermerhorn, "Parsis and Jews in India: A Tentative Comparison," *Journal of Asian Affairs* 1 (1976): 119–122. On the Parsis, *see also* E. Kulke, *The Parsees of India,* (Munich: Weltforum Verlag, 1974)

75. Waterbury, *North for the Trade.*

76. Robert K. Merton, "The Self-Fulfilling Prophecy," in his collection *Social Theory and Social Structure* (Glencoe, Ill.: Free Press, 1957), 421–436.

Chapter 2

1. This discussion concentrates on traditional societies because of the pervasiveness of large bureaucratic banks that makes for a very different structure in modern industrial society, although enclaves of traditionalism persist in urban slums and remote rural areas, as well as in underdeveloped peripheral societies.

2. Robert Chazan, *Medieval Jewry in Northern France: A Political and Social History* (Baltimore: Johns Hopkins Press, 1973), 17.

3. G. Lenski, *Power and Privilege* (New York: McGraw-Hill, 1966), 266.

4. Marshall Sahlins, *Stone Age Economics* (Chicago: Aldine, 1972), 191; Zosa Szajkowski, *Agricultural Credit and Napoleon's Anti-Jewish Decrees* (New York: Editions Historiques Franco-Juives, 1954), 55; W. Cahnman, "Pariahs, Strangers, and Court Jews—A Conceptual Classification," *Sociological Analysis* 35 (1974): 158; and Georg Simmel, *Soziologie* (Leipzig: Drucker & Humbolt, 1908). For a similar argument, *see* Raymond Firth, "A Viewpoint from Economic Anthropology," in *Capital, Saving and Credit in Peasant Societies,* R. Firth and B. S. Yamey, eds. (Chicago: Aldine, 1964), 29–31. Firth, however, terms reciprocal obligations of kin and the like as "social loans" and sees them as being generally short-term. Thus, he places them in the context of credit.

5. Benjamin Nelson, *The Idea of Usury* (Chicago: University of Chicago Press, 1969).

6. Brian L. Foster, "Minority Traders in Thai Village Social Networks," *Ethnic Groups* 2 (1980): 221–240.

7. David H. Wu, "To Kill Three Birds with One Stone: The Rotating Credit Associations of the Papua New Guinea Chinese," *American Ethnologist* 1 (1974): 565–584.

8. For Malaya, *see* Raymond Firth, *Malay Fishermen* (London: Routledge & Kegan Paul, 1964), 162–164; and "A Viewpoint from Economic Anthropology," 20–31. For Chiapas, *see* Evon Z. Vogt, *The Zinacantecos of Mexico* (New York: Holt, Rinehart & Winston, 1970), 59–61. For India, *see* Millard F. Long, "Interest Rates and the Structure of Agricultural Credit Markets," *Oxford Economic Papers* 20 (1968): 275–288. For elsewhere, *see* Ralph Beals, "Gifting, Reciprocity, Savings and Credit in Peasant Oaxaca," *Southwestern Journal of Anthropology* 26 (1970): 231–241; and Sutti Ortiz, "The Structure of Decision-Making," in *Themes in Economic Anthropology,* R. Firth, ed. (London: Tavistock, 1967). For the United States, *see* M. Sussman and Lee G. Burchinal, "Parental Aid to Married Children," *Marriage and Family Living* 24 (1962): 320–332; Ivan Light, Ethnic Enterprise in America (Berkeley: University of California Press, 1972), 19–20; and W. E. Mitchell and H. J. Leichter, *Kinship and Casework* (New York: Russell Sage Foundation, 1967), 30, 136–145. A discussion of lending to relatives, giving pros and cons including those used here, appeared in an article by Patricia Schiff Estess, "Should You Lend to a Relative? When to Say 'Yes,' How to Say 'No'," *Parade* magazine, *Sunday Times Union,* July 24, 1988, 45.

9. Shirley Ardener, "Comparative Study of Rotating Credit Associations," *Journal of the Royal Anthropological Institute* 94 (1964): 201–229; Ivan Light, *Ethnic Enterprise in America;* Donald V. Kurtz, "The

Rotating Credit Association: An Adaptation to Poverty," *Human Organization* 32 (1973): 44–58; and Wu, "Rotating Credit Associations of the Papua New Guinea Chinese," 565–584.

10. W. F. Wertheim, *Indonesian Society in Transition* (The Hague: W. Van Hoeve, 1969), 107. On the stigma of pauperism among the respectable poor in nineteenth-century Britain, *see* Melanie Tebbutt, *Making Ends Meet: Pawnbroking and Working-Class Credit,* (New York: St. Martin's, 1983), 23–24. This book is particularly good at describing pawnbroking and women in a modern industrial setting. *See also* John B. George, "Indian Weekend," *American Universities Field Staff Reports, East Africa Series,* I, I, 1952. George notes that impoverished British officers and aristocrats in East Africa borrowed secretly from Asian businessmen for reasons of status.

11. Alice Dewey, "Capital, Credit and Saving in Javanese Marketing," in *Capital, Saving and Credit in Peasant Societies,* R. Firth and B. S. Yamey, eds. (Chicago: Aldine, 1964), 230–255; Laurence D. Loeb, "*Dhimmi* Status and Jewish Roles in Iranian Society," *Ethnic Groups* 1 (1976): 89–105; Brian Pullan, *Rich and Poor in Renaissance Venice* (Oxford: Blackwell, 1971), 435, 538–578; and R. de Roover, *Money and Banking in Medieval Bruges* (Cambridge: Medieval Academy of America, 1948), 120, 149–167.

12. Loeb, "*Dhimmi* Status and Jewish Roles in Iranian Society." *Ethnic Groups* 1 (1976): 89–105.

13. Dewey, "Capital, Credit and Saving in Javanese Marketing," 244. In addition to this advantage, the inflation of the period made repayment of debts which were incurred earlier much cheaper.

14. N. Charlesworth, "The Myth of the Deccan Riots of 1875," *Modern Asian Studies* 6 (1972): 401–421; Joel Halpern, "Capital, Saving and Credit among Lao Peasants," in *Capital Savings and Credit in Peasant Societies,* R. Firth and B. S. Yamey, eds. (Chicago: Aldine, 1964), 102–103; and Loeb, "*Dhimmi* Status and Jewish Roles in Iranian Society."

15. Mattison Mines, "The Muslim Merchants of Pallavarum, Madras," (Doctoral thesis, Cornell University, 1970); Charlesworth, "The Myth of the Deccan Riots of 1875"; J. Tobias, "Buddhism, Belonging and Detachment—Some Paradoxes of Chinese Ethnicity in Thailand," *Journal of Asian Studies* 36 (1977): 303–325; Pullan, *Rich and Poor in Renaissance Venice,* 431–442; de Roover, *Money and Banking in Medieval Bruges;* Loeb, "*Dhimmi* Status and Jewish Roles in Iranian Society," 89–105; Laurence D. Loeb, *Outcast: Jewish Life in Southern Iran* (London: Gordon & Breach, 1977); Dewey, "Capital, Credit and Saving in Javanese Marketing," in *Capital, Saving and Credit in Peasant Societies,* R. Firth and B. S. Yamey, eds. (Chicago: Aldine, 1964), 247–250; and Burton Bene-

dict, "Capital, Saving and Credit among Mauritian Indians," in *Capital, Saving and Credit in Peasant Societies*, R. Firth and B. S. Yamey, eds. (Chicago: Aldine, 1964), 330–346.

16. S. W. Baron, *Social and Religious History of the Jews*, 12 (New York: Columbia University Press, 1967): 49–150, 315.

17. Brian L. Foster, "Ethnicity and Commerce," *American Ethnologist* 1 (1974): 437–448; and "Minority Traders in Thai Village Social Networks," *Ethnic Groups* 2 (1980), 221–240. While Foster relates ethnicity to trade in general, his arguments apply with particular force to borrower-lender relations. Joseph Shatzmiller, *Shylock Reconsidered: Jews, Moneylending, and Medieval Society* (Berkeley and Los Angeles, University of California, 1990) argues that minority moneylenders were sometimes accepted as upstanding members of the community. He uses the example of a case where a Provencal Jewish moneylender had to defend his reputation against a lower-class Christian. Christian witnesses testified on behalf of the former. While Shatzmiller poses a counterpoint to the usual interpretation of Jewish moneylenders and pawnbrokers in medieval times, campaigns against Jewish and other moneylenders both preceded and succeeded this case by only a few years. Shatzmiller's more favorable view of the relationship of moneylending to Jewish-Christian relations should be seen as a corrective, not as the final word on this matter.

18. Benedict, "Capital, Saving and Credit among Mauritian Indians," 344.

19. Millard Long, "Interest Rates and the Structure of Agricultural Credit Markets," *Oxford Economic Papers* 20 (1968), 275–288; Anthony Bottomley, "The Cost of Administering Private Loans in Underdeveloped Areas," *Oxford Economic Papers* 15 (1963): 154–163; "Monopoly Profit as a Determinant of Interest Rates in Underdeveloped Rural Areas, *Oxford Economic Papers* 16 (1964): 431–437; *Factor Pricing and Economic Growth in Underdeveloped Rural Areas* (London: Crosby, Lockwood, 1971); C. R. Wharton, Jr., "Marketing, Merchandising, and Moneylending: A Note on Middleman Monopsony," *Malayan Economic Review* 7 (1962): 24–44; A. B. Chandavarkar, "The Premium for Risk as a Determinant of Interest Rates in Underdeveloped Rural Areas: A Comment" (with reply by A. Bottomley), *Quarterly Journal of Economics* 79 (1965): 322–327; and S. Ghatok, "Rural Interest Rates in the Indian Economy," *Journal of Development Studies* 11 (1975): 190–201.

20. Technically, a *monopoly* is with a single seller and many buyers. The opposite, in which there is a single purchaser of a commodity and a multiplicity of sellers, is a *monopsony. See* Wharton, "Marketing, Merchandising and Moneylending." There are important technical ramifications implicit in this distinction. For present purposes, however, both will be designated as monopolies. In many cases, the same merchant is, in fact,

both seller of goods from the outside and purchaser of local commodities.

21. J. Katz, *Tradition and Crisis* (New York: Schocken, 1961), 59–62.

22. Wharton, "Marketing, Merchandising and Moneylending."

23. Wharton, "Marketing, Merchandising and Moneylending"; Martin W. Wilmington, "Aspects of Moneylending in the Northern Sudan," *Middle Eastern Journal* 9 (1955): 139–146; Y. O. Kielstra, "Credit Facilities in an Iranian Village," *Man* N.S. 8 (1973): 110; Beals, "Gifting, Reciprocity, Savings and Credit in Peasant Oaxaca," 231–241; Ortiz, "The Structure of Decision-Making"; Firth, *Malay Fishermen*, 169–172; Long, "Interest Rates and Structure of Agricultural Credit Markets"; and Benedict, "Capital, Saving and Credit among Mauritian Indians," 342–344.

24. Bottomley, *Factor Pricing and Economic Growth*, 8–89; Chandavarkar, "The Premium for Risk as a Determinant of Interest Rates"; Kielstra, "Credit Facilities in an Iranian Village"; Beals, "Gifting, Reciprocity, Savings and Credit in Peasant Societies"; Firth, *Malay Fishermen*, 169–172; and Long, "Interest Rates and the Structure of Agricultural Credit Markets."

25. Bottomley, *Factor Pricing and Economic Growth*, 90–100; Frank W. Moore, "Moneylenders and Cooperators in India," *Economic Development and Culture Change* 2 (1953): 139–159; and "A Note on Rural Debt and the Control of Ceremonial Expenditure," *Economic Development and Culture Change* 2 (1953): 408–415; Ortiz, "The Structure of Decision-Making"; Dewey, "Capital, Credit and Saving in Javanese Marketing, 247–250; and Szajkowski, *Agricultural Credit and Napoleon's Anti-Jewish Decrees*. On the relationship of consumption and pawnbroking in nineteenth-century England, *see* Tebbutt, *Making Ends Meet*, 65–67 and *passim*.

26. Wharton, "Marketing, Merchandising and Moneylending."

27. Marshall G. S. Hodgson, *The Venture of Islam*, Vol. III (Chicago, University of Chicago Press, 1974), 211–212.

28. H. Kellenbenz, "Banking and Bankers," in *Economic History of the Jews*, N. Gross, ed. (New York: Schocken, 1975), 211–225; H. H. Ben Sasson, "Moneylending," in *Economic History of the Jews*, N. Gross, ed. (New York: Schocken, 1975), 247–269; and de Roover, *Money and Banking in Medieval Bruges*, 113–120.

29. The interest rates in both agricultural credit and pawnbroking are on the high side, but they are comparable to rates charged in modern developed nations. The average for interest rates charged by commercial lenders in underdeveloped nations today is 20 percent *per annum*. Until

the 1970s, while other lenders charged an average of 24 percent per year, in France in the 1950s, some installment credit sales went up to 40 percent. In thirteenth-century Perpignan, the legal rate of interest was 20 percent, but the actual rate was probably much higher. The rate could, however, go much higher. In the northern Sudan during World War II, it went up to 100 percent, while in rural Oaxaca, Mexico, estimated rates on short-term commercial transactions were 10 to 30 percent per month, which would be well over 100 percent on the annual basis. In fourteenth-century Austria, the maximum legal rate was $173^{1/3}$ percent. *See* Bottomley, "The Cost of Administering Private Loans in Agricultural Marketing"; Wilmington, "Aspects of Moneylending in the Northern Sudan"; Wharton, "Marketing, Merchandising and Moneylending"; Beals, "Gifting, Reciprocity, Savings and Credit in Peasant Oaxaca"; Richard W. Emery, *The Jews of Perpignan in the Thirteenth Century* (New York: Columbia University Press, 1959), 80; de Roover, *Money and Banking in Medieval Bruges,* 128; Tebbutt, *Making Ends Meet,* 123–131; and Ben Sasson, "Moneylending." For present-day costs of pawnbroking, *see* Figure 1, p. 38.

30. de Roover, *Money and Banking in Medieval Bruges,* 128; Pullan, *Rich and Poor in Renaissance Venice,* 525, 538–575; Isidore Loeb, *"Reflexions sur des juifs," Revue de les Etudes Juives* 28 (1894): 1–31; Emery, *The Jews of Perpignan in the Thirteenth Century,* 80, 87; and Berthold Altmann, "Jews and the Rise of Capitalism—Economic Theory and Practice in a Westphalian Community," *Jewish Social Studies* 5 (1943): 163–186.

31. Michael Adas, "Immigrant Asians and the Economic Impact of European Imperialism: The Role of South Indian Chettiars in British Burma," *Journal of Asian Studies* 33 (1974): 385–401; Altmann, "Jews and the Rise of Capitalism"; Benedict, "Capital Savings and Credit among Mauritian Indians," 344; Charlesworth, "The Myth of the Deccan Riots of 1875"; de Roover, *Money and Banking in Medieval Bruges,* 116; Emery, *The Jews of Perpignan in the Thirteenth Century,* 14–16; Loeb, *Outcaste,* 125; Pullan, *Rich and Poor in Renaissance Venice,* 443–459, 476–509; S. Simonsohn, *Toldot Ha Yehudim be Duksot Mantova* (Jerusalem, 1963), 72–76; K. S. Sandhu, *Indians in Malaya—Immigration and Settlement, 1786–1957* (Cambridge: Cambridge University Press, 1969), 291–202; K. D. Thomas and J. Panglaykin, "The Chinese in the South Sumatran Rubber Industry," in *The Chinese in Indonesia,* J. A. C. Mackie, ed. (Honolulu: University Press of Hawaii, 1976), 139–198; Wharton, "Marketing, Merchandising and Moneylending"; and Wu, "Rotating Credit Associations of the Papua New Guinea Chinese."

32. Ben Sasson, "Moneylending"; Sandhu, *Indians in Malaya,* 292. *See also* Baron, *Social and Religious History of the Jews,* 430–447; S. W. Baron, "General Survey," in *Economic History of the Jews,* N. Gross, ed.

(New York: Schocken, 1975), 132–197; Loeb, *"Reflexions sur les juifs" Revue des Etudes Juives* 38 (1894) 1–31; Emery, *The Jews of Perpignan in the Thirteenth Century;* and J. Lee Shneidman, *The Rise of the Aragonese—Catalan Empire* (New York: New York University Press, 1970). The progression of the Lombards' entry into pawnbroking is obscure. It seems that they also started as general moneylenders and bankers in the twelfth century, competing with the Jews and other Italians. In Bruges, they became specialized as pawnbrokers by the thirteenth and fourteenth centuries. Despite stigmatization as only nominal Christians, however, assimilation was easier for them than it was for Jews. *See* de Roover, *Money and Banking in Medieval Bruges,* 100, 117, and 153–155; and J. Imbert and H. Lejoberel, *Histoire economique des origines a 1789* (Paris: Presses Universitaire de France, 1965), 222–223.

33. Adas, "Immigrant Asians and the Economic Impact of European Imperialism"; Mines, "The Muslim Merchants of Pallavarum, Madras"; and Sandhu, *Indians in Malaya,* 291–292. For histories of the Chettiars and other business communities in India, see Dwijendra Tripathi, *Business Communities of India: A Historical Perspective* (New Delhi, Manohar, 1984). *See also* David Rudman, *Caste and Capitalism in Colonial India* (Berkeley and Los Angeles, University of California Press, forthcoming) who presents a historical ethnography of the Chettiars.

34. K. Polanyi, C. Arensberg, and K. Pearson, eds., *Trade and Markets in Early Empires* (New York: Columbia University Press, 1957), 259.

35. Jerome Halberstadt, in a personal communication, made the generalization about the relationship between the professionals' status and that of people to whom they give service.

36. *See* William Chester Jordan, "Jews on Top: Women and the availability of Consumption Loans in Northern France in the Mid-Thirteenth Century," *Journal of Jewish Studies* 29 (1978):39–56. Jordan also points out that many of the Jewish pawnbrokers were women as were their customers. *See also* Jordan, "Women and Credit in the Middle Ages: Problems and Directions," *Journal of European Economic History,*17 (1988): 33–60. Jordan's interpretation would support Horowitz's "positional psychology" as a factor aggravating ethnic conflict. *See* Horowitz, *Ethnic Groups in Conflict,* (Berkeley: University of California Press, 1985): 216–219.

37. The situation of the minority moneylender again points up the paradoxical relationship between legitimate authority and wealth. Some social scientists have applied the analogy of creditor-debtor relationships to other asymmetrical social relationships, suggesting that leadership is rooted in usury. On the basis of personal experience in a Lebanese village, Emrys Peters has challenged this figure of speech. He points out that few usurers are leaders and respond to the demands of others as well as make claims on their followers. See Emrys Peters, "Shifts in Power in a

Lebanese Village," in *Rural Politics and Social Change in the Middle East,* R. Antoun and I. Harik, eds. (Bloomington: Indiana University Press, 1972), 182. While the fact is that traders and lenders in peasant communities are often isolated this is no simple matter. Even in peasant societies, political leaders may, through various ruses, profit from the interest payments of peasants to moneylenders.

38. Pullan, *Rich and Poor in Renaissance Venice,* 435–442; and Wharton, "Marketing, Merchandising and Moneylending."

39. Kielstra, "Credit Facilities in an Iranian Village"; and Benedict, "Capital, Saving and Credit among Mauritian Indians," 344.

40. Shneidman, *The Rise of the Aragonese-Catalan Empire,* 444.

41. Baron, *Social and Religious History of the Jews,* 138–140, 152, and 312; Pullan, *Rich and Poor in Renaissance Venice,* 5–8; and Szajkowski, *Agricultural Credit and Napoleon's Anti-Jewish Decrees,* 30.

42. On the other hand, the immigrant lenders apparently wanted to gain profits more quickly and sued their debtors in the courts of law established by the British. *See* Charlesworth, "The Myth of the Deccan Riots of 1875."

43. It should not be forgotten that, often, the wealthier peasants (expanding their landholdings) or impoverished nobility, rather than the very poor, are the borrowers. *See* Szajkowski, *Agricultural Credit and Napoleon's Anti-Jewish Decrees,* and Charlesworth, "The Myth of the Deccan Riots of 1875."

44. This obviously was what was happening in India in the nineteenth century. *See* Charlesworth, "The Myth of the Deccan Riots of 1875." *See also* Eric Wolf, *Peasant Wars of the Twentieth Century* (New York: Harper & Row, 1964), 63–65, 175–176; Shneidman, *The Rise of the Aragonese-Catalan Empire,* 444; Baron, *Social and Religious History of the Jews,* 138–140; Barrington Moore, Jr., *Social Origins of Dictatorship and Democracy* (Boston: Beacon Press, 1966), 358–361; and Moore, "Moneylenders and Cooperative in India,"; and "Rural Debt and the Control of Ceremonial Expenditure."

45. Szajkowski, *Agricultural Credit and Napoleon's Anti-Jewish Decrees,* 30.

46. Pullan, *Rich and Poor in Renaissance Venice,* 431–442, 451–470.

47. I. J. Cattanach, "Agrarian Disturbances in nineteenth-century India," *Indian Economic and Social History Review* 3 (1966): 65–84; and Adas, "Immigrant Asians and the Economic Impact of European Imperialism."

48. Rudolph C. Blitz and Millard F. Long, "The Economics of Usury Regulations," *Journal of Political Economy* 73 (1965): 608–619.

49. See Szajkowski, *Agricultural Credit and Napoleon's Anti-Jewish Decrees*, 47–48; de Roover, *Money and Banking in Medieval Bruges;* F. L. Bailey, "Capital, Saving and Credit in Highland Orissa [India]," in *Capital, Saving and Credit in Peasant Societies*, R. Firth and B. S. Yamey, eds. (Chicago: Aldine, 1964); Pullan, *Rich and Poor in Renaissance Venice*, 470–471; and Moore, "Moneylenders and Cooperators in India"; and "Rural Debt and the Control of Ceremonial Expenditure."

50. Bailey, "Capital, Saving and Credit in Highland Orissa," 127–128.

CHAPTER 3

1. For a general review of such theories, *see* Robert A. LeVine and Donald T. Campbell, *Ethnocentrism* (New York: John Wiley, 1972). The term *pure prejudice* comes from Edna Bonacich and John Modell, *The Economics of Ethnic Solidarity: The Case of the Japanese-Americans* (Berkeley: University of California Press, 1981).

2. Dean Peabody, "Group Judgments in the Philippines: Evaluation and Descriptive Aspects," *Journal of Personality and Social Psychology* 10 (1968): 290–300; and "Evaluative and Descriptive Aspects of Personality: A Reappraisal," *Journal of Personality and Social Psychology* 16 (1970): 636–646.

3. Peter Marris and Anthony Somerset, *African Businessmen* (London: Routledge & Kegan Paul, 1971), 96–97.

4. Michael Taussig, "The Genesis of Capitalism among a South American Peasantry: The Devil's Labor and the Baptism of Money," *Comparative Studies in Society and History* 19 (1977): 130–155. With regard to the development of similar ideas in Africa, *see* Parker Shipton, *Bitter Money: Cultural Economy and Some African Meanings of Forbidden Commodities*, (Washington D.C.: American Ethnological Society Monographs, No.1, 1989). Shipton views the Kenya Luo response to the monetary economy, both in terms of an autochthonous response to capitalism and as influenced by foreign ideas.

5. Gerhard Lenski, *Power and Privilege* (New York: McGraw-Hill, 1966). Lenski's "priestly class" also must be seen as including charismatic prophets, such as Amos, who are outside the official priestly class. Medieval churchmen were among the bearers of this ethic in their denunciation of usury. The Cauca-peasant view of "baptised money" bears some similarity to the scholastic view of usury. *See* Taussig, "Genesis of Capi-

talism among a South American Peasantry." The anti-Jewishness of the Christian church, however, preceded the medieval association of Jews with moneylending and was theologically based. *See* James Parkes, *The Conflict of the Church and the Synagogue* (New York: Atheneum, 1979).

6. Lenski, *Power and Privilege,* 70–71.

7. Willem Wertheim, *East-West Parallels* (Chicago: Quadrangle, 1964), 79–82. For portraiture of different classes of bankers and moneylenders, see the illustrations of Raymond de Roover, *Money, Banking and Credit in Medieval Bruges* (Cambridge, Mass.: Medieval Academy of America, 1948).

8. Wertheim, *East-West Parallels;* Edna Bonacich, "A Theory of Middleman Minorities," *American Sociological Review* 38 (1973): 583–594; and S. Andreski, "An Economic Interpretation of Anti-Semitism," *Jewish Journal of Sociology* 5 (1963): 201–213.

9. On the anticapitalistic strain in German thinking which was both anti-British and anti-Semitic, *see* H. D. Schmidt, "Anti-Western and Anti-Jewish Tradition in German Historical Thought," *Leo Baeck Yearbook* 4 (1959): 37–60. Anti-Americanism certainly partakes of this tradition. On the parasite metaphor common to both anti-Semitism and anti-Sinicism in the West, *see* Alex Bein, "The Jewish Parasite—Notes on the Semantics of the Jewish Problem with Special Reference to Germany," *Leo Baeck Yearbook* 9 (1964): 3–40.

10. Comparative studies of nationalism abound. Recent examples include Benedict Anderson, *Imagined Communities: Reflection on the Origin and Spread of Nationalism* (London: Verso, 1983); and Anthony D. Smith, *Theories of Nationalism* (London: Duckworth, 2nd Ed. 1983).

11. Representative of this approach is Leon Poliakov, *The History of Anti-Semitism* (New York: Schocken, 1965). On theology as the original base of Jew-hatred preceding economic motivation in time, *see* Parkes, *Conflict of the Church and the Synagogue.*

12. The "hooked nose" which is so characteristic of the Jewish stereotype can also be found in the Count of the television program *Sesame Street.* The Count, who is a toned-down Dracula with cape and Hungarian accent, "loves to count," a form of compulsive behavior akin to love of money. For a comparison of Jewish and Arab stereotypes, *see* James J. Zogby, *The Other Anti-Semitism: The Arab as Scapegoat,* ADC Issues No. 3 (Washington, D.C.: American Arab Anti-Discrimination Committee, n.d.). For the Soviet portrayal of Uncle Sam, *see* the picture accompanying "How Communist Economies Fall Short," *New York Times,* Dec. 17, 1989, E–3.

13. Poliakov, *History of Anti-Semitism,* 183–204.

14. Walter P. Zenner, "Ethnic Stereotyping in Arabic Proverbs," *Journal of American Folklore* 83 (1970): 417–429; and "Some Aspects of Ethnic Stereotype Content in Galilee: A Trial Formulation," *Middle Eastern Studies* 8 (1972): 405–416. *See also* Robert Canfield, "What They Do When the Lights Are Out? Myth and Social Order in Afghanistan," Paper delivered at the Conference on Symbols and Social Differentiation, Joint Committee on the Near and Middle East of the American Council of Learned Societies and the Social Science Research Council (May 25–28, 1978).

15. Poliakov, *History of Anti-Semitism;* and Parkes, *Conflict of the Church and the Synagogue.*

16. S. W. Baron, *Social and Religious History of the Jews,* Vol. 15 (New York: Columbia University Press, 1973), 78–80, 414; and Poliakov, *History of Anti-Semitism,* 190–197. *See also* Robert Anchel, "Early History of the Jewish Quarters of Paris," *Jewish Social Studies* 2 (1940): 45–60, who sees in these events a sign that Jews, albeit secretly, continued to live in Paris after the fourteenth-century expulsion. He also cites an earlier satire in which the *fripiers* comically affirm their Jewishness. Others do not support this view. Indeed, the Jewishness may derive more from a stereotypic occupation more typical of Jews in the seventeenth century than the fourteenth, and residence in a former Jewish quarter than actual ancestry.

17. Obviously, these are overlapping, but not identical, categories.

18. Ruth Pike, "The Image of the Genoese in the Golden Age of Literature," *Hispania* 46 (1963): 705–714. Micaela de Leonardo notes that Italians in California "frequently repeated the epithet that the Genovesi are the Jews of Italy," then worried about its anti-Semitic connotation. Tony Ripetto, a Genovese himself, said, "Like the Genovesi are supposed to be the Jews of Italy... that's a bad title, I'm not defending it. They were the great financiers." Micaela de Leonardo, *The Varieties of Ethnic Experience, Kinship, Class and Gender among California Italian-Americans* (Ithaca: Cornell University Press, 1984), 171–172.

19. Giovanni Paolo Marana, *Letters Writ by a Turkish Spy,* 6 (1984): 17, cited by Frederick B. Tolles, *Meeting House and Counting House* (Chapel Hill: University of North Carolina Press, 1948), 47. Marana was an Italian resident in Paris.

20. Anis Frayha, *Modern Lebanese Proverbs* (Beirut: American University, 1953), Proverbs 1725, 2139–2141, 3100. As will be indicated later, Frayha's proverbs do not associate Jews with moneymaking, but rather with poverty. *See also* Zenner, "Ethnic Stereotyping in Arabic Proverbs."

21. *See* Thomas Alfred Fischer, *The Scots in Germany* (Edinburgh:

O. Schulze, 1902), 38–39; and *The Scots in Eastern and Western Prussia* (Edinburgh: O. Schulze, 1903), 20–23, 32–35, and 118–119, for a description on how Germans and Poles lumped Scots and Jews together. *See also* John Kenneth Galbraith, *The Scotch* (Boston: Houghton Mifflin, 1946), 27–28, 94, who speaks of Scots not having collection plates in church because they do not wish to mingle their respect for the two deities, and of Scots loving money more than their wives. Of course, there is a Scottish proverb, "Count like Jews, gree (master?) like brothers" (Allan Ramsay, *A Collection of Scots Proverbs* (Edinburgh 1750), chapter 8, 23).

22. R. A. Fink, "Harvey Burch: The Yankee Peddler as an American Hero," *New York Folklore Quarterly* 3 (1974): 137–152; and Lewis Harap, *The Image of the Jew in American Literature* (Philadelphia: Jewish Publication Society, 1974).

23. Rudolf Glanz, "Jew and Yankee: A Historic Comparison," *Jewish Social Studies* 6 (1944): 3–30.

24. Bette Denich, personal communication.

25. Schmidt, "Anti-Western and Anti-Jewish Tradition in German Historical Thought"; and Paul R. Mendes-Flohr and Werner Sombart, "The Jews and Modern Capitalism: An Analysis of its Ideological Premises," *Leo Baeck Yearbook* 21 (1976): 87–108.

26. John Buchan, *The Thirty-Nine Steps* (London: Blackwood, 1915); and Norman Cohn, *Warrant for Genocide* (London: Eyre Spottiswoode, 1967).

27. *See* Edmund Scot, in S. Purchas, *Hakluytus Posthumus or Purchas His Pilgrims, Containing a History of the Work in Sea Voyages and Land Travels by English and Others,* Vol. 2 (Glasgow: MacLehase, 1905), 439–443.

28. Peter Garlick, "The Development of Kwahu Business Enterprise in Ghana since 1874: An Essay in Recent Oral Tradition," *Journal of African History* 8 (1967): 463–480; and T. Shibutani and K. Kwan, *Ethnic Stratification* (New York: Macmillan, 1955), 192. Another western tradition seeks parallels between ancient Israelite practices as found in the Old Testament and the rituals of modern Africans.

29. Rev. Robert Fellowees, *The History of Ceylon From the Earliest Period to the Year 1815* (London, 1817), cited in Dennis B. McGilvray, "Dutch Burghers and Portuguese Mechanics: Eurasian Ethnicity in Sri Lanka," *Comparative Studies in Society and History* 24 (1982): 239. Peter Kalm, a Swedish traveler in North America, applied a similarly "Hollandophobic" stereotype to the people of colonial Albany, N.Y.; *see* P. Kalm, *Peter Kalm's Travels in North America Prepared from the 1770 English Edition* Adolph Benson, ed. (New York: Dover, 1937). For a general discussion of

"Hollandophobia", which was at its height in the "Dutch Golden Age" in the seventeenth csentury and which used an image of the Dutch as crafty, frugal, and untrustworthy merchants, *see* Simon Schama, *An Embarrassment of Riches: An Interpretation of Dutch Culture in the Golden Age* (Berkeley: University of California Press, 1988), 257–288, 295. The identification of Holland as a land of Canaan and of the Dutch with Israel was part of both the Dutch self-image and their stereotyping by others.

30. See note 19.

31. Neville Mandel, *Arabs and Zionism Before World War I* (Berkeley: University of California Press, 1967), 49–55, 90, and 227–228; Sylvia Haim, "Arabic Anti-Semitic Literature: Some Preliminary Notes," *Jewish Social Studies* 17 (1955): 307–342; and Moshe Pearlman, "Arabic Anti-Semitic Literature: Comments on Sylvia Haim," *Jewish Social Studies* 17 (1955): 313–314. *See* Bernard Lewis, *Semites and Anti-Semites* (New York: W. W. Norton, 1986) *passim*.

32. H. Warrington Smythe, *Five Years in Siam* (New York: Scribners, 1898), *See also* Alice Tay Erh Soon, "Chinese in South-East Asia," *Race* 4 (1962): 34–48.

33. Kenneth P. Landon, *The Chinese in Thailand* (London: Oxford University Press, 1941), 32–47.

34. W. F. Vella, *Chaiyo! King Vajiravudh and the Development of Thai Nationalism* (Honolulu: University of Hawaii Press 1978), 186–196; and S. J. Tambiah, *World Conqueror and World Renouncer* (Cambridge: Cambridge University Press, 1976), 474–476.

35. Soon, "Chinese in South-East Asia."

36. Jacob Riis, cited by Harap, *Image of the Jew in American Literature*, 442.

37. Karl Marx, "On the Jewish Question" (1843), in *The Marx-Engels Reader*, Robert Tucker, ed. (New York: Norton, 1972), 48. *See also* Galbraith, *The Scotch*, 27–28, 94.

38. David Kranzler, *Japanese, Nazis and Jews: The Jewish Refugee Community of Shanghai, 1938–1945* (New York: Yeshiva University Press, 1976).

39. Ellen Hammer, *The Struggle for Indochina, 1940–1954* (Stanford, Calif.: Stanford University Press, 1955), 137–138.

40. William Roff, *Origins of Malay Nationalism* (New Haven: Yale University Press, 1967), 228. In a personal communication, Roff wrote that various Shakespeare plays, including *The Merchant of Venice*, were part of the curriculum of Malay schools. While the curriculum in British India

was undoubtedly similar to that in Malaysia, the Hindu reinterpretation took a different turn. Hindus saw the Christian reaction to Pharisaic Judaism as a parallel to their own anti-Brahminist reaction to the caste system. *See* Ariel Glucklich, "Brahmins and Pharisees: The Roots of India's Anti-Zionism," *Midstream*, vol. 39, no. 1 (January, 1988):12–15.

41. Soon, "Chinese in South-East Asia."

42. Mahathir bin Mohammed, *The Malay Dilemma* (Singapore: Asia Pacific Press, 1970), 84–85. *See also* Peabody, "Group Judgments in the Philippines."

43. Paul Theroux, "Hating the Asians," *Transition* 33 (1967): 46–51.

44. Denis Hills, *The White Pumpkin* (London: George Allen & Unwin, 1975), 183.

45. Republic of Uganda, *Speeches by His Excellency President Idi Amin Dada: Message to the Nation of British Citizens of Asian Origin* (1972), and *Speech by His Excellency Al-Haji, Marshall Idi Amin Dada to Thirteenth Session of the United Nations General Assembly* (1975).

46. June E. Hahner, "Jacobinos versus Galegos: Urban Radicals versus Portuguese Immigrants in Rio de Janeiro in the 1890s," *Journal of Inter-American Studies and World Affairs* 18 (1976): 125–154.

47. An example of this is the way that successive Polish governments continue to blame the shrinking Jewish community for their own troubles. In like manner, the Vietnamese government persists in linking the much-diminished ethnic Chinese community with Peking and its own economic woes. *See* Colin Campbell, "Vietnamese Blame Chinese for Woes," *New York Times* (June 15, 1982), A–3. It would be worthwhile in a general way to compare the manifest stereotypes of different minorities over time. On one Asian group in the United States, *see* Dennis Ogawa, *From Japs to Japanese: An Evolution of Japanese-American Stereotypes* (Berkeley: McCutheon, 1971).

CHAPTER 4

1. Fortunately, comprehensive studies exist which summarize much of this material, such as Kuznets, "The Economic Life and Structure of the Jews," in *The Jews: Their History, Culture and Religion*, L. Finkelstein, ed. (New York: Harper, 1960); Sen-do Chang, "The Distribution and Occupations of Overseas Chinese," *Geographical Review* 58 (1968): 89–107; and Chandra Jayawardena, "Migration and Social Change: A Survey of Indian Communities Overseas," *Geographical Review* 58 (1968): 426–229. *See also* Daniel J. Elazar, "The Reconstruction of Jewish

Communities in the Post–War Period," *Jewish Journal of Sociology* 11 (1969): 187–226; Lawrence W. Crissman, "The Segmentary Structure of Urban Overseas Chinese Communities," *Man* 2 (1967): 185–205; and Mary F. S. Heidhues, *Southeast Asia's Chinese Minorities* (Longman, Australia: Hawthorn Victoria, 1974).

2. Names and terms used here are those used in the sources, not what is used today. Sources on Chinese generally used pre–*pinyin* transliteration. The terms overseas Indians and Asians are synonymous with overseas South Asians and include Pakistanis, Bangladeshis, and Sri Lankans.

3. Use suggested by Max Weinreich, *History of the Yiddish Language* (Chicago: University of Chicago Press, 1980).

4. Jacob Lestschinsky, "Jewish Migrations, 1840–1956," in *The Jews: Their History, Culture and Religion*, L. Finkelstein, ed. (Philadelphia: Jewish Publication Society, 1960), 1536–1596. For the period before 1800, *see* J. Israel, *European Jewry in the Age of Mercantilism, 1550–1750*, (Oxford: Clarendon Press, 1985).

5. Kuznets, "Economic Life and Structure of the Jews," 1625–1634; and S. W. Baron, "General Survey," in *Jewish Economic History*, N. Gross, ed. (New York: Schocken, 1975).

6. W. J. Cahnman, "Adolf Fischoff and His Jewish Followers," *Leo Baeck Yearbook* 4 (1959): 114–115; and "A Regional Approach to German Jewish History," *Jewish Social Studies* 5 (1943): 211–224. *See also* William O. McCagg, "Jewish Nobles and Geniuses of Modern Hungary," *East European Quarterly, Eastern European Monographs* 3 (1972); and Nicholas Spulber, *The State of Economic Development in Eastern Europe* (New York: Random House, 1966), 89–151.

7. J. Barthys, "Grand Duchy of Poznan under Prussian Rule—Changes in the Economic Position of the Jewish Population, 1815–1848," *Leo Baeck Yearbook* 17 (1972): 191–204; Raphael Mahler, *A History of Modern Jewry, 1780–1815* (New York: Schocken, 1971), 54–77, 281–282, 299–313, and 406–409; Zosa Szajkowski, *Agricultural Credit and Napoleon's Anti-Jewish Decrees* (New York: Editions Historiques Franco-Juifes, 1954); S. W. Baron, *Jews Under Tsar and Soviet* (New York: Columbia University Press, 1964), 39–40, 90–118; and Celia S. Heller, *On the Edge of Destruction: Jews of Poland Between the Two World Wars* (New York: Columbia University Press, 1977), 77–142.

8. Kuznets, "Economic Life and Structure of the Jews," 1612–1614; Jacob Lestschinsky, The Relationship of the Industrialist to the Jewish Worker," in *Klal-Yisrael—Chapters in the Sociology of the Jewish People*, B. Z. Dinur, A. Tartakover, and J. Lestschinsky, eds.

(Jerusalem: Mosad Bialik, 1954); and Heller, *Edge of Destruction*, 100–106.

9. Kuznets, "Economic Life and Structure of the Jews," 1614–1615. *See also* Spulber, *State and Economic Development in Eastern Europe*, 106–107, who suggests for Romania that, as discrimination declined and assimilation strengthened, Jews turned from trade to secular intellectual pursuits.

10. On Germany, see E. Hamburger, "Jews in Public Service under the German Monarchy," *Leo Baeck Yearbook* 9 (1964): 206–238. On Poland, *see* Raphael Mahler, "Jews in Public Service and the Liberal Professions in Poland, 1914–1939," *Jewish Social Studies* 6 (1944): 291–350. On Romania, *see* Spulber, *State and Economic Development in Eastern Europe*, 107. On Hungary, *see* McCagg, "Jewish Nobles and Geniuses."

11. Jacob Katz, *Tradition and Crisis* (Glencoe, Ill.: Free Press, 1961), 24–25.

12. Ibid., 29–42; and Azriel Shohet, *Im Hilufei Tekufot (Beginning of the Hashkalah in German Jewry)* (Jerusalem: Mosad Bialik, 1960), 49–71. [In Hebrew]

13. C. R. Snyder, *Alcohol and Jews* (Glencoe, Ill.: Free Press, 1958).

14. Walter P. Zenner, "Memorialism—Some Jewish Examples," *American Anthropologist* 67 (1965): 481–483; and "Lachrymosity: A Cultural Reinforcement of Minority States," *Ethnicity* 4 (1977): 156–166; and Joel Savishinsky and Harold Wimberly, "Ancestor Memorialism: A Comparison of Jews and Japanese," in *Community, Self and Identity*, B. Misra and J. Preston, eds. (The Hague: Mouton, 1978), 115–132. The Jewish view of history was reinforced by Christian interpretations of Jews as the original chosen people, cursed for their rejection of Christ.

15. Katz, *Tradition and Crisis*, 23, 55.

16. Ibid., 40–42. *See also* C. Dresser, "Is it Fresh? An Examination of Jewish American Shopping Habits," *New York Folklore Quarterly* 27 (1971): 153–160. Of course, this does not exhaust ethnocentric business behavior. Jewish patronage of certain shops, because they sell kosher or Jewish-style foods, is natural. Such shops also develop their own ways of dealing with customers. Jewish delicatessens and butcher shops have persisted well into the era of supermarkets in the United States. Such preferences are certainly in line with ritual practices and cultural preferences, as well as a desire to deal with one's own.

17. Eduard Rosenbaum, "M. M. Warburg & Co.: Merchant Bankers of Hamburg," *Leo Baeck Yearbook* 7 (1962): 121–152; W. Mosse, "Rudolf Mosse and the House of Mosse," *Leo Baeck Yearbook* 4 (1959): 237–259. W. Hamerlin, "Jews in the Leipzig Fur Industry," *Leo Baeck Yearbook* 9

(1964): 239–266; and Robert J. Cole, "The Old Guard Changes," *New York Times* (July 10, 1977).

18. If Glueckel of Hameln is seen as an exemplary Jewish businesswoman, one must see what type she really represents. She was a member of a merchant class, and she became a businesswoman as a widow with children. *See* Glueckel of Hameln, *Memoirs*, (New York: Schocken Books, 1977). A divorcee would have had a much more difficult time. *See* Katz, *Tradition and Crisis*, 135–136.

19. Ibid., 135–136.

20. Ibid., 156.

21. *See* "Lodz," *Jewish Encyclopedia* (New York: Funk & Wagnalls, 1904). In England and New York City, Jewish tailors were also hired for work in Jewish sweat shops and paid quite low wages in the beginning. *See* S. Aris, *Jews in Business* (Harmondsworth: Penguin Books, 1970), 69–84; and Irving Howe, *The World of Our Fathers* (New York: Harcourt Brace Jovanovich, 1976), 154–159. The employment of Jewish workers by Jewish entrepreneurs contradicts Max Weber's view of Jewish employers.

22. "Guenzburg," *Jewish Encyclopedia* and *Encyclopedia Judaica.*

23. Katz, *Tradition and Crisis*, 59–61.

24. A. G. Rabinbach, "The Migration of Galician Jews to Vienna, 1857–1880," *Austrian History Yearbook* 11 (1975): 1–55; and Howe, *World of Our Fathers* (1976), 183–190.

25. Heller, *Edge of Destruction*, 40, 186.

26. S. Sharot, "Native Jewry and the Religious Anglicization of Immigrants in London," *Jewish Journal of Sociology* 16 (1973): 39–56; Chaim Bermant, *Troubled Eden* (New York: Basic Books, 1969); and McCagg, "Jewish Nobles and Geniuses."

27. Mahler, "Jews in Public Service"; Jacob Toury, *Prolegomena to the Entrance of Jews into German Citizenry* (Tel Aviv: Tel Aviv University Institute for the Study of the Diaspora, 1972) [in Hebrew]; and McCagg, "Jewish Nobles and Geniuses."

28. Baron, *Jews under Tsar and Soviet*, 43–48; Heller, *Edge of Destruction*, 130–134, 158–186; and Howe, *World of Our Fathers*, 287–329. Marxist-Zionists, like Mahler, stress the internal class conflict within the Jewish community. This conflict, with the associated concept that the well-to-do betrayed Jewish interests to the gentile ruling elite, is a major theme in Mahler's *History of Modern Jewry.* Theses of oppression in eighteenth-century Germany, of internal class division in nineteenth-century Russia, and the assimilation of the "bourg-nobles" are present,

however, in the works of other non-Marxist historians, such as Baron, *Jews under Tsar and Soviet;* and Toury, *Prolegomena to the Entrance of Jews into German Citizenry.*

29. Shohet, *Im Hilufei Tekufot* (1960), 27–28.

30. McCagg, "Jewish Nobles and Geniuses" (1972); G. G. Scholem, *On Jews and Judaism in Crisis* (New York: Schocken, 1976), 1–53; and Heller, *Edge of Destruction,* 211–248.

31. Katz, *Tradition and Crisis,* 231–244; S. Poll, *The Hasidic Community of Williamsburg* (New York: Schocken, 1962); and Baron, *Jews under Tsar and Soviet* (1964), 145–148.

32. Elazar, "Reconstruction of Jewish Communities"; S. W. Baron, *The Jewish Community* (Philadelphia: Jewish Publication Society, 1942); and *Jews under Tsar and Soviet,* 119–134; 223–227; and Katz, *Tradition and Crisis,* 79–134. *See also* Bermant, *Troubled Eden.*

33. Katz, *Tradition and Crisis,* 248–250; Baron, *Jews under Tsar and Soviet,* 119–134; 201–214; and 318–326; Shohet, *Im Hilufei Tekufot,* 72–88; and Mahler, *History of Modern Jewry,* 62–78; 140–147; 247–252; 291–298; and 413–423.

34. Baron, *Jews under Tsar and Soviet,* 223–243; 268–298; and Heller, *Edge of Destruction,* 260–278.

35. *See* "Adolph Cremieux," "Paul Nathan," and "Horace Guenzberg," in *Jewish Encyclopedia* and *Encyclopaedia Judaica.*

36. McCagg, "Jewish Nobles and Geniuses"; Jacob Toury, "Organizational Problems of German Jewry: Steps Toward Establishment of a Central Organization (1893–1920)," *Leo Baeck Yearbook* 13 (1968): 57–90; Howe, *World of Our Fathers* (1976), 90–94; 230–235; and 360–362; and Bermant, *Troubled Eden,* 62–63; 97–110; and 168–169.

37. Daniel J. Elazar, *Community and Polity* (Philadelphia: Jewish Publication Society, 1976), 70–77.

38. Chang, "Distributions and Occupations of Overseas Chinese"; Norton Ginsburg and C. F. Roberts, *Malaya* (Seattle: University of Washington Press, 1958), 249–252; G. W. Skinner, *Chinese Society in Thailand* (Ithaca, N.Y.: Cornell University Press, 1957), 33–45; William Willmott, *The Chinese in Cambodia* (Vancouver: University of British Columbia Publication Center, 1967), 17–26; and F. L. K. Hsu, "Influence of Southseas Emigration on Certain Chinese Provinces," *Far East Quarterly* 5 (1945): 47–59. For a new survey, see Lynn Pan, *Sons of the Yellow Emperor: A History of the Chinese Diaspora* (Boston: Little Brown, 1990).

39. Skinner, *Chinese Society in Thailand* (1957), 28–96, 301–305;

Chang, "Distribution and Occupations of Overseas Chinese"; *Also see* M. H. Fried et al., eds., *Colloquium on Overseas Chinese* (New York: Institute of Pacific Relations, 1958); Luong Nhi Ky, "The Chinese In Vietnam: Chinese Relations with Special Attention to the Period 1862–1961" (Doctoral thesis, University of Michigan, 1973), 83–107; V. G. Nee and B. D. B. Nee, *Longtime Californin'* (New York: Pantheon Books, 1972); James W. Loewen, *The Mississippi Chinese Between Black and White* (Cambridge: Harvard University Press, 1971); Paul C. P. Siu, *The Chinese Laundryman* (New York: New York University Press, 1987); James B. Watson, *Emigration and the Chinese Lineage* (Berkeley: University of California Press, 1975); Donald Willmott, *The Chinese of Semarang* (Ithaca, NY: Cornell University Press, 1960); and William Willmott, *Chinese in Cambodia* (1967), 44–63.

40. Loewen, *Mississippi Chinese.*

41. On United States, *see* S. W. Kung, *Chinese in American Life* (Seattle: University of Washington Press, 1962), 80–164, 293; Betty Lee Sung, *A Survey of Chinese-American Manpower and Employment* (New York: Praeger, 1976), 5–16; On Mexico, Charles Cumberland, "The Sonora Chinese and the Mexican Revolution," *Hispanic-American Review* 40 (1960): 191–212; David Weber, "Chinitos' Return to Mexico," *Christian Science Monitor* (November 26, 1960); On Southeast Asia, *see* Heidhues, *Southeast Asia's Chinese Minorities* (1973), 30–44, 59–86; J. A. C. Mackie and C. A. Coppel, "Preliminary Survey," in *The Chinese in Indonesia,* J. A. C. Mackie, ed. (Honolulu: University Press of Hawaii, 1976), 9–12; Judith Strauch, *The Chinese Exodus From Vietnam: Implications for Southeast Asian Chinese,* occasional paper no. 1 (Cambridge: Cultural Survival, 1980); and G. Porter, "Vietnam's Ethnic Chinese and the Sino-Vietnamese Conflict," *Bulletin of Concerned Asian Scholars* 12 (1980): 55–59.

42. Fried et al., *Colloquium on Overseas Chinese* (1958); Cumberland, "Sonora Chinese and the Mexican Revolution" (1960); and Nee and Nee, *Longtime Californin'* (1972).

43. Heidehues, *Southeast Asia's Chinese Minorities* (1973), 8–29; Spulber, *State and Economic Development in Eastern Europe* (1967), 121–138.

44. K. D. Thomas and J. Panglayakin, "The Chinese in the South Sumatran Rubber Industry," in *The Chinese in Indonesia,* J.A.C. Mackie, ed. (Honolulu: University Press of Hawaii, 1976), 138–198; and Janet T. Landa, *The Economics of the Ethnically Homogeneous Middleman Group* (Toronto: University of Toronto Institute for Policy Analysis, 1979).

45. On Mississippi, *see* Loewen, *Mississippi Chinese* (1969), 83–89. The overseas Chinese supported initial revolutionary activity in the Mainland early in the century, and they felt the impact of a half-century of war and internal civil conflict. *See* Lea Williams, *Overseas Chi-*

nese Nationalism (Glencoe, Ill.: The Free Press, 1960), 56–57; 63; and 69–70. This was especially true after World War II, when the Chinese governments vied for support from both the diaspora's host-states and the overseas communities as well.

46. F. L. K. Hsu, *The Challenge of the American Dream: The Chinese in the United States* (San Francisco: Wadsworth, 1971), 6–7; Rose Hum Lee, *The Chinese in the United States of America* (Hong Kong: Hong Kong University Press, 1960); Heidhues, *Southeast Asia's Chinese Minorities* (1974), 17, 28; William E. Maxwell, "Modernization and Mobility into the Patrimonial Medical Elite in Thailand," *American Journal of Sociology* 81 (1975): 564–590; and Nee and Nee, *Longtime Californin'*.

47. Charles Coppel, "Patterns of Chinese Political Activity in Indonesia," in *The Chinese in Indonesia*, J. A. C. Mackie, ed. (1976), 57, 71; Heidhues, *Southeast Asia's Chinese Minorities* (1974), 30–44; Stephen F. Tobias, "Buddhism: Belonging and Detachment—Some Paradoxes of Chinese Ethnicity in Thailand," *Journal of Asian Studies* 36 (1977): 303–325; and Giok-Lan Tan, *The Chinese of Sukabumi: A Study in Social and Cultural Accommodation* (Ithaca, NY: Cornell University Southeast Asia Program, 1963), 44.

48. Tobias, "Buddhism, Belonging and Detachment"; Willmott, *Chinese in Cambodia* (1967), 38–39; and Skinner, *Chinese Society in Thailand* (1957), 131–132, 138–139, 150–151, 257–258, and 314.

49. Willmott, *Chinese of Semarang* (1960), 247–248; Heidhues, *Southeast Asia's Chinese Minorities* (1974), 30–44; Mackie and Coppell, "Preliminary Survey" (1974), 4–12; and J. A. C. Mackie, ed., Outbreaks in Indonesia, 1959–1968," in *The Chinese in Indonesia*, J. A. C. Mackie, ed. (Honolulu: University Press of Hawaii, (1976), 79, 82, and 129–138.

50. There were instances, where individuals of mixed Chinese and other ancestry were not acknowledged, such as the exclusion of Chinese-black offspring in Mississippi. In that highly segregated state, the Chinese felt under pressure to exclude partly Negro individuals from the community, in order to demonstrate to the dominant whites their own concern for "racial purity" and a higher social status. This was part of a tacit agreement between the Mississippi Chinese and the whites during the 1920s and 1930s. *See* Loewen, *Mississippi Chinese* (1969), 135–153; R. H. Lee, *Chinese in the United States* (1960), 250–251; and Hsu, *Challenge of the American Dream* (1971), 5–6, 31, and 120. This contrasts sharply with the situation in Peru, where Spanish-Chinese offspring are accepted into the community, although there is an internal hierarchy with pure Chinese on top, followed by Spanish-Chinese and with the Indian-Chinese offspring being lowest. *See* Alice J. Kwong, "The Chinese in Peru," in *Colloquium on Overseas Chinese*, M. H. Fried ed. (New York: Institute of Pacific Relations, 1958), 41–48.

51. Skinner, *Chinese Society in Thailand* (1957), 126–127; Nee and Nee, *Longtime Californin'* (1972), p. 13; and R. H. Lee, *Chinese in the United States of America* (1960), 45–47, 69–85, 103–112, 185–251, and 300–307. John R. Clammer claims that there was relatively little intermarriage between the Straits ("baba") Chinese, who were veteran residents of Malacca and Singapore, and the local population, despite claims by others to the contrary. *See* J. R. Clammer, *Straits Chinese Society* (Singaore: Singapore University Press, 1980), pp.20–21.

52. Skinner, *Chinese Society in Thailand* (1957), 172–212; and Heidhues, *Southeast Asia's Chinese Minorities* (1974), 30–44. Since most studies stress the social, structural, and economic position of the overseas Chinese, less attention has been given to the cultural adjustments which the Chinese have made. One work which is devoted to a detailed ethnography of an overseas community is Giok-lan-Tan, *The Chinese of Sukabumi*, which describes the acculturation of the Peranakan Chinese in that West Javanese community from 1956 to 1957. For the behavior patterns of Chinese Americans, *see* Hsu, *Challenge of the American Dream* (1971), and Lee, *Chinese in the United States of America*, which offer contrasting views. For a focus on religion among Malaysian Chinese, *see* S. E. Ackerman and R. L. M. Lee, *Heaven in Transition* (Honolulu: University of Hawaii Press, 1988).

53. Wilmott, *Chinese of Semarang*; Tobias, "Buddhism, Belonging and Detachment"; Harold Crouch, "Generals and Businessmen in Indonesia," *Pacific Affairs* 48 (1976): 519–540; G. W. Skinner, *Leadership and Power in the Chinese Community of Thailand* (Ithaca, N.Y.: Cornell University Press, 1958), 302–320; and Coppel, "Patterns of Chinese Political Activity," (1976), 63, 71. The much desired individualism of the Chinese is, of course, familistic by American standards.

54. Willmott, *Chinese of Semarang* (1960), 71. For an economic interpretation of this Confucian ethic, *see* Landa, *Economics of the Ethnically Homogenous Middleman Group.*

55. Skinner, *Chinese Society in Thailand* (1957), 118–123; Heidhues, *Southeast Asia's Chinese Minorities* (1974), 101–102; and Louis Golomb, "Brokers of Morality: The Thai Ethnic Adaptation in a Rural Malaysian Setting," *Asian Studies at Hawaii*, no. 23 (Honolulu: University Press of Hawaii, 1973).

56. Ivan Light, "From Vice District to Tourist Attraction," *Pacific Historical Review* 43 (1974): 367–394. On the continuing power of the *tongs* in a manner comparable to discussions of the Mafia as an organized conspiracy, *see* Lee, *Chinese in the United States of America* (1960), 161–183, 300–307, and 352–372. Light views it in a more realistic manner. *See also* Hsu, *Challenge of the American Dream* (1971), 48, 95–108; and Nee and Nee, *Longtime Californin'*. Chinese-organized criminal organiza-

tion persists and are allegedly involved in the drug business today.

57. F. L. K. Hsu, *Americans and Chinese* (New York: Doubleday, 1970); *Challenge of the American Dream* (1971), 19–39; D. Willmott, *Chinese of Semarang* (1960), 47–50; and Skinner, *Chinese Society in Thailand* (1957), 28–76.

58. Watson, *Emigration and Chinese Lineage, passim.*

59. Nee and Nee, *Longtime Californin'*; Lee, *Chinese in the United States of America* (1960), 185–252; 325–352; Jacques Amyot, *The Manila Chinese: Familism in the Philippine Culture* (Ateneo de Manila University, 1973), 121–141; Burton Benedict, "Family Firms and Economic Development," *Southwestern Journal of Anthropology* 24, (1968): 1–19; and "Family Firms and Firm Families: A Comparison of Indian, Chinese and Creole Families in the Seychelles," in *Entrepreneurship of Cross-Cultural Context*, S. M. Greenfield, A. Strickton, and R. Aubey, eds. (Albuquerque: University of New Mexico Press, 1975); and Ivan Light, *Ethnic Enterprise in America* (Berkeley: University of California Press, 1972). Benedict has concluded that the patriarchal, virilocal joint family ideology with an authoritarian father is better suited for the success of family firms than a more conjugal type of family. This certainly fits the Chinese, although, as he has pointed out, much more comparative study is needed. The role of women in particular requires further investigation. A recent review of literature confirms many views of strong familism in Chinese societies, Nan Lin, "Chinese Family Structure and Chinese Society" *Bulletin of Institute of Ethnology Academia Sinica*, No. 65 (1988) 59–129. *See also* Siu-lun Wong, "The Chinese Family Firm: A Model," *British Journal of Sociology* 36 (1985):58–72, who includes the commercial aspects of Chinese firms in Hong Kong and Taiwan, as well as overseas firms.

60. Ju Kang Tien, *The Chinese of Sarawak: A Study of Social Structure* (London: London School of Economics, 1953), 80. *See also* Amyot, *Manila Chinese* (1973), 82–106; Lee, *Chinese in the United States of America* (1960), 173–175; and Hsu, *Challenge of the American Dream* (1971), 43–44.

61. Tien, *Chinese of Sarawak* (1953), 35–68; and Thomas and Panglaykin, "Chinese in the South Sumatran Rubber Industry."

62. Tien, *Chinese of Sarawak* (1953), 71; and Lee, *Chinese in the United States of America* (1960), 185–230. In the United States, as elsewhere, Chinese continue to immigrate illegally. Employers of such undocumented immigrants may exercise great powers as their patrons.

63. Light, *Ethnic Enterprise in America*; and David H. Wum, "To Kill Three Birds with One Stone: The Rotating Credit Associations of the Papua, New Guinea Chinese," *American Ethnologist* 1 (1974): 564–584.

64. Crouch, "Generals and Businessmen in Indonesia"; and Tien, *Chinese of Sarawak.*

65. Tien, *Chinese of Sarawak*, 10–19, 45–58; Skinner, *Leadership and Power in the Chinese Community of Thailand*, 315–319. *See also* Lee, *Chinese in the United States of America*, 144–147.

66. Tan, *Chinese of Sukabumi*; Willmott, *Chinese of Semarang*; Lee, *Chinese in the United States of America*, 103–112, 232–249; Hsu, *Challenge of the American Dream*, 6–8; and Sung, *Chinese-American Manpower and Employment*, 10–14, 211–213.

67. Thomas and Panglaykin, "Chinese in the South Sumatran Rubber Industry." The conflict between aliens and WNI may have been less severe, however, since citizenship was often assumed opportunistically, so that some family members may have held one citizenship different from others. The citizenship status of the Chinese in Vietnam was also complicated. The Republic of South Vietnam forced many Chinese to assume Vietnamese nationality, while the Chinese in the North had a special status. When the Socialist Republic of Vietnam was formed in 1975, the status of the Chinese in the South was a bone of contention between China and Vietnam. *See*, for example, Ky, "Chinese in Vietnam"; and Porter, "Vietnam's Ethnic Chinese." On citizenship of Chinese, *see* Heidhues, *Southeast Asia's Chinese Minorities*; Mackie and Coppel, "Preliminary Survey," (1976), 9–12; and Coppel, "Patterns of Chinese Political Activity in Indonesia." On southeast Asia, *see* Skinner, *Chinese Society in Thailand*, 165, 185–186, 219, and 263. On the United States, *see* Lee, *Chinese in the United States of America*, 7–19; Nee and Nee, *Longtime Californin'*; and Sung, *Chinese-American Manpower and Employment*, 16–18, 109. *See also* Roger D. Waldinger, *Through the Eye of the Needle: Immigrants and Enterprise in New York's Garment Trade* (New York: New York University Press, 1986). On Hong Kong immigrants in Britain, *see* Watson, *Emigration and Chinese-Lineage*, 96–100.

68. Tan, *Chinese of Sukabumi*, 75–77; Lee, *Chinese in the United States of America*; H. W. Gardiner and D. Lematawekul, "Second Generation Chinese in Thailand: A Study in Ethnic Identification," *Journal of Cross-Cultural Psychology* 1: 333–344; and Hsu, *Challenge of the American Dream*, 83–92. Hsu presents a construct of Chinese values in which generational and ideological struggle would be less sharp among Chinese, even overseas Chinese, than among Americans, although he does not deny some conflict. Lee and Tan seem to contradict this. Perhaps the experience of these two women, both born overseas and in the penumbra of "the ancestor's shadow" makes them more critical than Hsu, a China-born male scholar. Gardiner and Lematawekul's study begins to penetrate this problem through a battery of psychological tests, but the study reported is still an exploratory one.

69. J. Nagata, "The Status of Ethnicity and the Ethnicity of Status," *International Journal of Comparative Sociology* 17 (1976): 242–260. On the politicization of ethnicity, *see* A. Rabushka, *Race and Politics in Urban Malaya* (Stanford, Calif.: Hoover Institute, 1973), 97–101; and Ginsburg and Roberts, *Malaya*, 457–460.

70. Ching Hwang Yen, *The Overseas Chinese and the 1911 Revolution* (Kuala Lumpur: Oxford University Press, 1976); and Williams, *Overseas Chinese Nationalism.*

71. Tien, *Chinese of Sarawak*, 86; Stephen Fitzgerald, *China and the Overseas Chinese: A Study of Peking's Changing Politics, 1949–1950* (Cambridge: Cambridge University Press, 1972); Ky, "Chinese in Vietnam," 176–182.

72. Coppel, "Chinese Political Activity in Indonesia"; Skinner, *Chinese Society in Thailand*, 155–159; 261–297; 322–344; and 365–382.

73. Maurice Freedman, "Immigrants and Associations: Chinese in Nineteenth-Century Singapore," *Comparative Studies in Society and History* 3 (1960): 25–48; Lee, *Chinese in the United States of America*, 161–173; and Light, "Vice District to Tourist Attraction."

74. Williams, *Overseas Chinese Nationalism*, 38; G. W. Skinner, "Overseas Chinese Leadership: Paradigm for a Paradox," in *Leadership and Authority*, G. Wijayewardene, ed. (Singapore: University of Malaya Press, 1968), 191–207; Edgar Wickberg, *The Chinese in Philippine Life* (New Haven: Yale University Press, 1965), 38; Ky, "Chinese in Vietnam," 131–140, 175–176; and William Willmott, *The Political Structure of the Chinese Community in Cambodia* (London: Athlone Press, 1970), 32–45, 58–69.

75. Freedman, "Immigrants and Association," 25–48; Skinner, "Leadership and Power in the Chinese Community of Thailand"; Willmott, *Chinese of Semarang*, 129–168; and *Political Structure of the Chinese Community of Thailand*, 70–84, 147–149; Heidhues, *Southeast Asia's Chinese Minorities*, 45–58; Yen, *Overseas Chinese and the 1911 Revolution*; Williams, "Overseas Chinese Nationalism"; Hsu, *Challenge of the American Dream*, 43–50.

76. Rabushka, *Race and Politics in Urban Malaya*; Heidhues, *Southeast Asia's Chinese Minorities*, 59–86; and Coppel, "Patterns of Chinese Political Activity in Indonesia."

77. *See*, for example, Willmott, *Political Structure of the Chinese Community in Cambodia*, 118–120; Nee and Nee, *Longtime Californin'*; and Coppel, "Patterns of Chinese Political Activity in Indonesia." Despite such voluntary organizations, Chinese organize nonprofit voluntary organizations less than do Korean and Japanese immigrants in the United States, according to Lin, Chinese Family Structure, 54–57.

78. Willmott, *Chinese of Semarang*, 141–159. A factor making for fragmentation in the United States has been the dispersal of Chinese from their Chinatown ghettoes. This is true of both upwardly mobile Chinese-Americans and the scientific-professional segment of the new immigrants. The latter never experienced "Chinatown" and have little to do with the old immigrants. Student associations and the Chinese Engineers and Scientists Association of Southern California are the organizational markers of this group. *See* Hsu, *Challenge of the American Dream*, 48–50; Lee, *Chinese in the United States of America*, 181–183; and Sung, *Survey of Chinese-American Manpower and Employment*, 33–51.

79. Crissman, "Segmentary Structure of Urban Overseas Chinese Communities."

80. Hsu, *Challenge of the American Dream*, 45–50, 123–134.

81. Jayawardena, "Migration and Social Change"; Hilda Kuper, *Indian People of Natal* (Westport Conn.: Greenwood Press, 1970), 59–60; H. S. Morris, *The Indians in Uganda* (Chicago: University of Chicago Press, 1968), 8–9; and Usha Mahajani, *The Role of Indian Minorities in Burma and Malaya* (Westport, Conn.: Greenwood Press, 1973), 1–10, 16–29, and 95–105. For political reasons, the term South Asian is preferred to that of overseas Indians or the more ambiguous term, Asian. The latter can, of course, be used in reference to East Africa and Britain, where Asians from the Indian subcontient predominate. In this section, unless otherwise specified, Indian and South Asian will be used interchangeably as synonyms.

82. Jayawardena, "Migration and Social Change"; Leo A. Despres, "The Implications of Nationalist Politics in British Guiana for Cultural Theory," *American Anthropologist* 66 (1964): 1051–1077; and *Cultural Pluralism and Nationalist Politics in British Guiana* (Chicago: Rand McNally, 1967), 230–231; and Kuper, *Indian People of Natal*, 59.

83. *See* Morris, *Indians in Uganda*, 92–99; D. Pocock, *Patidar and Kanbi* (Oxford: Clarendon Press, 1972), 56–63; K. Sandhu, *Indians in Malaya Immigration and Settlement 1786–1957* (Cambridge: Cambridge University Press, 2969), 125–129, 241–243. Some overseas communities were "business communities" in India. For the history of such castes and communities in India proper, *see* D. Tripathi, ed., *Business Communities of India: A Historical Perspective* (New Delhi: Manohar, 1984). On the Chettiars in particular, *see* D. Rudner, *Caste and Capitalism in Colonial India* (Berkeley: University of California Press, forthcoming), which is based on Rudner's dissertation.

84. Some of this is drawn from the unpublished research of Ann Eskesen. Also see note 89.

85. Kuper, *Indian People of Natal,* 44–79; and Despres, *Cultural Pluralism and Nationalist Politics in British Guiana,* 4.

86. Barton Schwartz, *Caste in Overseas Indian Communities* (San Francisco: W. H. Freeman, 1967).

87. Richard Basham, "The Caste System Upside Down," *Current Anthropology* 16 (1975): 291–293; Nagata, "Status of Ethnicity and the Ethnicity of Status"; and Kuper, *Indian People of Natal.*

88. Agehananda Bharati, *The Asians in East Africa: Jayhind and Uhuru* (Chicago: Nelson-Hall, 1972), 33–94, 166; F. Dotson and L. O. Dotson, *The Indian Minority of Zambia, Rhodesia and Malawi* (New Haven: Yale University Press, 1968), 261–297.

89. R. Desai, *Indian Immigrants in Britain* (London: Oxford University Press, 1963), 11, 14–16, 18, 40, 70–71, 123, 139, and 142–143. Since Desai is dealing with newly arrived immigrants, many of whom have wives back in India, the question of cross-caste marriages in Britain does not arise frequently. He does indicate, however, that commensalism is tolerated. The most salient group is that of kin and others from one's own village, followed by friendships along regional-linguistic lines. It seems that, in Britain, these divisions may even cross religious and national lines, so that Punjabi Pakistanis are closer to Sikhs and Hindus from the Indian Punjab than to Kashmiri and Bengali Muslims (the latter, Bangladesh, formerly East Pakistan). For recent analysis on Asian small businessmen, *see* C. Zimmer and H. Aldrich, "Resource Moblization Through Ethnic Networks: Kinship and Friendship Ties of Shopkeepers in England," *Sociological Perspectives* 30 (1987): 422–445; and P. Werbner, "Business on Trust: Pakistani Entrepreneurs in the Manchester Garment Trade," in R. Ward and R. Jenkins, *Ethnic Communities in Business* (Cambridge: Cambridge University Press, 1984).

90. Bharati, *Asians in East Africa,* 79–80, 160. *See also* Desai, *Indian Immigrants in Britain,* 122–144.

91. Bharati, *Asians in East Africa,* 161; Dotson and Dotson, *Indian Minority of Zambia, Rhodesia, and Malawi,* 280–291; and K. S. Sandhu, *Indians in Malaya,* 167–168.

92. D. Pocock, *Patidar and Kanbi;* Bharati, *Asians in East Africa,* 126–127.

93. Dotson and Dotson, *Indian Minority of Zambia, Rhodesia, and Malawi,* 65–66; Desai, *Indian Immigrants in Britain,* 63–64, 70; and Howard Aldrich, "Asian Shopkeepers as a Middleman Minority: A Study of Small Business in Wandsworth," in *The Inner City: Employment and Industry,* A. Evans and D. Eversley, eds. (London: Heinemann, 1980).

94. Dotson and Dotson, *Indian Minority of Zambia, Rhodesia, and Malawi,* 64, 118, and 253–259; Bharati, *Asians in East Africa,* 140–145.

95. Dotson and Dotson, *Indian Minority of Zambia, Rhodesia, and Malawi,* 254–256; and Desai, *Indian Immigrants in Britain,* 75.

96. D. P. Ghai, "An Economic Survey," in *Portrait of a Minority: Asians in East Africa,* D. P. Ghai and Y. P. Ghai, eds. (Nairobi: Oxford University Press, 1970), 115–116; Donald Rothchild, *Racial Bargaining in Independent Kenya* (London: Oxford University Press, 1973), 175–176; Dotson and Dotson, *Indian Minority of Zambia, Rhodesia, and Malawi* (1968), 202–205, 269–273; Bharati, *Asians in East Africa,* 158–160; Peter Marris and Anthony Somerset, *African Businessmen* (London: Routledge and Kegan Paul, 1971), 93–98. Marris and Somerset suggest that, while some of the charges made against Asians by African businessmen on these matters are correct, the Africans also accept an unfavorable image of the Asians, while being more favorably disposed to the more distant European businessmen. They also suggest that European bureaucratic corporations can integrate Africans into their organizations more easily than can smaller Asian family firms. *See also* Aldrich, "Asian Shopkeepers as a Middleman Minority" who finds few differences between the white and Asian shopkeepers in Wandsworth, England. He even finds similar use of family members. The Asians do work longer hours. *See also* Zimmer and Aldrich "Resource Mobilization." Africans, however, did not all resent the Asian traders equally. When Baganda traders organized a boycott of Indian traders in Uganda in 1959–60, they received little support and some opposition from other Africans. *See* D. P. Ghai, "The Bugandan Trade Boycott," in *Power and Politics in Black Africa,* R. I. Rotberg and A. A. Mazrui, ed. (New Jersey: Oxford University Press, 1970).

97. Benedict, "Family Firms and Economic Development"; Morris, *The Indians in Uganda,* 125–132, 139; Dotson and Dotson, *Indian Minority of Zambia, Rhodesia, and Malawi,* 155–164; John Zarwan, "The Social and Economic Network of an Indian Family Business in Kenya, 1920–1970," *Kroniek van Afrika* 6:3(1975): 219–235; and Benedict, "Family Firms and Firm Families." On Muslims in India, *see* Mattison Mines, "The Muslim Merchants of Pallavarum, Madras" (Doctoral thesis, Cornell University, 1970), 61, 64. Benedict has compared East-African Indian firms with the House of Rothschild, and Indian and Chinese family firms with Creole firms in the Seychelles. He finds that the Rothschilds, the Indians, and the Chinese all share a strong patriarchically oriented familism which is useful in capitalistic enterprise. There are some differences. The Creoles differ from the others because of their conjugal family structure. The Chinese and Indians are similar, but differ with regard to the role of women. In the Chinese family, they are more likely to work in the store than in the Indian family; in addition, Chinese are more able to form kinship ties with the local population, since some intermarriage is per-

mitted. On contemporary Britain, *see* Werbner, "Business on Trust," and Zimmer and Aldrich, "Resource Mobilization."

98. They are the descendants of Cutchi-speaking members of the Lohanna (Hindu) caste who converted to the Khoja Ismaili sect. *See* Bharati, *Asians in East Africa* (1972), 80–81; Benedict, "Family Firms and Economic Development"; and J. S. Mangat, *A History of the Asians in East Africa* (Oxford: Clarendon Press, 1969), 52–53.

99. Jayawardena, "Migration and Social Change"; Sandhu, *Indians in Malaya* (1969), 74–140.

100. See Desai, *Indian Immigrants in Britain,* 88, 94. Pakistani activity is especially visible in certain areas, such as Bradford in Yorkshire. Pakistanis and other Muslims have, together with orthodox Jews, opposed a ban on the ritual slaughter of meat. This is based on my observation in 1987 and a personal communication from my colleague, Sucheta Muzumdar.

101. Mangat, *History of the Asians in East Africa,* 141–142; Morris, *Indians in Uganda;* and D. P. Ghai and Y. P. Ghai, *Portrait of a Minority: Asians in East-Africa* (Nairobi: Oxford University Press, 1970), 10.

102. Donna Nelson, "Problems of Power in a Plural Society: Asians in Kenya," *Southwestern Journal of Anthropology* 23 (1972): 255–264.

103. Kuper, *Indian People of Natal;* and Sandhu, *Indians in Malaya,* 75–140.

104. Despres, *Cultural Pluralism and Nationalist Politics in British Guiana;* Sandhu, Indians in Malaya, 288–289; Mahajani, *Role of Indian Minorities in Burma and Malaya,* 198–218; and Kuper, *Indian People of Natal,* 45–67.

105. Kuper, *Indian People of Natal,* 40–42, 133–139.

106. Bharati, *Asians in East Africa,* 252–256.

107. Despres, *Cultural Pluralism and Nationalist Poliics in British Guiana;* Nagata, "Status of Ethnicity and the Ethnicity of Status"; and Cynthia H. Enloe, *Ethnic Conflict and Political Development* (Boston: Little, Brown, 1973), 87–88; 175–179.

108. Bharati, *Asians in East Africa,* 152–153; 159–160; Marris and Somerset, *African Businessmen;* Bert H. Adams and Mike Bristow, "The Politico-Economic Position of Ugandan Asians in the Colonial and Independent Eras," *Journal of Asian and African Studies* 13 (1978): 151–156.

109. Dotson and Dotson, *Indian Minority of Zambia, Rhodesia and Malawi,* 89, 221.

110. Morris, *Indians in Uganda;* H. H. Patel, "Power, Race, Class and Citizenship: Toward a Conceptual Integration of Indian Political Activity in Uganda," a paper presented at the international seminar on Asian Trading Minorities in Africa (Leiden: Afrika-Studiecentrum, December 15–19, 1975).

111. Mangat, *History of the Asians in East Africa,* 97–131. It is unclear from Mangat or other sources whether the Indian political leadership during this period was much more than the factional leaders described by Dotson and Dotson. Certainly, they did achieve greater recognition, but they might still have been an essentially self-appointed leadership.

112. Mangat, *History of the Asians in East Africa* (1969), 178.

113. Adams and Bristow, "Politico-Economic Position of Ugandan Asians." In Uganda, most Ugandan citizens were Ismaili Muslims, while Hindus were generally British or Indian citizens, and there were also Pakistanis.

114. India and Pakistan did not necessarily stick to that position. *See* Rothchild, *Racial Bargaining in Independent Kenya,* 389–407.

115. *See* Rothchild, *Racial Bargaining in Independent Kenya;* Dotson and Dotson, *Indian Minority of Zambia, Rhodesia and Malawi,* 298–379; Bharati, *Asians in East Africa,* 149–178; H. H. Patel, "Power, Race, Class and Citizenship," and Adams and Michael Bristow, "Politico-Economic Position of Ugandan Asians."

116. There do seem to be some differences between the English-speaking countries and the continental European states, such as France. The latter seem to prefer formal recognition of minorities, as symbolized by the *Kultusgemeinde* in Germany, the *chef de congregation* in French Indochina and the Kapitan system in the Netherlands East Indies. The Anglophone states allow more room for voluntary organization of minorities. Also newly independent states, such as interwar Poland or Romania, Cambodia in the past twenty years, Indonesia since 1949, and the East African states seem to be particularly sensitive to "foreign interference" in their internal affairs and insensitive to the feelings and reactions of minorities. Of course, poverty and unemployment in all of these states is very much involved in this drive to sovereignty.

117. On Jews in Nazi Europe, *see* Lucy S. Dawidowicz, *The War Against the Jews, 1933–1945* (Philadelphia: Jewish Publication Society, 1975), 223–278. On Anglo-American Jewish communities, *see* Elazar, *Community and Polity,* (1976), 13; and Bermant, *Troubled Eden* (1969), 168–169. On Indonesia, *see* Coppel, "Patterns of Chinese Political Activity in Indonesia," and Mackie, "Anti-Chinese Outbreaks in Indonesia" (1976), 95. On Indians in Uganda, *see* Adams and Bristow, "Politico-Eco-

nomic Position of Ugandan Asians." *See also* Skinner, *Chinese Society in Thailand;* and Crouch, "Generals and Businessmen in Indonesia" (1975–76), 519–540.

118. See Shohet, *Im Hilufei Tekufot* (1960), 72–88, 113–122; Heidehues, *Southeast Asia's Chinese Minorities* (1974), 45–48; Skinner, "Overseas Chinese Leadership"; Williams, *Overseas Chinese Nationalism* (1960), 124; and Willmott, *Political Structure of the Chinese Community in Cambodia* (1970), 61–64.

119. Baron, *Jews under Tsar and Soviet* (1964), 41–56, 50, 56, and 63–64; Heller, *Edge of Destruction* (1977), 77–142; Porter, "Vietnam's Ethnic Chinese"; and Strauch, "Social Structure and Prejudice." For a good overview of Peking and the Chinese, *see* Fitzgerald, *China and Overseas Chinese. Also see* Robert S. Ross, *The Indochina Tangle* (New York: Columbia University Press, 1988), 194–198. For a comparison of persecution, *see* W. P. Zenner, Middleman Minorities and Genocide, *Genocide and the Modern Age,* I. Wallimann and M. N. Dobkowski, eds. (Westport, Conn.: Greenwood, 1987), 253–252.

120. Elazar, "Reconstruction of Jewish Communities in the Post-War Period"; *Community and Polity;* and Crissman, "Segmentary St_ucture of Urban Overseas Chinese Communities."

CHAPTER 5

1. On the contrast between pariah and modern capitalism, *see* Max Weber, *Ancient Judaism* (Glencoe, Ill.: The Free Press, 1952), 343–345; and *Economy and Society* (New York: Bedminster, 1968), 498–499, 615–623; and W. Sombart, *The Quintessence of Capitalism (Der Bourgeois)* (New York: E. P. Dutton, 1915). *See also* Howard P. Becker, "Constructive Typology in the Social Sciences," in *Contemporary Social Theory,* H. E. Barnes, H. P. Becker, and F. B. Becker, eds. (New York: Appleton-Century, 1940), 17–46; *Through Values to Social Interpretation* (Durham, N.C.: Duke University Press, 1950); and *Man in Reciprocity* (New York: Praeger, 1956); I. Rinder, "Strangers in the Land," *Social Problems* 6 (1958): 253–260; Gershon Hundert, "An Advantage to Peculiarity? The Case of the Polish Commonwealth," *Association for Jewish Studies Review* 6 (1981): 21–38; and S. Stryker, "Social Structure and Prejudice," *Social Problems* 6 (1958): 340–354. In dealing with Catholic entrepreneurs, *see* on the Galegos, or the Portuguese natives in Brazil, read June E. Hahner, "Jacobinos versus Galegos: Urban Radicals versus Portuguese Immigrants in Rio de Janeiro in the 1890s," *Journal of Inter-American Studies and World Affairs* 18 (1976): 125–154. On the Antioqueños (natives of the province of Antioquia, Columbia), *see* E. E. Hagen, *On the Theory of Social Change* (Homewood, Ill.: Dorsey Press, 1962), 353–384. On Berber groups in North Africa, such as

the Sousis, and on the Faasis natives of Fez, *see* John Waterbury, *North for the Trade* (Berkeley: University of California Press, 1972). On Muslim sectarians, such as Djerbans and Mzabites, *see* Russell Stone, "Religious Ethic and the Spirit of Capitalism," *International Journal of Middle Eastern Studies* 5 (1974): 260–273; and E. A. Alport, "The Mzab," in *Peoples and Cultures of the Middle East*, L. E. Sweet, ed. (Garden City, N.J.: Natural History Press, 1970), 225–241. Most of these groups are distinguished from their neighbors by region, religion or language, but they also have claims of nativity which mitigate their alienation. Some, such as the Galegos, evidently assimilate quickly, while others, such as the Djerbans, maintain their separation over a long period of time.

2. Weber sees the Protestant entrepreneur as universalistic with regard to his monetary dealings, but not in employment practices. In fact, he points to Puritan entrepreneurs who set up factories for devout Christian workers and contrasts them with Jewish entrepreneurs who did not do this. *See* Weber, *Economy and Society*, 613–614.

3. See Hagen, *Theory of Social Change*, 185–199; and S. Andreski, "An Economic Interpretation of Anti-Semitism," *Jewish Journal of Sociology* 5 (1963): 210–213. In addition, *see* Edna Bonacich, "A Theory of Middleman Minorities," *American Sociological Review* 38 (1973): 583–594.

4. On the Huguenot church in New York City, *see* John A. F. Maynard, *The Huguenot Church of New York* (New York: French Church of Saint Esprit, 1938). *See also* G. Elmore Reamon, *On the Trail of the Huguenots* (Baltimore: Baltimore Genealogical Society, 1966). For a history of Balfour, Williamson & Co., Ltd., *see* Wallis Hunt, *Heirs of Great Adventure: The History of Balfour, Williamson & Co., Ltd.* (London: Balfour, Williamson, 1951, 1960). *See also* J. R. Dolan, *The Yankee Peddlers of Early America* (New York: Bramhall, 1964).

Anniversaries such as the Tercentenary of the Revocation of the Edict of Nantes have been occasions for some new publications. Still, the flagging interest in the Huguenots and similar groups is discussed in Robin D. Gwynn, "Patterns in the Study of Huguenot Refugees in Britain: Past, Present, and Future," *Huguenots in Britain and Their French Background, 1550–1800*, Irene Scouloudi, ed. (London: Macmillan, 1987), 217–235.

5. On Scottish immigration to Canada, *see* Douglas A. Hill, *Scots to Canada* (London: Gentry Press, 1972).

6. Warren C. Scoville, *The Persecution of Huguenots and French Economic Development, 1680–1720* (Berkeley: University of California Press, 1960); and Frederick A. Norwood, *The Reformation Refugee as an Economic Force* (Chicago: American Society of Church History, 1942).

Also several of the articles in I. Scouloudi, *Huguenots in Britain,* and in Michelle Magdelaine and Rudoff von Thadden, *Le Refuge huguenot* (Paris: Armand Colin, 1985). *See also* Jon Butler, *The Huguenots in America: A Refugee People in the New World* (Cambridge, Harvard University Press, 1983).

7. F. B. Tolles, *Meeting House and Counting House* (Chapel Hill: University of North Carolina Press, 1948); Philip J. Benjamin, *The Philadelphia Quakers in the Industrial Age, 1865–1920* (Philadelphia: Temple University Press, 1976); and M. Magdalaine and R. von Thadden, *Le Refuge Huguenot* (Paris: Armand Colin, 1985) are examples.

8. Norwood, *Reformation Refugees as an Economic Force,* is the main source used in this section.

9. Ibid., 2, 146–148. Like Hagen, McClelland, and Scoville, Norwood focuses his attention on entrepreneurship and technological innovation, rather than on interethnic relations. He attributes innovation to the Protestant immigration from the Netherlands, both because this immigration helped break down the conservative guild system and the attributes of these immigrants as hardworkers and innovators. He suggests that Protestant nations flourished, in part, on account of these Protestant refugees. Why did the considerable number of Catholic refugees and immigrants not produce similar results? One answer is the Weberian one attributing change to Calvinist doctrine. Another is the difference in occupational background. The Catholic refugees were more likely to be unproductive scholastics. Norwood gives only scant attention to the whole range of mercantile and labor migrations which took place in sixteenth-century Europe, which produced similar results in the short term. There was an Italian presence, including merchants, workmen, architects, and masons, in Poland and Transylvania, as well as France. France continually dispatched artisans, itinerant merchants, water carriers, and farm workers to Catalonia, as well as a rural-urban migration. It is possible that Norwood is, here, overrating the role of the Protestant refugees. *See also* F. Braudel, *The Mediterranean and the Mediterranean World of the Age of Philip II* (New York: Harper and Row, 1972), 220, 222, 334–348, and 416–418. Also, on the seventeenth century, *see* Irene Scouloudi, "The Stranger Community in the Metropolis, 1558–1640" in *The Huguenot in Britain,* 42–55.

10. Norwood, 28, 38.

11. Norwood, 73–92.

12. Norwood, *Reformation Refugee,* 96–97, 100–101; and Robert T. Anderson, "The Danish and Dutch Settlements on Amagor Island: 400 Years of Socio-Cultural Interaction," *American Anthropologist* 60 (1958): 683–701. There were also agricultural immigrants from the Netherlands

in Prussia and even in Denmark. While Norwood treated them as Protestant refugees, it is possible that some were not. Of course, Anabaptists, of whom the Mennonites and Hutterites were a good part, did become agriculturalists in Eastern Europe. *See also* Ruth E. Baum, "The Ethnohistory of Law: The Hutterites Case," (Doctoral thesis, State University of New York at Albany, 1977), 80–93. Baum suggests that the early Hutterites were, in fact, craft specialists in the early period of their history. Eastern Europe was, of course, something of an agricultural frontier in that era and provided an outlet for agricultural settlement, while Western Europe was more densely populated.

13. Norwood, 87–89, 110–111, 117–119, 122–123.

14. Norwood, 3–5, 159–177.

15. Scoville, *Persecution of Huguenots and French Economic Development,* is the primary source here.

16. Ibid., 142–162.

17. Ibid., 46–47, 142–152.

18. Ibid., 153. For the description of a single pre–Revocation emigre's circle, *see* H. G. Roseveare, "Jacob David: A Huguenot London Merchant of the Late 17th Century and His Circle," in *Huguenots in Britain,* 72–88. On post–Revocation, international circles, *see* G. A. Rothrock, *The Huguenots: Biography of a Minority* (Chicago: Nelson-Hall, 1979), 184–185.

19. Scoville, *Persecution,* 151–152. *See also* M. Prestwick, "The Huguenots under Richelieu and Mazarin," in *Huguenots in Britain,* 175–197.

20. Scoville, *Persecution,* 150–151.

21. Ibid., 321–357.

22. Ibid., 357–361. *See also* Remy Scheurer, *"Passage, Accueil et Integration des Refugies Huguenots en Suisse,"* in *Le Refuge Huguenot,* Magdelaine and von Thadden, 45–62.

23. Scoville, *Persecution,* 321; Maynard, *Huguenot Church of New York,* 89–90; Henri and Barbara van der Zee, *William and Mary* (New York: Knopf, 1973); Elisabeth Labrousse, "Great Britain as envisaged by the Huguenots of the 17th Century," *Huguenots in Britain,* 143–157; B. Cottret, *"Glorieuse Revolution, Revocation Honteuse? Protestant Francais et Protestants d'Angelterre,"* in *Le Refuge Huguenot,* 83–96.

24. Scoville, *Persecution,* 362.

25. Maynard, *Huguenot Church of New York;* Labrousse "Great Britain," in *Huguenots in Britain,* 151–152.

26. Reaman, *Trail of the Huguenots,* 104; and Labrousse, "Great Britain," 151–152, 156. On Germany, *see also* Magdelaine and von Thadden, *Le refuge Huguenot,* 97–260.

27. Scoville, *Persecution,* 150.

28. A retention of the Huguenot heritage among their assimilated descendants is seen in family names such as Jay, Revere, and Sombart. *See* Stryker, "Social Structure and Prejudice," and the discussion of "Huguenots' associations" in Britain and Germany in the nineteenth and twentieth centuries, F. Centurier, *"Les Descendants de Huguenot et L'Association des Huguenots Allemand,"* in *Le regue,* Magdelaine and von Thadden, 245–253. *Also see* Raymond Vigne, "Preface" to *Huguenots in Britain,* xxi–xxiii, and Robin D. Gwynn, "Patterns in the Study of Huguenot Refugees in Britain, Past, Present and Future," ibid, 217–235. In 1990, the leader of the East German Christian Democratic party was Lothar de Maiziere, a Protestant of Huguenot origin (Serge Schmemann, "An Uneager Leader: Lothar de Maiziere, *New York Times,* March 21, 1990, A–l6. U. Haarmann has suggested that Prussian families of Huguenot heritage were part of the Prussian elite. Whether they did this through intermarriage combined with retention of patronyms is worth investigating.

29. The "fixed-price policy" which epitomized Puritan capitalism for Weber was actually a Quaker innovation, not originally utilized by other Protestant sects. For a discussion of Weber and the sociopolitical context of the Quaker fixed-price policy, *see* Stephen A. Kent, "The Quaker Ethic and the Fixed Price Policy: Max Weber and Beyond," *Sociological Inquiry* 53 (1983): 16–32. *See also* B. Nevaskar, *Capitalists without Capitalism: The Jains of India and the Quakers of the West* (Westport, Conn., Greenwood, 1971), 217, who suggests that their sectarianism, in effect, made early Quakers pariahs.

30. *See* Arthur Raistrick, *Quakers in Science and Industry* (New York: Augustus Kelley, 1968 [1950]), *passim;* Richard T. Vann, *The Social Development of English Quakerism, 1655–1755* (Cambridge, Mass.: Harvard University Press, 1969); Stephen A. Kent, "Relative Deprivation and Resource Mobilization: A Study of Early Quakerism," *British Journal of Sociology,* 33(1982):529–544.

On nineteenth-century British Quakers, *see* M. W. Kirby, *Men of Business and Politics: The Rise and Fall of the Quaker Pease Dynasty of North East England 1700–1943* (London: George Allen and Unwin, 1984); Leonore Davidoff and Catherine Hall, *Family Fortunes: Men and Women of the English Middle Class 1780–1850* (London: Hutchinson, 1987), 52–91, 216, 219, and 386–388. Ron Helfrich suggested the last reference to me.

31. Tolles, 33, 43; and Benjamin, *Philadelphia Quakers in the Industrial Age,* 30–41.

32. Tolles, 85–89, 91.

33. Benjamin, 49–72.

34. Tolles, 91–108.

35. Benjamin, 51, 56.

36. Benjamin, 51, 58–59; and Tolles, 47.

37. Max Weber, *The Protestant Ethic and the Spirit of Capitalism* (London: George Allen & Unwin, 1930). Weber erroneously believed that the Boston-born Franklin was a Quaker. He also demonstrated the pervasive interweaving of Protestant religious achievement with the business ethic of Americans. *See* Max Weber, "The Protestant Sects and the Spirit of Capitalism," in *From Max Weber: Essays on Sociology,* H. Girth and C. W. Mills, eds. (New York: Oxford University Press, 1946), 302–322.

38. Dolan, *Yankee Peddlers of Early America,* 229–230.

39. Ibid., 233–241. Dolan defends the reputation of the peddlers in his book by pointing to the conditions of the times and the hostility of settled shopkeepers to itinerant peddlers, as well as a general suspicion of strangers.

40. Rudolf Glanz, "Jew and Yankee. A Historic Comparison," *Jewish Social Studies* 6 (1944): 3–30.

41. Weber, *Protestant Ethic and the Spirit of Capitalism,* and "Protestant Sects and the Spirit of Capitalism."

42. Becker, "Constructive Typology in the Social Sciences," 32–33.

43. John K. Galbraith, *The Scotch* (Boston: Houghton Mifflin, 1964), 27–28, 94.

44. Becker, "Constructive Typology in the Social Sciences"; A. Frances Stewart, *Papers Relating to the Scots in Poland,* vol. 59 (Edinburgh: Scottish History Society, 1915). *See also* Thomas A. Fischer, *The Scots in Germany* (Edinburgh: O. Schulze, 1902), and *The Scots in Sweden* (Edinburgh: O. Schulze, 1907).

45. W. C. MacKenzie, *The Highlands and Isles of Scotland* (London: Moray Press, 1937).

46. Charles H. Anderson, *White Protestant Americans* (Englewood Cliffs, N.J.: Prentice Hall, 1970); Galbraith, *The Scotch;* Hill, *Scots to Canada;* and Hagen, *Theory of Social Change,* 296–297.

47. J. Douglas Porteous, "Easter Island—The Scottish Connection," *Geographic Review* 68 (1978): 145–156; and Hunt, *Heirs of Great Adventure.*

48. Dotson and Dotson, *Indian Minority of Zambia, Rhodesia, and Malawi*, 21–22, 79–80. *See also* Harold Barclay, "An Arab Community in the Canadian Northwest," *Anthropologica* 10 (1968): 143–156; W. Hamerlin, "Jews in the Leipzig Fur Industry," *Leo Baeck Yearbook* 9 (1964): 239–266; Erik Munsterhjelm, *The Wind and the Caribou* (New York: Harcourt Brace Jovanovich, 1976), 338–339; and R. D. Hershey, Jr., "Demand Soars at Fur Auction," *New York Times* (January 2, 1979), D2–3. Ethnic specialization and succession in the fur trade and industry must still be traded, but Scots, Jews, Greeks, and Lebanese have all played important roles both on the fur-trading frontiers of the United States, Canada, and Russia and in the manufacture and trade of hats and coats in the "metropole."

49. *See* William Steward Wallace, *Documents Relating to the Northwest Company* (Toronto: Champlain Society, 1934). Of the prominent "Nor'westers" listed in this biographical dictionary, approximately one-third were born in Scotland and a fair number of the Canadian-born and others were part Scot by descent. Among the key figures in the Northwest Company were Simon McTavish, his nephew William McGillivray, and the explorer Alexander MacKenzie, all Scottish highlanders.

50. Margaret William Campbell, *McGillivray—Lord of the Northwest* (Toronto: Clark-Irwin, 1962); and Douglas MacKay, *The Honourable Company* (Indianapolis: Bobbs-Merrill, 1936), 112–113, 118–119, and 133–448. In addition to wildness, laziness is sometimes attributed to Highlanders. In a recent mystery, a Lowland Scot says the following of a Highlander constable, "Never had to do any real work before, and, like all these Highlanders, fights shy of it as much as possible." (M. C. Beaton, *Death of a Gossip* (New York: St Martin's, 1985), 81. The Highlander in question is also portrayed as a heavy drinker.

51. MacKay, *Honourable Company*, 231; and Harold A. Innis, *The Fur Trade in Canada* (New Haven: Yale University Press, 1962). In the period of the Northwest Company and of Hudson's Bay Company under Simpson, family connections were of some importance. The Nor'westers were often related to each other. Sir George Simpson himself found his way into the Company through a relative who employed him. He was accused on one occasion of nepotism. On family ties in these two companies, *see* Jennifer S. H. Brown, *Strangers in the Blood: Fur Trade Company Families in Indian Company* (Vancouver: University of British Columbia Press, 1980).

52. R. Jarvenpa and W. P. Zenner, "Scot Trader/Indian Workers Relations and Ethnic Segregation: A Subarctic Example," *Ethnos* 44 (1979): 58–77.

53. Jarvenpa and Zenner, "Scot Trader/Indian Workers Relations." *See also* W. P. Zenner and R. Jarvenpa, "Scots in the Northern Fur Trade," *Ethnic Groups* 2 (1980):189–210.

CHAPTER 6

1. An earlier version of this interpretation is Walter P. Zenner, "American Jewry in the Light of Middleman Minority Theories," *Contemporary Jewry* 5 (1980): 11–30. Some minor citations to previously published literature will be found there and is omitted here. The interpretation of the transformation of American Jewry found here parallels, in many respects, that of Edna Bonacich and John Modell, *The Economic Basis of Ethnic Solidarity: Small Business in the Japanese-American Community* (Berkeley: University of California Press, 1980).

2. See Edna Bonacich, "A Theory of Middleman Minorities," *American Sociological Review* 38 (1973): 585–594; and *Economic Basis of Ethnic Solidarity;* and S. Kuznets, "The Economic Life and Structure of the Jews," in *The Jews: Their History, Culture and Religion,* L. Finkelstein, ed. (New York: Harper, 1960).

3. On Europe and North American pioneering, *see* N. Gross, ed., *Jewish Economic History* (New York: Schocken, 1975), 199–205, 237–249; Stephen Aris, *Jews in Business* (Harmondsworth: Penguin Books, 1970); Kuznets, "Economic Structure of the Jews"; and D. J. Elazar, *Community and Polity* (Philadelphia: Jewish Publication Society, 1976), 36. On the needle trade and urban slums, *see* Judd L. Teller, *Strangers and Natives* (New York: Delacorte, 1968), 79–93; and Irving Howe, *The World of Our Fathers* (New York: Harcourt, Brace Jovanovich, 1976), 77–84 and Roger D. Waldinger, *Through the Eye of the Needle: Immigrants and Enterprise in New York's Garment Trade* (New York: New York University Press, 1986) *passim.*

4. James W. Loewen, *The Mississippi Chinese between Black and White* (Cambridge: Harvard University Press, 1971), 12–13, 49–53, 55–57, and 112–117, refers to such ethnic succession in Mississippi.

5. Lucy S. Dawidowicz, "A Century of Jewish History, 1881–1981: The View from America," *American Jewish Yearbook* 82 (1982): 17; J. S. Fauman, "The Jews in the Waste Industry in Detroit," *Jewish Social Studies* 3 (1941): 41–56; and Murray Schumach, "The City's Most Exclusive Club," *New York Times Magazine* (May 6, 1979), 108–113.

6. S. Kuznets, *Economic Structure of the United States Jewry: Recent Trends* (Jerusalem: Institute of Contemporary Jewry, Hebrew University, 1972); W. P. Zenner and J. S. Belcove-Shalin, "The Cultural Anthropology of American Jewry," *Persistence and Flexibility,* (Albany, N.Y.: State University of New York Press, 1988), 12–14; Richard Alba and Gwen Moore, "Ethnicity in the American Elite," *American Sociological Review* 47 (1982); and Richard Zweigenhaft, "Recent Patterns of Jewish Representation in the Corporate and Social Elites," *Contemporary Jewry* 6

(1982): 36–46. Here, I am stressing change, while others have emphasized the continuation of discrimination in the upper class/ruling elites. While both views have validity, change is not negligible. For the other view, *see* A. Leibman, *Jews and the Left* (New York: Wiley, 1979), 602–611. *See* Charles E. Silberman, *A Certain People: American Jews and Their Lives Today* (New York: Summit Books, 1985), 82–156; S. L. Slavin and M. A. Prudt, *The Einstein Syndrome: Corporate Anti-Semitism in America Today* (Lanham, Md.: University Press of America, 1982); and Abraham Korman, "Anti-Semitism and the Behavioral Sciences: Toward a Theory of Discrimination in Work Settings," *Contemporary Jewry* 9 (1988): 63–86. On the assimilation of contemporary young executives, *see* Samuel Z. Klausner, *Succeeding in Corporate America: The Experience of Jewish M.B,A.s* (New York: American Jewish Committee, 1990).

7. The severity of anti-Jewish discrimination in universities prior to World War II is documented by Leonard Silk, *The Economists* (New York: Basic Books, 1976); Diana Trilling, "Lionel Trilling: A Jew at Columbia," *Commentary* 67 (1979): 40–46; and Sidney Hook, "Anti-Semitism in the Academy: Some Pages of the Past," *Midstream* 20 (1979): 49–54. Anthropology departments dominated by Franz Boas and his students were an exception, although he and his *coterie* downplayed their Jewishness. Still, they were perceived as discriminating against various male gentile anthropologists. On Boas, *see* Leslie White, *The Social Organization of Ethnological Theory,* (Houston: Rice University Studies, 52, 1966): 4; and Leonard Glick, "Types Distinct from Our Own: Franz Boas on Jewish Identity and Assimilation," *American Anthropologist* 84 (1982): 545–565. Some points regarding "old boy networks" and visibility strategies are applicable to this group. For data on Jews in academia in the 1970s, *see* Everett C. Ladd and Seymour Martin Lipset, *The Divided Academy* (New York: McGraw-Hill, 1975), 149–167.

8. On Poland, *see* R. Mahler, "Jews in Public and the Liberal Professions in Poland, 1914–1939," *Jewish Social Studies* 6 (1944): 241–350; on New York, *see* Howe, *World of Our Fathers,* 166–167; David Rogers, *110 Livingston Street* (New York: Random House, 1968), 285–289; and Walter P. Zenner, *Jewish State Employees in the Albany Area: A Research Report* (Albany, N.Y.: State University of New York, Department of Anthropology, 1978). On Federal Service, *see* Stephen Isaacs, *Jews in American Politics* (New York: Doubleday, 1974).

9. Kuznets, *Economic Structure of U.S. Jewry;* Calvin Goldscheider, *Jewish Continuity and Change: Emerging Patterns in America* (Bloomington: Indiana University Press, 1986), 107–150; and William L. Yancey, Eugene P. Ericksen, and George H. Leon, "The Structure of Pluralism: We're All Italian Around Here, Aren't We, Mrs. O'Brien?" in *Ethnicity and Race in the U.S.A.—Toward the 21st Century* R. D. Alba, ed. (Boston and London: Routledge & Kegan Paul, 1985), 94–116.

10. Betty Boyd Caroli, *Italian Repatriation from the United States, 1900–1914* (New York: Center for Migration Studies, 1973).

11. Howe, *World of Our Fathers,* 135–168; Aris, *Jews in Business,* 93–112.

12. Of course, traditional Jews have always prayed for a return to Zion, for a restoration of the Temple, and the reestablishment of the Davidic monarchy. The immediacy of such utopian and millenarian visions varied in importance.

13. Louis Harap, *The Jew in American Literature* (Philadelphia: Jewish Publication Society, 1976), 303–376; Eli Evans, *The Provincials* (New York: Atheneum, 1973); Elazar, *Community and Polity;* S. Adler and T. E. Connelly, *From Ararat to Suburbia* (Philadelphia: Jewish Publication Society, 1960), 135–136, 237, and 259; Dawidowicz, "Century of Jewish History,"

14. S. Poll, *The Hasidic Community of Williamsburg* (New York: Schocken, 1969); Schumach, "City's Most Exclusive Club"; and J. Gutwirth, "Antwerp Jewry Today," *Jewish Journal of Sociology* 10 (1968): 121–138. The lack of rootedness may, however, change over time. The Chabad or Lubavicher have come to function in a way that is parallel to American Protestant evangelical movements. On such adaptation, *see* Janet S. Belcove-Shalin, "The Hasidim of North America: A Review of the Literature," in *Persistence and Flexibility,* 183–207.

15. Walter P. Zenner, "Syrian Jews in Three Social Settings," *Jewish Journal of Sociology* 10 (1968): 101–120; "The Cross-National Web of Syrian Jewish Relations, in *Urban Life: Readings in Urban Anthropology,* G. Gmelch and W. P. Zenner, eds. (Prospect Heights, Ill.: Waveland Press, 1988), 381–390; "Arabic-Speaking Immigrants in North America as Middleman Minorities," *Racial and Ethnic Studies* 5 (1982): 457–477; and "Syrian Jews in New York City Twenty Years Ago," in *Fields of Offering: Essays in Honor of Raphael Patai,* V. Sanua, ed. (New York: Herzl Press, 1983). *See also* Joseph A.D. Sutton, *Magic Carpet: Aleppo-in-Flatbush* (Brooklyn: Thayer-Jacoby, 1979).

16. Herbert A. Strauss, "The Immigration and Acculturation of German Jews in the United States of America," *Leo Baeck Yearbook* 16 (1971): 63–96.

17. On Hollywood, *see* Howe, *World of Our Fathers,* 164–166. and Neal Gabler, *An Empire of Their Own: How Zukor, Laemle, Fox, Mayer, Cohn and Warner Bros, Invented Hollywood* (New York: Crown, 1988). In the Watergate tapes, Nixon made some disparaging comments about Jews, yet he appointed Jews to high positions in his administration. One of his most loyal supporters after Watergate was a rabbi, Baruch Korff. On

Kissinger and Nixon, *see* Seymour M. Hersh, "Kissinger and Nixon in the White House," *Atlantic Monthly* (May 1982), 35–68.

18. *See* E. Leyton, "Composite Descent Groups in Canada," in *Readings in Kinship in Urban Society,* C. C. Harris, ed. (New York: Pergamon Press, 1970), 179–186; W. E. Mitchell and J. Leichter, *Kinship and Casework* (New York: Russell Sage Foundation, 1967), 135–145; and Myrna Silberman, "Family, Kinship and Ethnicity: Strategies for Social Mobility," in *Persistence and Flexibility: Anthropological Perspectives on the American Jewish Experience,* W. P. Zenner, ed. (Albany, N.Y.: SUNY Press, 1988), 165–182. *See also* R. Winch, S. Greer, and Rae Lesser Blumberg, "Ethnicity and Extended Familism in an Upper-Middle Class Suburb," *American Sociological Review* 32 (1967): 265–272, who connect the more intense kin ties to a value on familism and attribute occupational choice and failure to migrate to this value, rather than seeing occupation and migration as intervening variables. The fact that their study was done in a Chicago suburb, in an old northeastern city, rather than in Los Angeles, where more Jews are secondary migrants, may explain some of their results. They also had difficulty with such factors as perception of occupational opportunity, discrimination, and a division which they suggest between "bureaucrat" and "entrepreneurs."

19. In diamonds, of course, there is a Diamond Club which performs such tasks. Jewish organized crime helped enforce price-fixing in the garment industry, which was a more sinister connection. *See* Alan Block, *East Side, West Side: Organizing Crime in New York, 1930–1950* (Cardiff: University College of Cardiff Press, 1980).

20. On agriculture, see *Jewish Encyclopedia* (New York: Funk & Wagnalls, 1903); Gross, *Jewish Economic History,* 119–222; Howe, *World of Our Fathers,* 84–87; and J. Brandes, *Immigrants to Freedom* (Philadelphia: Jewish Publication Society, 1971). On *Lantsmanshaften,* see Howe, *World of Our Fathers,* 188; and Teller, *Strangers and Natives,* 15–16. On the "cousinhood," *see* Abner Cohen, *Two Dimensional Man* (Berkeley: University of California Press, 1974), 110–114. On anthropologists, *see* White, *Social Organization of Ethnological Theory.* On psychoanalysts, *see* H. Wilensky and J. Ladinsky, "From Religious Community to Occupation Group: Structural Assimilation Among Professors, Lawyers and Engineers," *American Sociological Review* 32 (1967): 541–561. On subtle strategies, *see* L. Plotnicov and M. Silverman, "Ethnic Signalling: Social Bonding among Jews in Contemporary American Society," *Ethnology* 17 (1978): 407–423. On state workers, *see* Zenner, *Jewish State Employees in the Albany Area.*

21. Robert K. Merton, "The Self-Fulfilling Prophecy," in his collection, *Social Theory and Social Structure,* 2nd ed. (Glencoe, Ill.: The Free Press, 1957), 432–434; and Sherry Gorelick, "The Jewish Success and the Great American Celebration: The Cold War vs. The World War in

Social Science," *Contemporary Jewry* 5 (1980): 34–55.

22. *See* Milton Matz, "The Meaning of the Christmas Tree to the American Jew," *Jewish Journal of Sociology* 3 (1961): 129–137; A. G. Duker, "On Religious Trends in American Jewish Life," *YIVO Social Science Annual* IV (1949): 51–63; *idem* "Emerging Cultural Patterns of American Jewish Life: The Psychocultural Approach to the Study of Jewish Life in America," *Publications of the American Jewish Historical Society* 40 (1950): 351–389; *idem* "Notes on the Cultural Life of American Jewry," *Jewish Journal of Sociology* 2 (1960): 98–102; Charles E. Silberman, *A Certain People*, 230–240; and J. M. Cuddihy, *The Ordeal of Civility* (New York: Basic Books, 1975). While not discussing the American scene directly, *see* the discussion of such ambivalence in Sandor Gilman, *Jewish Self-Hatred: Anti-Semitism and the Hidden Language of the Jews* (Baltimore: Johns Hopkins University Press, 1986). Samuel Z. Klausner, *Succeeding in Corporate America*, has noted the very thin "Jewishness" of sucessful Jewish corporate executives.

23. Modern Orthodox Jews—that is, those who pass fairly freely between the modern intellectual world of science and traditional institutions such as the synagogue—are profoundly ambivalent about the orthopraxis. *See* Samuel Heilman, *Synagogue Life* (Chicago: University of Chicago Press, 1976); and "Inner and Outer Identities: Sociological Ambivalence Among Orthodox Jews," *Jewish Social Studies* 39 (1977): 227–240. In some circumstances, for example, modern Orthodox men will wear skullcaps and eat kosher food, but skip the blessings before and after the meal. *See* M. Himmelfarb, "Plural Establishment," *Commentary* 59 (1974): 69–73, and Diane Axelrod Pariser, "The Shtibl Congregation: The Celebration of Passover among One Group of Orthodox Jews" (Masters thesis, State University of New York at Albany, 1973).

24. Robert Weisbrot, *The Jews of Argentina* (Philadelphia: Jewish Publication Society, 1979).

25. On traditional Jewish officials, *see* W. P. Zenner, "Jewish Retainers as Power Brokers," *Jewish Quarterly Review* (1990), forthcoming. A major source for this section is Isaacs, *Jews in American Politics*. For specific information on Jewish politicians mentioned here, *see Encyclopaedia Judaica* (Jerusalem: Keter Publishing, 1971), and *National Cyclopedia of American Biography* (1929–1943). On Jewish politicians in the American South, *see* Evans, *Provincials*.

26. Isaacs, *Jews in American Politics*.

27. On Kissinger, *see* M. Kalb and B. Kalb, *Kissinger* (Boston: Little, Brown, 1974). Kissinger's Jewishness has been a factor in his diplomacy. Minority status can have its effects on the minority when a prominent member becomes a scapegoat. Certainly this potential exists here. For

instance, Greek disappointment with America's role in the Cyprus war of 1974 was expressed through anti-Kissinger demonstrations with anti-Semitic overtones. Kissinger's Jewishness had been manipulated by himself and by his Arab and Israeli counterparts during negotiation. *See also* M. Golan, *Conversations with Kissinger* (New York: Quadrangle, 1976); and Walter Z. Lacquer, *Confrontation* (New York: Quadrangle, 1974). Regarding the salience of his Jewishness in his relationship with Nixon, *see* Hersh, "Kissinger and Nixon in the White House."

28. Some of the dilemmas faced by Jewish elected and appointed officials emerged in the career of Herbert H. Lehman, who served as Governor of New York (1933–1942), as director of the United Nations Relief and Rehabilitation Agency (UNRRA) after World War II, and who was the first directly elected United States Senator of Jewish origin. He entered politics after a career in business. As a politician Lehman was a New Dealer and a reformer. Throughout his life, Herbert Lehman was an active participant in the Jewish community, a member of a Reform temple, volunteer in lower East Side settlement houses, and a philanthropist. Like most German Jews of his generation, he was a non-Zionist, although he became known later as an ardent, but critical, supporter of Israel during his term as senator and in retirement. *See* Allan Nevins, *Herbert H. Lehman and His Era* (New York: Scribners, 1963). Despite this, very little in Nevins's portrayal of Lehman's career indicates any special patronage for the Jews during his terms as governor. While the number of Jews employed by the state government increased during his term, this was due more to the New Deal than to Lehman's patronage. He was evidently as silent as other Jewish leaders in the United States in not protesting American and Allied indifference to the German genocide. Later, in 1946, in UNRRA, Lehman absolved a subordinate accused of anti-Semitic prejudice of these charges, despite Jewish protests. *See* Nevins, 292–296. Here, Lehman was consistent with the general impartiality which was a hallmark of his public career. The point that Jewish political leaders in the general sector serving majority or general interests is as applicable to Lehman as it is to others is made by R. Gordis, "Jews as Political Figures," *Judaism* 22 (1973): 100–108. Only as senator from a state with a large Jewish voting population could he appear to be a "special pleader" for pro-Israel policies. *See* Nevins, 369. *See also* articles in the *National Cyclopedia of American Biography* on Bamberger and Horner, two Jewish governors. On Henry Horner, *see also* Edward Mazur "Jewish Chicago: From Diversity to Community," *Ethnic Chicago,* M. G. Holli and P. A. Jones, eds. (Grand Rapids, Mich.: W. B. Eerdmans, 1984), 46–68.

29. The image of the Jew preceded large-scale Jewish immigration to North America, as shown by Louis Harap, *The Image of the Jew in American Literature* (Philadelphia: Jewish Publication Society, 1974); and Rudolf Glanz, "Jew and Yankee: A Historic Comparison," *Jewish Social Studies* 6 (1944): 3–30. While the United States and modern Great Britain

have been spared the more violent manifestations of anti–Semitism, there is no doubt that anti-Semitic sentiment shaped public policy, such as British and American immigration laws. This was especially true in the period between 1920 and 1950. For a full historical review of anti-Semitism in the United States, including regional and ethnic variations, *see* Leonard Dinnerstein, *Uneasy at Home: Anti-Semitism and the American Jewish Experience* (New York: Columbia University Press, 1987). Since many Jewish businesses were looted during the ghetto riots in the 1960s, and this period was often marked by fierce exchanges between Jews and blacks, anti-Semitism was also involved. Some see these as classic anti-Semitism and antimiddleman pogroms and point to anti-Semitic rhetoric and expression in the black middle class. *See* Loewen, *Mississippi Chinese Between Black and White,* 176–177; Bonacich, "Theory of Middleman Minorities," 583–594; and J. R. Cayton and S. C. Drake, *Black Metropolis* (New York: Harper and Row, 1962), 435–456. One may see such looting and gutting during a riot as a general manifestation of anti-white feeling and a desire for plunder made possible by the riot itself; perhaps the stores were plundered because they were there, not because they were owned by Jews. On black-Jewish tensions in the 1980s, *see* Charles E. Silberman, *A Certain People,* 339–343, 351–3; and Taylor Branch, "The War Between Blacks and Jews," *Esquire* (May 1989). These authors suggest that ideology and symbolic politics play a role beyond immediate economic interests in these actions. For a critique of Bonacich's "sojourner" theory as it relates to American Jews *vis a vis* blacks, see Robert Cherry, "Middleman Minority Theories: Their Implications for Black-Jewish Relations," *Journal of Ethnic Studies* 17 (1989): 117–138.

30. *See* S. M. Lipset, "The Study of Jewish Communities in a Comparative Context," *Jewish Journal of Sociology* 5 (1963); 157–166; and Ben Halpern, *The American Jew* (New York: Herzl Press, 1956). On anti-Semitism, I have modified the proposition of S. Andreski, "An Economic Interpretation of Anti-Semitism," *Jewish Journal of Sociology* 5 (1963): 201–213.

Conclusion

1. *See* Walter P. Zenner, "Middleman Minorities in the Syrian Mosaic: Trade, Conflict and Image Management," *Sociological Perspectives* 30 (1987):400–421.

2. *See* Clifford Geertz, *Social History of an Indonesian Town* (Cambridge, Mass.: MIT Press, 1965), 28–29, 57–60, 77–78, 146–148. Also: Sartono Kartodirjo, *Protest Movements in Rural Java* (Singapore: Oxford University Press, 1973), 151–168.

3. *See* John Waterbury, *North for the Trade* (Berkeley and Los Angeles: University of California Press, 1972).

4. *See* Zenner, "Middleman Minorities in the Syrian Mosaic." *Also see* W. P. Zenner, "Jewish Retainers as Power Brokers," *Jewish Quarterly Review* (forthcoming).

5. *See* W. P. Zenner, "Middleman Minorities and Genocide," in *Genocide and the Modern Age: Etiology and Case Studies of Mass Death,* I. Wallimann and M. N. Dobkowski, eds. (Westport Conn.: Greenwood, 1987), 253–282. Documentation of the above is given there. The Wallimann and Dobkowski volume discusses other cases as well.

6. H. Smith, *The Russians,* 106–134; Konstantin Simis, "Russia's Underground Millionaires," *Fortune* (June 1981), 36–50. Simis was an attorney who represented entrepreneurs from the countereconomy.

7. *See* Elizabeth Schillinger and John Jenswold, "Cooperative Business Ventures in the Soviet Union." *Sociology and Social Research* 73 (1988): 22–30. This study, an early result of Soviet openings to Western researchers, is obviously exploratory.

8. Edna Bonacich and Ivan Light, *Immigrant Entrepreneurs: Koreans in Los Angeles: 1965–1982* (Berkeley: University of California Press, 1988); and Pyong G. Min, *Ethnic Business Enterprise: The Case of Korean Small Business in Atlanta* (Staten Island, N.Y.: Center for Migration Studies, 1988). I am also relying here on my own observations in New York City, Philadelphia, and other cities.

On press reaction to the Brooklyn boycott, *see New York Times,* "Sonny Carson, Koreans, and Racism," May 8, 1990, A–28; Seth Mydans, "On the Same Job, Koreans and Blacks," *New York Times,* May 27, 1990, 18 (deals with Los Angeles). *Also see* a nationally syndicated writer, Mike Royko, "New York blacks should organize like Koreans," *Albany Times-Union,* May 22, 1990, A–11.

9. In 1989 and 1990, there were reports of increased anti-Semitic activities in the Soviet Union, as well as riots against Armenians in Baku and in other parts of the USSR.

10. "Violence against Mauritanians in Dakar," *New York Times,* May 1, 1989, A–6; Kenneth B. Noble, "Hundreds Die in Months of Clashes on Two Sides of West African Border," *New York Times,* May 1, 1989, A–1, A–6; Greg Myre (Associated Press), "Generals declare Ciskei emergency," *Philadelphia Inquirer,"* March 7, 1990, 14–A.

Subject Index

D

E

F

G

H

I

J

P

Q

R

S

T

U

V

W

Y

AUTHOR INDEX

M

N

O

P

Y

Z